Client/Server over ATM

Client/Server over ATM

Making use of broadband to support client/server applications

DAN MINOLI
Teleport Communication Group
Stevens Institute of Technology

ANDREW SCHMIDT

MANNING

Greenwich
(74° w. long.)

For electronic browsing of this book, see http://www.browsebooks.com

The publisher offers discounts on this book when ordered in quantity. For more information, please contact:

Special Sales Department
Manning Publications Co.
3 Lewis Street
Greenwich, CT 06830

Fax: (203) 661-9018
email: orders@manning.com

Library of Congress Cataloging-in-Publication Data
Minoli, Daniel, 1952 -
    Client/server applications on ATM Networks / Daniel M. Minoli, Andrew G. Schmidt.
        p.   cm.
    Includes index
    ISBN 1-884777-32-5
    1. Client/server computing. 2. Local area networks (Computer networks)
3.Asynchronous transfer mode. I. Schmidt, Andrew G.
QA76.9.C55M56   1996
004'.36--dc20   96-43993
                                    CIP

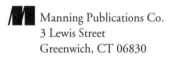 Manning Publications Co.
    3 Lewis Street
    Greenwich, CT 06830

    Copyeditor: Margaret Marynowski
    Typesetter: Dorothy Marsico
    Cover designer: Leslie Haimes

Printed in the United States of America
1 2 3 4 5 6 7 8 9 10 – CR – 00 99 98 97 96

contents

Part III ATM-based approach to client/server 191

5 LAN Emulation and Classical IP over ATM 192

preface

When talking about Information Technologies (IT), *the client/server approach* is the contemporary buzzword. Client/server computing is a popular subject of discussion, important to every corporation. Client/server techniques, if implemented correctly, can change the way companies do business, so they can enhance their competitive position and do business more profitably.

In the contemporary paradigm, IT is established around workgroup computing, whether the workers are in a building, in a campus, around town, around the nation, or around the world. We have reached a stage of development where "the corporation-is-the-network." Therefore, deployment of client/server technology across an enterprise will increasingly require a robust broadband communication infrastructure which can support the required grade of service and availability that are dictated by the productivity expectations of the organization. Also, there is now significant interest in deploying intranets, which not only utilize client/server technology, but also necessitate broadband backbones and broadband desktop access. Having placed most if not all of the employees on an entreprise network, any communication delays, quirks, or inefficiencies can significantly degrade overall company productivity, and, ultimately, business viability. (Naturally, server-level bottlenecks are equally undesirable.)

To achieve the desired worker productivity enhancements sought through communication technology, workgroups will increasingly be interconnected over an enterprise-wide high-speed networks. Large corporations find themselves with a growing need to extend high-speed communications beyond key sites, in order to support applications such as client/server-based company processes (order processing, inventory management, etc.), distributed cooperative computing, business/scientific imaging, video conferencing, video distribution, multimedia, (corporate) distance learning, etc.

Asynchronous Transfer Mode (ATM) technology and cell relay service will play a major role in enterprise networks. ATM technology not only supports fastpacket services but also frame relay service, LAN emulation, cut-through IP connectivity, and video/multimedia services. It is anticipated that ATM services will transform the enterprise network from a data-only network, to an integrated data, voice, video, image, and multimedia corporate infrastructure. ATM is being positioned to meet these corporate needs now receiving CTO, CNO, and CIO attention.

A lot of discussion has occurred in the industry in the past five years about ATM's general evolution in support of wide area high-speed connectivity, support of legacy LANs and legacy protocols, and multimedia capabilities. However there has been no specific discussion of how ATM can support the client/server environment, now so prevalent.

Given these two conspicuous but so far unrelated technologies, client/server and ATM, this book aims at explaining how the inevitable marriage of the two will soon, have to, occur. The book is divided into three major sections. Section One (Chapters 1–3) covers the basics of client/server technology and the business importance of this IT paradigm. Chapter 1 provides an introduction to the concept. Chapter 2 discusses the use of this technology in the corporate environment. Chapter 3 looks at the more general topic of distributed databases and object-oriented methodologies. Section Two (Chapter 4) covers the basics of ATM, and the business needs the technology addresses. Section Three (Chapters 5–9) covers specific integration of client/server in an ATM environment. This critical section covers supporting classical IP-based client/server systems over ATM (Chapter 5). This chapter also discusses supporting new client/server applications using LAN Emulation. Multiprotocol Over ATM (MPOA) and its relationship to client/server systems is covered in Chapter 6. Internet client/server technology (HyperText Transfer Protocol—HTTP—and Java) is covered in Chapter 7, because of the evolving intranet requirements in many corporations. Finally, Chapter 8 discusses issues and measurements related to ATM usage for client/server applications.

acknowledgments

The authors would like to thank Mr. R. Graff, Intel Corporation, for providing the insightful treatment of the business importance of client/server technology which has been included in Chapter 2.

The authors would also like to thank David Raila, University of Illinois, for his consultation on realtime communication included in Chapter 7.

Mr. Minoli also acknowledges the support of R. D. Rosner, Vice President and General Manager, Teleport Communications Group, Private Lines and Internet & Data Services, for the insight, guidance, and assistance provided.

Mr. Minoli also thanks Mr. Ben Occhiogrosso, President, DVI Communications, for his suggestions and assistance based on DVI's extensive corporate practice in this field.

Ms. Jo-Anne Dressendofer, President, IMEDIA, is also thanked.

Mr. Schmidt would like to thank Clair Hilchie-Schmidt for her editorial comments and encouragement during the writing of this book, and Kimberly Price for her valuable guidance and support.

PART I

Business drivers and basic client/server concepts

chapter 1

Client/server: The business imperitives driving the search for new solutions

1.1 Overview

When talking about Information Technologies (IT), *the client/server approach* is the contemporary buzzword. Client/server computing is now a popular subject of discussion, important to every corporation. Client/server techniques, when implemented correctly, can change the way companies do business, so they can enhance their competitive position and do business more profitably. Successful applications impact company business both internally and externally: the client/server application model has the potential to improve business processes, add efficiencies, increase productivity and improve the bottom line.

A meaningful implementation of client/server technology across an enterprise invariably necessitates a robust communication infrastructure which can support the required grade of service and availability, and that is commensurate with the productivity expectations of the organization. Having placed most, if not all, of the employees on such a computing infrastructure, any communication delays, quirks, or inefficiencies can significantly degrade overall company productivity and, ultimately business viability. (Naturally, any similar pathologies related to the server or to the application itself can also adversely affect the company's posture.)

On a forward going basis, IT will be established around workgroup computing, whether the workers are in a building, in a campus, around town, around the nation, or around the world. To achieve the desired worker productivity enhancements sought through communication technology, workgroups will increasingly be interconnected over enterprise-wide high-speed networks. Specifically, many large corporations now have a growing need to extend high-speed communications beyond key sites, to support applications such as client/server-based company processes (order processing, inventory management, etc.), distributed cooperative computing, business/scientific imaging, video conferencing, video distribution, multimedia, (corporate) distance learning, etc.

Most communication practitioners by now agree that Asynchronous Transfer Mode (ATM) technology in general, and Cell Relay Service (CRS) in particular (obtainable with ATM), will play a major role in enterprise networks and intranets in the immediate future. ATM refers to a high-bandwidth, low-delay switching and multiplexing technology currently becoming widely available for both public and private networks. ATM supports voice, video, and data. While ATM in the strict sense is simply a (data link layer) protocol, the more encompassing ATM principles and ATM-based platforms form the foundation for a variety of high-speed digital communication services aimed at corporate users for high-speed data, LAN interconnection, imaging, video, and multimedia applications. CRS can be utilized for networks that use completely private, completely public, or hybrid communication facilities. A variety of vendors now have ATM products on the market. A significant number of carriers provide ATM-based services or are poised to do so in the near future. ATM supports both switched (Switched Virtual Circuit) and non-switched (Permanent Virtual Circuit) connections. ATM supports services requiring both circuit-mode and packet-mode information transfer capabilities. ATM employs fiber facilities as the transport medium, supporting data rates which are multiples of 155 Mbps; lower-speed rates are also available for specific applications.

What distinguished ATM from previous communication technologies is that ATM technology not only supports native services, specifically CRS, but also frame relay service, LAN emulation, Internet Protocol (IP) networking, and video/multimedia services. It is anticipated that ATM services will transform the enterprise network from a data-only network, to an integrated data, voice, video, image, and multimedia corporate infrastructure. ATM is being positioned to meet all of these corporate needs now receiving CTO, CNO, and CIO attention. When talking about evolving communication paradigms, *the ATM approach* is the contemporary buzzword.

A lot of discussion has occurred in the industry in the past five years about ATM's general evolution in support of wide area high-speed connectivity, support of legacy LANs and legacy protocols such as IP, and multimedia capabilities. However, there has been no specific discussion of how ATM can support the client/server environment, now so prevalent.

Given these two conspicuous, but so far nearly unrelated, technologies, *client/server* and *ATM*, this book aims at explaining how the inevitable marriage of the two will soon, have to, occur.

There is a lot of current interest in deploying *intranets* in corporate environments. Intranets use Internet communication, application, and browsing principles to provide corporate users with uniform access to the company's distributed data repository. This book should prove useful to planners exploring these requirements, in that the World Wide Web (WWW) model being imported into the intranet is intrinsically a client/server model. Furthermore, the use of ATM in the local and wide area network, is almost a given when hundreds, if not thousands, of corporate users will be transacting graphics-intensive but productivity-enhancing data now typical of WWW browser-based applications.

1.1.1 Scope of text

The book is divided into three major sections. Section One (Chapters 1–3) covers the basics of client/server technology and the business importance of this IT paradigm.

Chapter 1 provides an introduction to the concept. Chapter 2 discusses the use of this technology in the corporate environment. Chapter 3 looks at the more general topic of distributed databases and object-oriented methodologies. Section Two (Chapter 4) covers the basics of ATM, and the business needs the technology addresses. Section Three (Chapters 5–8) covers specific integration of client/server in an ATM environment. This critical section covers supporting classical IP-based client/server systems over ATM (Chapter 5). Chapter 5 also discusses supporting new client/server applications using LAN Emulation (LANE). The newer Multiprotocol Over ATM (MPOA), and its relationship to client/server systems, is covered in Chapter 6. Internet and intranet client/server technology (HyperText Transfer Protocol—HTTP—HyperText Markup Language—HTML—and Java) is covered in Chapter 7; this information is critical for planners contemplating the deployments of intranets. Finally, Chapter 8 discusses issues and measurements related to ATM usage for client/server applications.

The book is aimed at corporate planners who need to prepare for the introduction of ATM technology in their organizations in the 1997–99 timeframe to support client/server applications, intranets, and Internet access. The reader who is familiar with client/server technology may choose to skip the first three chapters and go directly to Section 2 (Chapter 4) and then Section 3 (Chapters 5–8). Readers familiar with ATM but not with client/server technology should concentrate on Section 1 (Chapters 1–3) and Section 3 (Chapters 5–8). Other readers should work through the book in linear fashion.

This introductory chapter looks at the current corporate environment along with the drivers that are propelling corporations into client/server technology. The chapter covers the topic from a *present-mode-of-operation* perspective, without the additional challenge of deploying client/server over ATM, which we call *second-generation client/server technology*. This *future-mode-of-operation* topic will be rejoined later in the book. In providing this panoramic description of the field, the chapter offers a motivation as to why finding a way to support client/server (over new communication infrastructures) is so important. This chapter offers the guidance and explores the leading techniques needed to enable successful applications of client/server computing. It explains important aspects of the underlying technologies and explores the business realities of practical applications. It will also explore some of the IT-related pitfalls to be avoided. All of the discussion in Chapter 1 focuses attention on the requirement to support client/server by the corporate communications infrastructure, which increasingly will be ATM-based. As the reader goes from Chapter 1 to Chapters 2 and 3, he or she will see that the approach taken in the book is to go from the general to the specific, from the macro business requirements to the microscopic "bit and bytes" details needed to ultimately support these business requirements.

1.2 An introduction and frame of reference

Client/server computing* is important because it represents a new way of doing business in the IT organization. Client/server requires a new set of programming and system implementation tools and skills that are not used or learned in traditional "mainframe computer and terminal-oriented" environments. Client/server computing even molds the IT organization structure into new shapes. As client/server computing proliferates in corporate environments, IT p3rofessionals need to learn more about the underlying technologies, including design, implementation, operation, and tuning. They also need to understand the business implications and the proper techniques for successful applications. Further, the subject of client/server computing is important to people working in the business departments; these are the clients of client/server computing and IT departments.

This chapter provides definitions and characteristics important to understanding client/server computing. It describes interrelated forms and flavors, including downsizing, rightsizing, and distributed computing. It points out the infrastructure needed before embarking on implementation. It focuses on what motivates companies to deploy client/server systems. The following chapters address the issues from a more technical perspective. Sections 2 and 3 then address the communication implications of this corporate migration, as they relate to the need for broadband communications.

1.2.1 Frame of reference

The goal of this section is to cover the business implications and aspects of client/server computing, from planning through implementation, including operational assurances for systems management and security. The technology used to build and implement client/server computing has been and will continue to be evolving. In fact, a term often applied to this phenomenon evokes images of short, quick movement: *leap-frogging*. Therefore, the technology samples used in this chapter should serve as examples, and are illustrative of principles and business implications having a much longer life. There are a number of approaches described in detail in the press which have proven successful. All have a common thread that will help the planner to succeed.

Management approval and buy-in is critical to the success of every client/server initiative. Financial support for hiring, training, infrastructure, development tools, and

---

* The authors thank Mr. Russ Graff for the input provided for this material.

implementation effort all hinge on management support. Likewise, the philosophy of client/server computing and the strategy for implementing it must be shared by those who will implement it and use it, including those people in the information technology department and the end-user community. Without buy-in at all of these organizational levels, a client/server initiative cannot succeed.

Client/server computing is more than merely the sum of its technological parts. To be successful, this migration must benefit the business. It is required that the planner formulate and follow a strategic vision for how client/server computing can be applied within the business, and for specific benefits the planner expects to derive. This is especially important if the organization's business computing roots are mainframe-based.

1.2.2 Computing evolution

We will begin with a quick look back at some of the history of computing. Recall the progression of computing over the last few decades. This historical perspective provides the frame of reference for understanding the influential roots and paradigm shifts that have shaped where we are today. This legacy also shows what we are trying to improve with client/server computing.

The 1960s were characterized as the age of mainframe computing, with centralized batch processing. These large business machines were typically located in special rooms. These rooms had a controlled environment that was cool and static-free, and had raised floors to accommodate required air flow, cables, and pipes. Data flowed in and out of this environment on punched cards, tape, and paper, created by the information worker and carried into the controlled environment in the hands of the computer operator or pushed in on a wheeled cart.

The 1970s saw a shift of emphasis and computing power to minicomputers. These scaled-down machines could be located in an office environment for greater convenience and at less cost. Mainframes saw the extension of access to electronic keyboards and monitors, or terminals, on primitive networks. Data were moving closer to the information worker, as well as becoming more available interactively. But the philosophy of central control of a single flow of data prevailed.

The 1980s witnessed the explosion of personal computers (PCs). As these small business machines replaced terminals on the desktop, the thirst for information grew. This shifted computing power to the desktop and fingertips of the information worker. Not only were the data close at hand, often they were put into many different forms to suit the particular needs and likes of the information worker. This increased availability of data and its transformation into information is continuing into the 1990s, which has become the age of client/server computing.

In recent years there has also been a significant interest in the Internet, not only at the personal level, but also at the corporate level. There are expectations that the Internet will support electronic business, and many corporations are now planning to take advantage of these new opportunities. In addition, there is an increasing requirement for the deployment of corporate intranets which will provide the same kinds of WWW-based services to the corporate user with regards to organization-generated information [2].

1.2.3 Definitions

As we continue setting the stage, it is important to share an understanding of some terminology as we are applying it. This common frame of reference provides the foundation for successive material. The word *business* is used often in this chapter. The context or scope in which this word is used should be understood to mean the whole business or company, as in the whole enterprise. This broad context spans all geography and organizational structure.

A precise definition of the term *client/server computing* continues to be a subject of broad debate. A specific definition (we offer one in Chapter 2) is less important than recognizing the opportunities where this concept should be applied, and understanding the implications of applying it. The intent of all computing is to turn data into information. Client/server computing is a particular type of computing that transforms the way information is used in business. A computing architecture is a particular set of computing elements that are arranged and operate in a particular fashion according to a particular set of precepts. Every computing architecture contains a number of underlying technologies and techniques that are combined into an application. Such an application typically automates a business process. Applications are also referred to as information systems. Client/server computing, then, is a technical way to design applications so that they take advantage of graphical desktop computers which are networked with a diversity of other computers housing the information needed at the desktop. The mechanism for getting and using this information is called an *application*. Client/server applications are characterized by the splitting of tasks that make up this application among multiple computers.

Client/server computing is an application implementation technique that is defined as the splitting of application functionality into two or more tasks. These tasks are performed on multiple computers, primarily personal computers or desktop workstations. The computers seeking information are known as *clients*. The computers providing information are known as *servers*. These servers provide information to more than one client. In addition to the client's and server's hardware, software, firmware, and middleware, the underlying technologies in client/server computing also include the *network*, the *database*, and all associated *development and operational tools*.

Client/server computing promises easy access to valuable business-wide information by a broad range of users. When used appropriately, it can provide the *Information Systems (IS) organization with the means to keep pace* with changing business requirements by enabling rapid application development, deployment, and modification. Client/server computing is not just a buzzword, but represents the future of the IS business, and a fundamental process for achieving effective computing in every corporation from today forward. Hence, CIOs, CTOs, CNOs, and other corporate technology planners will find this book of value.

Information systems applications can be grouped into two families or types. The first is decision support or executive information analysis applications. These tend to have unique aspects particular to each business, and therefore require more customization for each business. Client/server applications for this type are likely to be unique for each business, and even unique from one department to the next within the business. The second type is production applications, such as customer service, order entry, and records management. These contain more commonality from business to business. Common solutions for many businesses can even be bought off-the-shelf, already shrink-wrapped. Many specialty systems houses are highly experienced at building this type of application with client/server technologies, and are available as outsourcers. Client/server technology will also be important in intranets.

1.2.4 Related computing initiatives

There are forms and flavors of initiatives in IS that relate to client/server computing. Common definitions of many overlap with, and complement that of, client/server computing. *Down-sizing* is the term typically applied when IS applications are being scaled down in terms of the computer used to run them. The point of reference or perspective is the old environment. Generally, the term also implies migration away from proprietary systems and into open systems, such as UNIX, Windows, or NT. For example, this term is generally applied when one is evolving from a mainframe environment to "smaller" computing platforms. The benefits of this include cost savings for some software packages: for those with both mainframe and PC versions, the latter are cheaper, especially over time when the former are leased.

Right-sizing carries the connotation of sizing applications appropriately to the size of the computers on which they run. The point of reference or perspective is the new environment. The objective is efficiency. *Distributed computing* has perhaps the longest list of interpretations. This term has even been applied to the desktop or office computing environment, prevalently known as *end-user computing*. The term *distributed systems* is also applied by those who have evolved from mainframe environments: computers once kept in the backroom or glass house are now distributed to desktops in offices. It is interesting to observe the evolution of terminology associated with the evolution of technology.

1.2.5 Enabling technologies

Key elements in implementing a successful client/server computing solution need attention before embarking on the journey, because they are enablers. All of the elements discussed here are the raw materials used in the construction of client/server solutions. Principal key factors enabling rapid proliferation of the client/server phenomenon are the growth of raw computing power on the desktop, the advances of network and communication technologies, and the growth of relational databases. Separately, any one of these would not have been sufficient to trigger significant reaction, but in combination, they represent a powerful catalyst for significant change.

Many people needing to understand and use enabling technologies are ill-prepared to do so. This condition can seriously inhibit successful client/server implementations. Further insights into the most important implementations are provided in the following sections. After discovering the variety of technological elements and forces that are the foundation of client/server computing, it will become increasingly evident to the planner that the key to successful business implementations is integration.

Standards are evolving and change is occurring at an accelerating rate. Those who get going now will be the ones able to take significant steps forward toward changing culture and preparing for the future. Those who take as many cost-justifiable steps as possible today will be in the best position later for new technologies entering the marketplace, ie., intranets.

Enabling technologies span the application development side of client/server as well as the communications side. This is one of the motivations for looking at ATM, as it provides a likely platform for broadband support of traditional and evolving (e.g., intranet) client/server applications.

Open systems Open systems provide flexibility and transparency, and can save the organization money. Applications can be made portable across computing platforms, lowering the barriers between technologies. Open systems and databases provide the foundation for meeting business requirements for faster, more responsive, and less expensive information systems. Open systems approaches enable interoperability among products from multiple providers. Technologies rooted in open systems facilitate rapid information technology innovation and introduction to the marketplace. Increases in performance and processing speed are achievable in enterprise-wide networks which are based on open systems and distributed processing.

Open systems integrate diversity and heterogeneity. *Integration* means interoperability: any piece works together interchangeably, in a "plug and play" fashion. *Diversity* includes various hardware, operating systems, networks, and databases. *Interoperability* means transparent access to computing resources and information. Competitive advantage can be achieved from new technology that comes along in the future, when today's client/server solutions are quickly adapted to it without a complete retooling of hardware and software. In general, the benefits of open systems include increased interoperability, flexibility, portability, interchangeability, and cost containment.

How and when do all of these characteristics and lofty concepts become real? An example of this reality is when one has distributed the data and applications, the applications work together, and the data are available from any location on the network. The user of the data does not have to know or care about where the data come from, or how they get to where they are needed, or what transformations they go through before appearing in a report or query response. Some of this information might come to the user in Seattle from an IBM mainframe in New York, and more of it might come from a Sybase database on a UNIX server in Atlanta.

Graphical user interface (GUIs)   An important feature of client/server applications intended to be understandable and useful to the user is the human interface, or presentation layer. In simple terms, this human interface refers to its appearance to the person looking at it—the "look"—and the interaction characteristics with that person—the "feel"—or the way the application interacts with the user. A successful human interface is friendly and intuitive. It is easy to use by less computer-sophisticated people. An interface that is visual or graphical rather than textual or character-based is today's typical manifestation of this phenomenon. Pictures are easier and simpler to understand than exclusive use of words. Eventually Virtual Reality (VR) interfaces may become available.

Applications with a GUI often are larger in size, contain more built-in intelligence, and require more powerful computers to run them efficiently. The development tools are plentiful to facilitate the creation of GUI applications. The tools themselves often have a graphical interface, making them simpler to use by the application developer. These tools also provide sets of predefined objects to serve particular functions, easing standardization of appearance and function. On the downside, developers have a learning curve to overcome when developing a GUI application: they must translate the task to be done by the application into the GUI elements.

Using client/server technology is easier and faster with GUIs, resulting in lower training costs and increased productivity. GUIs can help users find files quicker, organize their data better, and move information more efficiently between applications and across networks. The recent explosion of Internet access via browsers such as Mosaic, Netscape, and Explorer is a testimonial to the power of GUIs.

GUIs, however, are not always the right answer. The best example of where a GUI is inappropriate is for high-volume data entry applications. Productivity is decreased if users required to keep their hands on the keyboard extensively must now shift back and forth between the keyboard and a mouse, and move their eyes to and from the screen to see where the cursor is located.

The importance of GUIs is further reinforced by the recent success of the Internet and the WWW. Only the development of what we call Network GUIs (NGUIs) has made that technology accessible to the average user and the average employee. NGUIs are now facilitating the introduction of intranets in the corporate environment.

Relational database management systems   A relational database management system manages the creation, organization, modification, and access to a database. The database is organized and accessed based on relationships between data elements. Structured Query Language (SQL) is a standardized set of rules used to manipulate and access data. Implementations from different vendors vary slightly.

Again, the intent of all computing is to turn data into information. Information is the life-blood of today's business environment. Access to and control of this data, as it is turned into information, is accomplished by employing database management systems. This is often referred to as the data management layer. In a client/server environment, data are often distributed across a variety of computing platforms connected by an enterprise-wide network and through the services of distributed database management systems. These systems, although distributed, must also be integrated and cooperative, meaning that they operate as one in a common model or architecture.

The leading Relational Database Management Systems (RDBMS) include Oracle, Informix, Ingres, and Sybase. In terms of market share, Oracle leads the pack by a large margin, and the others mentioned are neck-and-neck with each other for second in most surveys and by most measures. These vendors have begun to do more than just supply database software. They are going a step further and successfully generating revenue by selling services: professional consulting, training, and software development tools and applications. They are entering the client/server technology integration business. The future plans for all of them include embracing massively-parallel processing to enhance performance, and object-orientation to enhance scalability and transportability across a wide range of server processors and desktops.

Personal computers   Computing power has made phenomenal progress since the introduction of the personal computer. The traditional basic unit of measure for computing power is one million instructions per second, (MIPS). In all computer categories, from mainframes to personal computers, those with greater power, or more MIPS, cost more money. Of significance here is that the introduction of the PC led to an order of magnitude reduction in the cost per MIPS. A few years ago, a mainframe MIPS cost approximately $100,000, and a PC MIPS cost approximately $5,000, or 20 times less. These ratios are now much higher because the cost of PCs has remained at the same relative price while their performance has increased significantly. This price/performance characteristic of PCs has made them an instrumental enabler in the client/server movement, both as a desktop client and as an information server.

Desktop computers come in many flavors and types. The end-user's tool of choice for a desktop computer has a very direct correlation with productivity. With adequate planning, it is possible to allow and accommodate heterogeneity on the desktop. Open systems and the increasing availability of cross-platform tool sets are the key to enabling the integration of any and all preferred desktops into a common environment. A common mistake is to allow the IT department to select and support a single desktop computer. The motivation for this is that it may take the IT application development staff more effort to develop and support two different computers (a PC and a Macintosh, for example). The end-user community buy-in is critical to the success of every client/server computing initiative. The risk of alienating this community can be high if users are forced to change computing platforms.

Distributed processing   In a business, information typically resides in many places. Creating an enterprise system linking these many places enables access to distributed information from any point in the enterprise. In this way, information is available to anyone who needs it, and is authorized to access it from wherever one is in the enterprise. This link consists of networks, computers, and applications joined in a cohesive communications system, where each desktop computer is a person's window into the environment containing the business information needed. Parts of an application can run as separate processes on separate clients and servers that interact across this link using a structured predefined protocol.

Object technology   Object-oriented programming (OOP) techniques represent a more flexible approach to programming that is key to the client/server philosophy. It is a way to construct applications as a collection of code segments or objects that interact with each other. This interface can range from a simple set of parameters to a complex application protocol, such as X.400 or the Object Management Group's Common Object Request Broker Architecture (CORBA). Different interactions can create different results, without changing the object's underlying identity. These interactions between objects take the form of messages that contain requests for services and responses to those requests. Objects constructed as common functions or methods can be stored in libraries and reused in new applications. This feature of reusability is a compelling attraction, since developers do not have to recode the same functionality over and over again. The resulting applications are more flexible and adaptable to change. Future application development can be cheaper, faster and of higher quality.

The power of object-oriented technology for both developers and end-users is realized when they are used in combination with GUIs. It is then possible to achieve real productivity increases and to provide more complex tasks to users in a form that can be understood and performed efficiently. OOP is covered in more details in Chapter 3.

It was inevitable that sharing objects throughout a business would converge with distributed processing initiatives, resulting in distributed object libraries. These two key enabling technologies in client/server computing are merging into one, combining the best characteristics of each. Even the terminology used in each discipline has similar meanings: protocols and interfaces, processes and objects, communications links and messages, and functions and methods. Evolving standards are facilitating client/server applications that are transparently portable and interoperable, and that can be developed in a fraction of the time previously required.

Network infrastructure   Network infrastructure is the basic technological foundation upon which these raw materials can be used to build solutions. The proper network and systems infrastructure is one that allows continual innovation in a controlled and affordable manner. Care must be taken when planning and realizing network infrastructure investments. The best approach is to take a systematic and strategic view. Scrimping and fragmenting may seem affordable and expeditious up front, but beware in the future when patching and reconstructing becomes necessary. Above all, do not base purchases exclusively on initial cost. The longer term cost of ownership and the cost of making it all work together as future changes are introduced will likely be more expensive than the initial savings.

Networks should be viewed as long-term strategic business investments. In every client/server computing architecture, the network ties all the other parts together. An enterprise network based on open architectures is a prerequisite for any client/server computing initiative. This book places emphasis on broadband support networks, as discussed in Sections 2 and 3.

Client/server enterprise activities (data transfers) take place both across Wide Area Networks (WANs) and Local Area Networks (LANs). Just looking at LANs, one notices that after a decade of relative stability at the fundamental platform level, LAN technology is now seeing burgeoning activity in several radically new directions. In addition to traditional technologies such as Ethernet, token ring, and Fiber Distributed Data Interface (FDDI), systems now reaching the market include the switched 10-Mbps

Ethernet, switched token ring, full-duplex Ethernet, 100-Mbps Ethernet, switched 100-Mbps Ethernet, ATM-based LANs at various speeds, virtual LANs, and (ATM) emulated LANs. Other proposed technology includes IsoEnet (IEEE 802.9), FDDI II, and Fibre Channel Standard (FCS). Corporate network planners are bewildered by the array of choices, as well as by the complexity of the new solutions, particularly internet-working. Ultimately, tens of billions of dollars are at stake within the North American corporate world, and millions of dollars within specific organizations. This textbook examines many of the recent LAN activities at the technical level, particularly in regards to ATM-based LANs, including LAN emulation, as this applies to client/server support. WAN technologies will also be discussed.

Internet/intranet technologies*   A few years ago, most networks were independent entities, established to serve the needs of a single group, whether in an intraenterprise or interenterprise environment. Users chose hardware technologies appropriate to their communication problems. In the past couple of decades, a technology has evolved that makes it possible to interconnect many disparate physical networks and make them function as a coordinated system. This technology, called *internetworking technology*, accommodates diverse underlying hardware by providing a set of communication mechanisms based on common conventions. The internetworking technology hides the details of network hardware and permits computers to communicate independent of their physical network connections.

An *internet* consists of a set of connected networks that act as an integrated whole. The chief advantage of an internet is that it provides universal interconnections, while allowing individual groups to use whatever network hardware is best suited to their needs. The trend, as we enter the first decade of the new century, is toward ubiquitous connectivity.

There is a large internet *par excellence*. This is the *Internet*. The Internet, with a capital *I,* is a massive world-wide network connecting a plethora of subnetworks and computing/information resources located on these subnetworks, including devices such as computers, servers, and directories. As a network of networks, it provides the capability for communication between research institutions, government agencies, businesses, educational institutions, and individuals. It is an effective, open and inexpensive inter-enterprise network. It is estimated that over 20 million users a day in 90 countries access the Internet.

A complex system of interlinked networks, the Internet includes millions of *server* computers, housing large volumes of all sorts of information. From 4 million *host*

---

* This section is based on [2].

computers around the world at press time, the Internet is expected to grow to more than 100 million systems in five years. The latest breakthrough began in 1993 with the creation of an Internet subnetwork called the WWW—really just a software apparatus for imposing order over the mass of freeform information on the Internet by organizing it in easily understood *pages*. What makes the Web such a powerful tool is a software technique known as *hyperlinking*. When composing a web page, an author can create hyperlinks—words that appear in bold type and indicate a path to some other information. Using a program known as web browser on a PC or workstation, one can read pages stored on any Web computer.

This type of intuitive access did not occur overnight. Internet development and deployment began in the late 1960s or early 1970s under the auspices of the US Department of Defense (DOD) as a means to connect government agencies with research companies, contractors, and academic institutions. In the recent past, the Internet was used mainly by nonprofit entities for research and development. More recently, the Internet has experienced significant growth as corporations, home users, and nongovernment academic and research entities have gained access, as a result of its commertialization.

There are a variety of ways for individuals, companies, or institutions to connect to the Internet. Large organizations usually connect by means of direct dedicated high-speed connections to give their users high bandwidth networking capabilities. Home users typically connect by means of telephone line and a modem. Users use the Internet to search for all types of information, including images, graphics, and sound and movie clips, in an ever growing number of remote host computers. When users retrieve and distribute this information to others, network activity becomes highly intensive in terms of file transfer times and traffic volume, especially when one considers how large multimedia files are even when they have been compressed. This is now fueling the upgrade of the Internet to wideband and broadband access and backbone facilities.

Interestingly, nobody *owns* the Internet or controls centrally what happens on the Internet. The networks within different countries are funded and managed according to local policies. The Internet allows any endsystem that is equipped with a minimal set of communication capabilities to connect to a large pool of information. Many details of the network hardware are hidden from the user. The physical connection to the network only mostly controls the speed of access. The specifications of the Internet technology are publicly available, allowing anyone to develop the software needed to communicate over the Internet.

As described earlier, Internet-based technology has now migrated to what are called *intranets*. These networks are corporate networks, basically portions of or overlays to traditional enterprise networks, which use the same lower layer and application level protocols as the Internet, specifically WWW-related technology. Companies are deploying intranet technology in increasing numbers. For example, Federal Express already has 60 internal Web sites, mostly created for and by employees. The company is equipping its 30,000 office employees around the world with Web browsers so they will have access to a plethora of new sites being set up inside the company headquarters. Corporations are seizing the Web as a swift way to streamline and transform their organizations. These private intranets use the structure and standards of the Internet and the WWW, but are separated from the public Internet by *firewalls*. This way, employees can access the Internet, but unauthorized users cannot come into the corporate intranet. The intranet Web is an inexpensive, yet very effective alternative to other forms of internal communications, in that is provides the mechanism to eliminate paper while increasing accessibility to information. Examples of applications of intranet-based information include internal telephone books, procedure manuals, training materials, requisition forms. All of this information can be converted to electronic form on the Web and updated in a low-cost manner. To prepare for a meeting, an executive could tap into the finance department home page, which has hyperlinks to information such as revenues, forecasts, etc. Employees can order supplies from an electronic catalog maintained by the purchasing department.

Most companies already have the foundation for an intranet—a network that uses the Internet set of networking and transport protocols. Computers using Web-server software store and manage documents built on the Web's HyperText Markup Language (HTML) format. With a Web browser on the user's PC, the user can call up any Web document, no matter what kind of computer it is on. Firewalls are another element that may already be in place. Intranets allow the presentation of information in the same format to every computer. It is a single system of universal reach.

Many client/server systems that will be deployed in the future will be in support of intranets. ATM will play a significant role in these intranets.

1.3 Market motivations and trends

This section provides some corporate statistics and trends regarding the proliferation of client/server computing and surveys some of the principal methodologies. Motivations for client/server computing discussed include the demand for immediate access to distributed information, the existence of overloaded IT organizations, demands to cut costs, the requirement to cut system development and implementation cycle times, and the desire to achieve computing economies of scale.

Industry surveys regularly cite results indicating that the majority of businesses are involved in some form or stage of client/server computing. Many survey respondents report doing this despite their feelings that tool technology is still not state of the art, and despite insufficient funding for the total life-cycle costs, including system management and support.

1.3.1 Motivations

Adopters of client/server methodologies and implementors of solutions are motivated to do so for a variety of reasons. In general, businesses today face increased competition, global influence and demand, pressure for more responsive customer service, pressure to bring products to market more quickly, and the need to provide faster access to increasing amounts of information in a growing variety of ways.

Specific benefits motivating the move to client/server include improved user productivity, improved programmer productivity, operational, and business decision-making improvements. Likewise, they do it for better access to information across the enterprise and to offset growing costs to support legacy systems. These legacy systems tend to be heavily customized, and therefore increasingly costly to maintain. The large majority of adopters are not out to completely dispose of legacy systems, but rather augment them with client/server implementations. In fact, they may be faced with a capacity problem on the mainframe and have chosen to move into client/server computing rather than face a multimillion dollar mainframe upgrade.*

A goal for using new client/server technologies is to gain competitive advantage for the business. Companies know they need to respond faster to market opportunities and to customer needs. Today's highly competitive business climate is driving many companies into client/server computing even if they are not ready. They cannot afford the luxury of an orderly, methodical migration. Applying new client/server technology can be a competitive weapon, or it can be a waste of resources if not done properly.

Productivity comes from getting the ultimate user to operate the application for information access. This eliminates the middlemen—other people and paperwork in the traditional chain of information access. It improves the company's ability to communicate and exchange data. It also instigates and facilitates resourcefulness on the part of end-users. They can shape their own reports and customize the interface they use. By participating in the development process, end-users can actually change the way their jobs are performed; in short, they can reengineer their own jobs. With prior

---

* In some cases the mainframe has become the server in the client/server environment, or the Web server in the intranet.

systems, they typically relied on "backroom" IS staff to run reports overnight or the next day. This improves customer service and improves the user's decision making process. These gains are made possible principally because of GUIs and user response times. Successful solutions depend on providing both in appropriate forms. Fast-prototyping software toolkits have also become available to further expedite this transition.

The computer trade press is often full of examples of client productivity improvements due to client/server computing. Depending on the type of processing involved, jobs that took two to three hours on a mainframe now take less than a minute on an engineering workstation. Three- to five-minute mainframe tasks now take several seconds. These are some easily measurable examples of productivity improvement. It is important to measure levels of productivity in areas affected by client/server computing both before the development effort starts and after the new application is in place.

Client/server computing is motivated by the desire to cut IT costs and reduce application development cycle times. Identified often as a less important objective is the desire to improve the efficiency of the application development staff. Although many view this as a secondary objective, keeping it in mind throughout the process will only enhance the outcome. Programmer productivity comes from the personal tools available. Speed and flexibility are achievable with the right integrated tool sets. Quick and efficient reaction to changing demands and market are possible and desired by many businesses.

Operational improvement brings competitive advantage. Proprietary systems, typically mainframe-based ones, limit efforts to move forward in a growing business. Many are overburdened by rising demands placed on them, their inflexibility, and the rising costs to operate and maintain them.

Cost displacement and avoidance are also achievable with client/server systems. Typical drivers include such things as reduced service bureau charges, mainframe costs and software/hardware maintenance and upgrade costs. The enabler here is price-performing PC microprocessor technology. When one can run an application on a computer that costs $150 per MIPS rather than on a computer that costs $15,000 per MIPS, it is not hard to build a business case around cost savings.

There are many value-added benefits available as a result of platform specialization in client/server technology. Having different types of platforms available that interoperate in standard ways provides a robust list of options for customizing the exact solutions needed to meet diverse requirements. The wide range of technology providers must meet competitive pressures to integrate with others, for their products to survive in the marketplace. Each must plug and play well with the technology of other vendors or they will not survive. This environment further promotes the availability of prepackaged applications to entice organizations away from the need to write their own. Buying, rather than building, can put a business ahead of those continuing to build.

Then there is the strategic imperative for every business organization to reinvent itself. Open, integrated and networked client/server solutions facilitate open, integrated and networked organizations that are quicker on their feet and able to compete in the new dynamic, volatile, and competitive business environment. Success and survival depend on reinvention and the ability to extend a computer systems to include customers, suppliers, and even competitors. This is achievable in client/server environments using open and interoperable technologies.

A situation very common to manufacturers is their process of building products based on marketing forecasts. The sales force then bases its delivery time commitments to customers on these same forecasts. In practice, these forecasts are typically either lucky or lousy, and the factory may or may not be able to meet committed delivery dates. There probably is no way to use actual sales orders to drive the manufacturing process. Their Material Requirements Planning (MRP) system running on a central mainframe is expensive, and ineffective at getting order data to the factories where those data are really needed. Motivated to improve this business process and save money at the same time, some have chosen to do away with their mainframe MRP systems and convert to a client/server solution.

1.3.2 Market trends

"Everybody is doing it," or says he will shortly. The aggressive movement to client/server computing is widespread, spanning all business segments and company sizes, all over the world. Hence, the desire of this book to describe how to do it over ATM.

Early implementors of client/server solutions were supplementing their existing computing environment. They were protecting prior computing investments. During the early 1990s, it became clear that adopters shifted their focus toward replacing prior investments, rather than supplementing them. This second stage of client/server computing signals an important shift in confidence, willingness to take risks, and maturity of the enabling technologies. Computing models and business models are changing, as they need to, in order to create the right climatic conditions for successful client/server solutions.

A variety of studies, interviews, articles, surveys, and anecdotal data suggest that upwards of 45% of corporations with mainframes will replace mainframe applications with client/server in the next few years. Most of these will use packaged solutions, rather than grow their own. Some report over 50% of businesses surveyed have already developed new applications on downsized, distributed systems, or have moved applications from proprietary computers like mainframes to smaller open systems. The process is not easy, but does entail rewards.

Many recent surveys point to the growing percentage of businesses responding that they are running client/server applications. The percentage is now over 50% and moving rapidly toward 60%. Those that are getting into it also report that their funding is growing.

The most common client/server solutions being selected for implementation are to improve customer service, to expand existing product lines, to support the development of new products, and to assist with business process reengineering efforts.

1.3.3 Obstacles and challenges

Planners will be alert for a number of obstacles and challenges. These range from unpleasant surprises to major problems. Be aware of them and prepare for dealing with them. Underestimating the costs of technology, both that which is specific to client/server application development and that which is for the requisite infrastructure, is a common mistake. Another dimension of this cost is the number of personnel needed to implement and support developed applications and infrastructure. Think of costs in terms of the systematic holistic life cycle. Oftentimes, budget restrictions can influence how much money is available, and in turn how much of the project plans can actually be implemented. More details on the cost implications of client/server computing can be found in the next section.

Obstacles and challenges include lack of expertise; network availability; underperforming and immature application development tools; underhorsepowered servers and workstations; coordinating and integrating products from multiple vendors; systems and network management deficiencies, including making open systems reliable and secure, cost-effective management in multivendor environments; security risks; scheduling blunders; lost and corrupted backups; file system saturation; forgotten promises to users; accounting difficulties; and IT department culture and structure.

End-user training is also critical. The best choice is classroom training; other supplementary offerings include training on demand using CD-ROM, computer-based training (CBT), interactive video, and videocassette. Delivery of quality application code is a significant challenge. Training and practice within the developer staff are important elements to overcoming it.

1.4 Financials impact

This section explores the financial aspects and considerations of client/server computing. Cost/benefit factors and methodologies are explored. The importance of business case justification is discussed. Examples of corporate experiences are used as illustrations. Some implementations end up being more expensive and others result in cost savings. There are many perceptions of the cost implications of client/server computing. Most are real, and some are accurate.

1.4.1 Financial realities

Eliminating a mainframe may reduce hardware costs by as much as 50% or more. In reality, this savings is offset by the costs of setting up and running a client/server environment. The hardware costs a lot less, but PCs and client/server networks cost more in labor than mainframes. Do not overlook this fact, and choose candidate implementations in areas that will provide the highest return on investment.

In the earlier days of client/server computing, the cost of the mainframe was a clear factor in deciding on a client/server alternative. The mainframes were priced so much higher. But now these prices are generally half of what they were, making this much less of a distinction, if not wiping out this advantage completely. This makes it even more important to look at a much wider view of total system costs, including all aspects of interrelated technology and the people involved. Then a proper analysis can be made to determine any cost advantage.

The appeal of client/server solutions is to provide ready access to information anywhere in the enterprise. Recognize that this information takes varied forms with corresponding varied demand for network bandwidth. This demand can come from anywhere in the enterprise. Therefore, network capacity and use can drive network/telecommunications cost up.

As mentioned in the previous section, the IT staff need training and tools for network and system capacity planning. This discipline is well-defined and provisioned in the mainframe environment, but remains rather sketchy and loose in a client/server environment, where the needed tools and techniques are not generally available or understood. This factor will impact support costs.

The cost of training is significant, both for business clients who will be using the new applications, and for the applications developers who will be creating and supporting them. Applications developers also need to be trained in PCs, network architectures and protocols, network and systems management, and prototyping. Training is essential; do not understate it, both in terms of dollars and time needed.

Although processing power on PCs and workstations is considerably cheaper than mainframes, and business applications can be developed much faster for the client/server environment, it is also true that costs are driven in the other direction by much larger support levels and lower reliability levels. Support costs are higher due to a number of factors. One is the sheer number of applications and devices that make up the typical client/server environment. Support people need to be familiar with many more parts, each having quirks of its own, their interactions and relationships with each other and with the various ways they may be customized or tweaked for each department.

Another important support cost factor is the increased numbers of support people needed because the applications and their clients are distributed throughout an enterprise. Support people get dispersed to all corners of a business. Centralized support specialists cannot provide all of the coverage and talent needed.

Lower client/server system reliability levels decrease the availability of the applications and the productivity of the people relying on them. All of this increases the cost of client/server computing to the business. But there are trends in the industry working feverishly toward reducing this cost challenge. Improvements in system management tools are increasing client/server system reliability and narrowing this cost difference. Similar improvements in network management tools and their convergence with systems management tools are enabling more efficient problem solving, and in turn lower support costs.

Some of the more readily identified costs associated with client/server computing include the necessary hardware and software, training and wiring. But these technology costs add up to only about 25% of the total costs. A much bigger fraction is labor costs, both for IS department people and for client department people. This labor includes application development, server operations, client support, and client effort to learn and operate their desktop systems. Such labor costs can exceed 70% of total costs. And over time, the unit cost for the technology will drop, while the unit cost of labor will increase. Since the labor component of total cost is so much larger, this means the cost of client/server systems will increase over time, all things being equal. But they never are, and the challenge for the planner is to recognize this reality and take responsibility for introducing efficiency wherever possible. Be sure to teach clients about GUI environments so they are familiar with them and know what to expect. These days almost everyone in the corporation will be using a computer; think in terms of the general user, not the computer-savvy. Identify and teach key clients how to design GUIs—these are the people who will be gathering the requirements and prototyping application functionality. Why focus so much on the GUI? Simply put, the GUI is the application to the client. Focus everyone there, make them good at it, and one gets labor efficiency, and in turn, lower total costs. On the flip side, however, also concentrate on the data needed to run the business, not just the form of the data when presented to the user.

One of the classical dilemmas facing businesses considering moving to client/server computing is also tightly coupled to training and cost. The dilemma is whether to retrain technical staffs or to hire new blood. Of course, this does not have to be an either/or decision. Most often, positions are adopted at many points along the continuum joining these two extremes. There are many important considerations in choosing a strategy appropriate for the planner.

1.4.2 Life-cycle costs

Many businesses are proceeding with client/server computing initiatives without sufficient funding for the total life-cycle costs. There are two major components of life-cycle costs. One is the development and initial implementation phase. The other is the ongoing support or sustaining phase. The lack of funding for total life-cycle costs is due to two principal factors. One is executive management reluctance. The other is the IT management inability to identify and quantify them accurately up front. In any case, most seem to be doing OK by handling or burying the costs at the business department level in the clients' budgets, rather than in the IT budget. This practice can have significant impact on the CIO when the CFO consolidates all of these individual business unit line items into one item for the executives. The CIO may not have been responsible for this phenomenon, but still may be held accountable. The fallout from this could be career-threatening.

As experience with client/server systems development and implementation mature, we are developing a clearer understanding of cost components, in terms of both advantages and disadvantages of client/server computing. For the development and initial implementation phase, the cost of acquiring and installing PC hardware and networks is less than for mainframes. This is primarily due to mass marketed parts and pieces. This provides a cheaper development platform with faster development cycle times. Observed results during the sustaining phase are different. Client/server systems are not as cost-effective as mainframes in terms of support, training, and manageability. These are recognized deficiencies. We are beginning to see tools emerging to address this. For now, these costs are higher, and less hidden and unplanned than in the recent past. The financial impact of these deficiencies also decreases further into the sustaining phase, as experience in support and application usage grows, and training efforts pay off.

1.4.3 Savings opportunities

Just as there are a number of unanticipated factors driving costs up, there are a number of opportunities and factors that can reduce the costs of client/server computing.

Many people in client departments have already been using desktop computers for a number of years and are familiar with PC applications, like word processors and spreadsheets. Rather than universally develop new applications with custom (GUI or otherwise) human interfaces, why not leverage that familiarity by taking advantage of suitable development tools to implement that human interface with the look and feel of a spreadsheet or word processor? This could result in more productive and satisfied users, improving the return on investment and in turn reducing the cost to the business.

Build everything in the development arena with an eye toward reusability and flexibility. Do everything with chosen standards, from programming interfaces to development tool sets. Thus, one programmer can easily understand the work of another and reuse elements of previous applications. This reduces the maintenance burden and speeds new development work, reducing the cost of client/server computing to the business. Standards are critical to the entire enterprise/intranet environment, from browsers, to languages (e.g., HTML), to communications (e.g., HTTP and TCP/IP), to communication "wires" (e.g., LANs, services, etc.).

1.5 Communications architectures

This section explores a variety of principal architectures upon which client/server computing depends. Network and infrastructure implications and preparations must be in place. Network architectures and standards are critical to a successful deployment of a client/server system that meets expected performance levels. This section also explores wide area network and remote network access considerations.

A network computer environment is essential for client/server computing. It is a key element of every information technology infrastructure. Since the network is such an integral part of every client/server architecture, it is essential for every developer to have a much greater understanding of network technologies and issues than was required in the past. This knowledge will be used in the screening and decision-making process for application development tools and databases.

1.5.1 Infrastructure

Network computing requires the building of an infrastructure that will support cooperative client/server computing throughout a business. This enterprise network is a managed facility formed by tying together desktop computers and servers, including any mainframes, with networking technology. Those who rely on a network or networks that have been patched together rather than systematically designed will find that their business needs cannot be met, and that their networks are difficult to modify and expensive to maintain.

High capacity networks are required for both the LAN and WAN segment of the enterprise networks. Increasingly, one will see ATM being deployed in the corporation. Network infrastructure can be constructed as a departmental entity in scope, and as a company-wide entity. For an effective business-wide client/server environment, an enterprise network infrastructure is needed. This infrastructure can be made up of a variety of network technologies. Local data link facilities can include Ethernet, switched Ethernet, fast Ethernet, token ring, FDDI, and ATM LANs. Longer distances over the wide area are linked using facilities such as private lines, packet switching, cell switching, and dial-up lines obtained from communications common carriers. Other important devices used to create a network include hubs, bridges, routers, firewalls, multiplexers, modems, and gateways. Actual communications on all of this gear is achieved with a variety of available transport protocols used between programs or applications. Network infrastructure also includes cabling and wiring necessary to tie all of these parts together. The materials used include fiber optic and copper. Each client and server computer needs a network interface card to attach to a network.

Building the requisite network infrastructure causes a cost spike up front. The network and services can be expensive, depending on what may already be in place when one starts. In every case, involve the network planning people in the process of planning any client/server solution. Applications plans should not be allowed to jeopardize the integrity or performance of the network. An increase in network traffic is a certainty, especially when data and processing are distributed across the network. Work together to minimize the traffic and load, and to size and provide sufficient infrastructure capacity ahead of time; working in isolation will almost guarantee problems later. On a mainframe one 9.6-kbps line once supported 100 users; now one user needs, or wants, 100 Mbps, or perhaps 10 Mbps.

The performance of a client/server solution on the network is impacted by many factors, including how an application is distributed. As an example, consider the transaction-oriented situation where response time is critical. Distributing application processing code to local servers can improve performance. These local servers can better process large amounts of data locally and send out the results, rather than sending all data across the network for central processing.

1.5.2 Network operating systems

A network operating system (NOS) is a multiuser system that provides network access and communication services, and manages network resource access and sharing, primarily for files and printers.

The role of the NOS in corporations is changing, due in large part to the new business emphasis on client/server computing. Client/server applications sprouting up around the network on application servers need to be as accessible as file and print sharing services, the standard fare of all NOSs. But the future need for NOSs may not be assured, as desktop operating system vendors move further down the continuum of providing networking as part of their core operating systems. The trend is toward transparent, location-independent, universal desktop communications. Ultimately, there may be no need for a NOS.

Novell's NetWare, Microsoft's LAN Manager, and Banyan's Vines are examples. The ideal would be to build client/server applications that are transparent to NOS. It would be unwise in the long run to build any with dependencies. The goal of open systems computing is, after all, to be able to swap around among these environments without impact on the planner's applications.

1.5.3 Network management

Managing all of the elements making up a client/server environment is one of the principal challenges facing businesses that are implementing client/server solutions. This is mainly due to the fact that there are a variety of products and vendors involved. There are a variety of tools available, but not all of the most likely ones needed work together seamlessly yet. Nor does any one include all of the needed functions. The challenge is much more significant than was the case in a traditional mainframe hierarchical network environment. Although the job is difficult, it can be done. With the help of standards and more open implementations of these products, integration and effective management is getting closer. SNMP (Simple Network Management Protocol) and CMIP (Common Management Information Protocol) are the standards, with SNMP having a wider presence and a solid industry backing.

1.5.4 Systems management

The management of distributed systems in client/server environments is more and more dependent on and interrelated with network management. As the network moves closer and closer to being "the system," this is not a surprise. The two will become one as the various elements become integrated. If there is an Achilles heel in client/server computing, it is systems management. Like network management, it is possible to knit together a patchwork of products to do the job. Eventually, standards, vendors, and products can be selected to construct a systems management architecture to compete with those available for mainframes. Systems management services will emerge as objects that can be distributed so they can communicate across the network and accomplish their mission. CORBA may play a big role here.*

The objective of systems management is to control and synchronize the operating systems and applications residing on network devices distributed around the entire geography of an enterprise. The categories of functions that need to be performed include software management (distribution and licensing), storage management (file systems, backup, recovery, and database administration), configuration management (authentication, authorization, ID/password, and change control), and operations management (events, problems, printing, scheduling, performance, capacity, and accounting).

There are a variety of products available in every category. Until standards and well-integrated products emerge, the best guidance is to select as few as possible to do as much as possible in concert with other elements in one's client/server strategy. Choose a mix that provides a balance of centralized and distributed (i.e., delegateable) controls, since completely centralizing all aspects of systems management will be totally ineffective in the typical business.

Performance management's aim is to enable the tracking and tuning of the behavior of computer systems. The object is to measure operating efficiency. The majority of the systems management tools available in the first wave of product offerings were geared toward administrative tasks, such as job scheduling, printer management, and backup services. None were geared toward detailed performance data gathering across multiple systems for central presentation and analysis. Providers of this type of functionality for mainframe environments have begun to make the transitions to client/server product offerings. These companies include Candle Corp., Legent Corp., IBM, Digital Equipment, and BGS Systems. Comprehensive performance management environments are beginning to emerge from the likes of IBM, Hewlett-Packard, and Tivoli Systems. These companies are working toward providing client/server products that meet the prevalent market attitude and expectation that functionality will match or exceed the capabilities taken for granted in the mainframe environment.

_____

* OSF's Distributed Management Environment (DME) seems to have fallen away.

The bulk of these products are real time server-based tools that track operating system response times, CPU cycle times, I/O activity, memory and disk use, application and database efficiency, and many other measures of performance for single and multiple systems. Many offer event notification and the ability to automatically respond with correction, notification or adjustment actions. For example, they might send email messages, initiate a pager call, or generate a UNIX file that triggers other actions, such as backing up files to free up disk space. Performance tools also allow interval sampling for off-line monitoring and analysis of trends and capacity over time. Some offer simulation and modeling capabilities. By mixing and matching, they generally will meet most of one's needs and desires. The quality of the information gathered is improving over time.

Needed functions include system monitoring, problem management, software distribution, and performance management. No single product meets all the demands of a multiplatform, multivendor client/server environment. Several offer products that integrate the processes of capturing, filtering, and responding to messages from a variety of platforms.

1.5.5 Impact of application networks on design

There are a number of choices that can be made in the client/server application design process that impact a network. Awareness of them will enable a proper and intelligent balancing of tradeoffs. The choices made regarding where to make the split between client and server functionality can impact the network bandwidth requirement and satisfactory application performance significantly.

Partitioning all processing functions to servers and only display functions to clients will result in a heavy network traffic load. This design may not tap the significant processing power of today's client computers. The database replication technique employed in a distributed database environment can impact network load in a variety of ways, depending on how often and how much information is communicated: the whole database or only changes, and only when changes occur or at scheduled intervals. In distributed object computing applications, requiring clients to continually ask servers for objects will result in heavy message traffic on the network. It is much more efficient to request clusters of objects in a single message. Further, distributing objects on servers around a network likewise spreads the messaging traffic.

With ATM being increasingly deployed for both LAN and WAN applications, planners need to know how to make the best use of this technology to support client/server applications. This critical question will be addressed in Part 3 of this book.

1.6 Technical foundation

This section describes the important principles, methodologies, tools, hardware and software products that provide the foundation for successful client/server computing. This includes development aids and environments, porting and cross-platform development, object-oriented technologies, distributed databases, intelligent processes across multiple computers, partitioning processes, synchronizing by replication at regular intervals—daily for time-critical data (financial, etc.). The foundation needed for network and remote data access, and data security is explored.

Is client/server computing ready for "prime time"? The state of the technology is certainly mature enough to implement fully effective solutions. There are many families of automated development environments and tools available from a wide assortment of vendors to help one do the job, whatever the complexity, budget, or time frame. One can select from several more sophisticated and better integrated families of technology products to help ensure success. A few examples are provided here to illustrate. We discuss a small sampling of products that is not intended to be comprehensive. Some general guidelines to apply in the selection process include looking for products that are scalable, flexible, portable, and maintainable. Look for the ability to prototype the human interface for the application in a short period of time. Then be sure to learn and understand how to use the products. In most cases, applying these new tools effectively further entails using new techniques for application development.

How does one find the right tools to do the job? There are certainly many of them out there. You will probably want to take a look at a number of them. It may be a noble objective to identify a single set to do everything you will need, but reaching that objective might mean you have now bought a hammer, and you will think that every problem is a nail. You will likely need a mix of tool sets to do the jobs you will face. But traditional advice to limit the total numbers and types is still prudent. Be selective; you do not need one of each. You want to be able to leverage knowledge, expertise, and expenditure across multiple projects.

Once you have a bunch of these new tools in hand, how well will they work together? They may work very well individually, but not work in combination with one or more of the others that one is depending on. In general, standards bodies and tool providers are aligning with two approaches to integrating development tools. One is integration at the data level, where design information can be shared among tools. This sharing can be by two-way interface, file transfer, or on multiple linked distributed repositories. The other approach is integration at the control level, where tools are connected and communicate in an integrated development environment by passing messages back and forth.

1.6.1 Observations on sample tool providers

Specification repositories are a common feature of application development tool sets. These provide shared storage for definitions of the nature of controls, events, and actions. Once in place and shared, these elements are reusable, decreasing the cost of the next development effort. For this reason, it is important to build quality into them at the beginning, so it is propagated later.

Some tool vendors provide development tools that are geared for use by clients not requiring the help of Information Technology professionals. This introduces some interesting implications and responsibilities for both the client organization and the IT organization. The significant observation here is that clients want this capability for development speed, flexibility, and ease to accommodate future change. Some vendors are able to satisfy this need with easy-to-use tools.

The latest available tools are higher level. There is a diminishing and disappearing need to learn how to program in third generation languages like C++ or Pascal, or how to use visual development environments like Microsoft Visual Basic. More and more toolsets provide a lot of visual objects, removing the requirement to write a lot of code.

Having all of the answers on which tools to use is perhaps less critical than having the right people available and trained, and defining the development methodology they will use.

Using GUI development tools for SQL front ends has advantages over doing the same work and dealing with the programming complexities of the Microsoft Windows Software Development Kit. Screens, menus, and dialog boxes can be completed in a matter of hours rather than weeks. Application interface code is isolated from the application's functionality code, simplifying future support and enhancements. It is often easier for programmers of other languages, such as FORTRAN and Cobol, to learn a GUI tool's language than to learn C from scratch. However, the applications produced with GUI tools may not be as quick to run as specific and optimized C code.

1.6.2 Product overviews

This section lists some of the tools available. These are discussed here only to document desirable features and capabilities. (This discussion is not meant to recommend any products or to attempt to provide an up-to-the minute review of release features.)

Powersoft Corp.'s PowerBuilder is a GUI builder with good data dictionary and report creation tools. It appeals to the generalist, visual-oriented programmer having a good handle on the big picture. It comes with a variety of object-oriented programming tools. To enhance team development, it provides module check in/out and supports direct links with third-party version control systems. It is used mostly for developing department-level applications. Powersoft scheduled the release of capabilities to directly access information from PC databases such as dBase, FoxPro, Paradox, and Access. By directly linking PC databases with SQL databases, such tools and capabilities further promote access to business information transparently wherever it resides, provides a migration path for PC databases and any applications developed to access them, and avoids the need for indirect access through ODBC or EDA/SQL gateways.

Gupta Technology Corp.'s SQL Windows family of products appeals to the bit-twiddling, get-into-the-details programmer who likes dealing with complexities and does not mind writing more code. To enhance team development, it provides a project management environment complete with standards enforcement, version control, and repository-managed templates.

Intersolv's APS for Client/Server is a GUI front-end builder. Another product is its Object-Oriented Analysis and Design tool for Excelerator II, which works with APS for Client/Server. This tool provides a repository of reusable information and designs that can be shared across a network of developers. Excelerator can also be interfaced with PowerBuilder and SQL Windows. Its PVCS is useful as a software version and configuration management tool.

PeopleSoft has concentrated on providing client/server solutions for the human resources and finance communities. Its first offering was the Human Resource Management System (HRMS) which appeared in 1988, the pioneer days of client/server computing. Its second product, Financials, was introduced in 1993. A third product, Distribution, integrates order processing, billing, inventory, and purchasing functions for materials management and distribution. Future vertical market plans are aimed at higher education, health care and government. Based on its PeopleTools development environment, the application architecture supports Microsoft Windows clients accessing PC, UNIX and mainframe servers, and databases from Oracle, Sybase, Microsoft, Gupta, Hewlett-Packard, IBM, and Digital. A new core technology called Open Workflow adds the productivity and intelligent routing capabilities needed to automate business processes and enable enterprisewide communication of information.

Unify's VISION is a development tool with a graphical interface that provides functions for forms design, database access, and GUI application development and testing. It provides for development across most popular environments, including UNIX, Microsoft Windows, Windows NT, and Macintosh. With VISION, it is possible to access multiple PC, server, and mainframe databases simultaneously, including dBase, DB2, Oracle, Informix, Sybase, and Ingres. Unify's technology allows the planner to develop the application anywhere and run it everywhere, purporting to be the ultimate development tool set for portable applications. The scope includes character-based and graphical tools.

KnowledgeWare Inc.'s ObjectView creates applications in a Windows environment that access multiple databases. Its Flashpoint product simplifies the development of GUIs for legacy mainframe applications.

IBM provides the POWERbench family of AIX-flavor software development tools. The list of tools includes a language-sensitive color program editor, a program debugger, a static analyzer, a desktop file manager and tool manager, a program builder, a development manager, language-specific libraries, a help utility, and tutorials. A GUI integrates all of these tools. This family comes in three language varieties: C++, FORTRAN and Cobol, all designed for optimal use of its RISC processor architectures. Further, the family includes work group support features like version control, project management, and distributed build facilities.

1.6.3 Foundation

Hardware providers are driven by market requirements for open, scalable platforms on which to run this new stuff.

1.6.4 Front-ends

The human interface, or presentation, is the application's front-end. It is what the user sees and feels. It is how the user interacts with and uses the application. It is where data are presented, manipulated, and displayed.

1.6.5 Middleware

The term *middleware* in the context of client/server computing is applied to a layer of software that sits between the application and the network, often in both the client environment and in the server environment. This layer provides a common application programming interface, or *API*, for exchanging messages among the various distributed pieces of the application running on client and server nodes. Disparate operating systems, like UNIX, VAX/VMS, CICS, Microsoft Windows and NT, and OS/2, and communications protocols and topologies, like Netbios, Netware, Named Pipes, and TCP/IP, introduce their own individual complexities that developers must accommodate. When these client and server nodes encompass such operating system and protocol diversity, middleware knits them together and shields the developer from having to understand them all. Middleware understands all of these details, and the application developer needs only to understand the intricacies of the API.

Middleware understands the information in the client request received through the front-end components, and performs format translations where needed to make the request comprehensible by the server back-end components. For example, everyone knows that SQL is the relational database "standard." But compliance is not universal nor entirely consistent. Database vendors vary their SQL implementations, and offer unique extensions. The role of middleware in this situation is to understand these differences, and accommodate them for the application developer and the user.

Middleware is important since it provides these connections between applications and diverse databases on back-end servers and mainframes. This is how the needed information flows around, from requestors to providers and back. It provides a common API for accessing information on servers and mainframes. It allows for integration and a single set of interface code. This simplifies application code maintenance.

One of the shortcomings of middleware products currently available is that each has its own API. There is yet no standard defined or agreed to for this interface. This, of course, affects the interchangeability and openness of the client/server solutions created with them. This is recognized and is being dealt with by the industry. A great deal of work has been done in this area. Improvements and conformance with evolving standards are forthcoming from a number of sources.

Microsoft has offered Open Database Connectivity (ODBC) as a standard. This API provides Windows clients with access to diverse databases, including DB2 from IBM, Rdb from Digital and its own SQL Server. Clients with Macintosh computers can participate with Apple Computer's Data Access Language (DAL) linkage to ODBC. Additional third party support for ODBC extends participation.

Some additional functions provided by middleware are transaction management support, security, global naming, version control, and network management. There are many examples of database middleware products available. Some are available from the database vendor (purchased separately, or included with the database), and others are available from third parties.

Oracle's SQL*Net provides an API for accessing any other Oracle environment, and non-Oracle environments through a gateway, using many network protocols. These protocols can be changed without requiring an application code change.

Micro Decisionware's Database Gateway is widely used in PC applications for access to DB2, Sybase, SQL/DS, Teradata, VSAM, IDMS, IMS, and CICS. Various SQL extensions in these products are also supported by Database Gateway (MDI has been acquired by Sybase Inc.).

Information Builder's Enterprise Data Access/SQL has the advantage of integrating non-relational back-ends with a long list of relational products. This is particularly useful for businesses with significant amounts of non-relational data.

Software AG of North America provides Entire Connection to support RPCs. Its Spirit methodology walks those with centralized mainframe processing through to a distributed computing environment.

Lotus Development Corp.'s Notes supports the distribution, location, and management of Object Linking and Embedding (OLE) objects, making them a player in the distributed object and object middleware arena.

Other examples include Data Access Language from Apple Computer, SequeLink from TechGnosis, AccessWorks from Digital Equipment (also a gateway product), and SQL Bridge from Microsoft. Momentum Software Corp. is an example of an up-and-coming player in this area. (They have merged with Horizon Strategies Inc.)

Middleware has become a key ingredient to successfully integrating the diversity of client/server technology. The application and its developers are insulated from the intricacies of platform-specific code, interplatform hardware and operating system inconsistencies, and network protocols. Development efforts are quicker because programmers can focus on programming applications code, not communications code. Middleware implementations improve application portability and facilitate flexible application partitioning. There are three types of middleware: remote procedure calls (RPCs), messaging, and object request brokers (ORBs).

RPCs are a mature technique based on a simplistic synchronous call-return API. Many vendors provide RPC support, as does the Open Software Foundation (OSF)'s Distributed Computing Environment (DCE). Basically, the RPC model is based on subroutine calls, and is therefore familiar to programmers. It is a communications mechanism built using a *sockets* interface that is widely available and accepted across many computing systems, including almost all UNIX systems. While the call is outstanding, the caller is blocked from performing any other logic until the call completes. This can be circumvented by launching other threads or tasks in parallel, with corresponding complexity of setup and management. The RPC technique risks obsolescence if it does not incorporate object technology.

The messaging model for distributed applications has emerged with a great deal of potential. Unlike RPCs, messaging is asynchronous, not depending on any direct connection with another program. Messages are queued out on the network for processing by a service responsible for managing that queue. Complex transactions are frequently broken into multiple messages. The messaging technique is readily adapted for use to connect legacy applications with client/server systems in an integrated fashion.

The Object Management Group's Common ORB Architecture has potential, but must achieve interoperability among its flavors.

Middleware is an important issue that is revisited in Chapter 3.

1.6.6 Back-ends

These are the database engine functions of storing, manipulating and protecting data. This usually occurs on a server. Do not forget that in some cases, this server could be the traditional mainframe.

1.6.7 Object-oriented technology

Object-oriented programming is the process of combining objects to produce a finished software application. Objects, the real work that an application performs, are developed to carry out specific tasks. Objects can be recycled from other applications and upgraded for new functionality. The short-term benefits include flexible systems and rapid application development. The long-term benefits include significant code reuse and reduced maintenance costs.

Object-oriented technology holds the promise of improvement in the speed with which applications can be developed and deployed. Methods based on this technology can enable users to respond quickly to changing business needs by giving them the means to program and enhance their own applications. Object technology is almost pervasive now. The promise of point-and-click logic integration allows quick on-the-spot changes in harmony with changing business needs.

Achieving success with object technology has more to do with the softer side of the process—things like analysis and design discipline, team structure and motivation, and other people issues, rather than object tools, language or methodology. A number of factors need to be addressed. Senior management support and sponsorship is gained by education in concepts and benefits, rather than technical details. The technology is particularly well suited for complex, highly interactive applications, and groups of applications that share common functionality. Development teams should consist of the curious and motivated rather than those with solid, traditional, programming backgrounds. One effective technique for assembling object teams is to allow self nomination. Investment in training of developers is essential, and should cover object concepts, analysis and design, development libraries and frameworks, and object languages. Typically, the learning curve covers four to six months, with true proficiency achievable in a year. Reinforcement is recommended by encouraging more reading and attendance at conferences and seminars. Those becoming the experts should begin training others as soon as possible, to reinforce their learning and to pull others into the process.

Object project teams will see the rise of new and different roles. These roles include a mentor/educator for process guidance, a methodology analyst/designer for modeling and methodology, an object librarian for object libraries and promoting their reuse, an advocate for strict adherence to object rules, an object constructor for building applications, and a specialist for understanding business processes.

1.6.8 Distributed databases

The debate is on going whether to house an application's data completely in one location or to distribute it across multiple locations while maintaining as much location transparency as possible. The context of locations includes multiple computers at the same physical site and at many distant sites, with an interconnecting network. This trend for databases follows that of processing: as information processing gets distributed across networks to servers and desktop computers, the same happens to the databases. It is important to understand and address the issues associated with this, and get comfortable with them. The key issues include data integrity, database synchronization, database management, and network impact.

Users and owners of data need assurances and certification that each copy of their data is not spoiled, but is current and is consistent. One aspect of this issue is illustrated simply as preventing more than one user at different locations from updating the same record at the same time. The solution to this problem is available from database providers in the form of two-phase commit capabilities. Two-phase commit is a transaction process that lets an update occur only when all sites where the database exists acknowledge the change. The process prevents changing one copy of the database if another copy of it is inaccessible due to access failure because of network or computer outage, for example. Instantaneous distributed updates, complete with table locking, roll-back, and recovery mechanisms, can be essential to multiuser time-critical update applications such as airline reservations or banking systems.

Another aspect of this issue is maintaining consistency across multiple copies of a database. Replication is another transaction process that copies the database to all locations instantaneously when changes occur, or at definable regular intervals. The complete database may be copied, or only changed portions. Those databases that communicate only the changes have obvious benefits from the perspectives of time to replicate and network impact. The time taken affects the whole user community. The impact on the network should be considered closely and jointly between application and network staffs. Database providers will work closely with the user to define the proper strategy and methodology for specific situations and requirements.

Once in use, the distributed database and user community need to be administered. Standardized management tools for distributed administration have been scarce, leaving plenty of room for improvement. There are database vendor-specific offerings that one can use to get started. Look for improvements in the near future. Standards will evolve, as is now the case in the network management arena, providing one set of management tools that can be used with database products from different vendors. Who should manage the distributed databases is frequently discussed. One alternative standards trend is to base future management tools on an SNMP specification. Database administration is not quite like network administration. Specialists in these two areas almost never report to the same organizational component. Then there is the issue of where to perform distributed database management—centrally or locally. Real knowledge of the insides of a local database resides locally. The lack of standards-based tools hinders central management. The issue revolves around control of an important corporate asset. Compromises and patience are recommended.

Finally, changes to the distributed database application code need to be managed. Tracking changes is tricky. Third-party tools are beginning to appear. Software distribution tools and processes are needed and should be considered in the total plan for client/server implementations. This topic is revisited in Chapter 3.

1.6.9 Application partitioning

Like the proverbial pie, there are many ways to divide an application and distribute the parts around the enterprise computing resources. Recall that the point of doing this in the first place is to take advantage of distributed computing power that delivers flexibility and economy.

Partitioning in client/server designs can take many forms. One way is to divide an application such that all processing is done on the server and only display functions are performed on the client. This method results in heavy network traffic loads. Another, fairly common, method is to put most of the application logic on the client and rely on remote servers for database services, running SQL transactions between them. Another method, characterized as distributed function or cooperative processing, divides the logic among multiple nodes around the network. When this type of application runs, the parts on the clients and servers interact to accomplish the functions of the application. The interprocess communications used to interact include remote procedure calls, messaging, and object brokering services. Advantages of this method include simplified software distribution and change management if one intelligently places logic likely to change often on servers, and logic less likely to change on clients.

Partitioning allows one to take advantage of computing technology scalability. Server or client computers can be upgraded and added independently for focused performance and capacity improvements. It may not be necessary to upgrade "the whole system" as may have been the case previously with mainframes.

1.7 Implementation strategies

This section describes the attributes of successful client/server implementations. It discusses the leading successful strategies for designing and delivering client/server solutions—departmental versus central development, steps for realigning traditional mainframe applications, identifying strategic business processes, determining cross-organization objectives, identifying opportunities for automating and reautomating processes, application-specific considerations (imaging, etc.), multiplatform integration, planning and project management, methodologies, teamwork and chemistry, project sign-up, transition. It also covers the importance of communicating: vision, participation, needs assessment and continued refinement, buy-in, status, and success stories. Off-the-shelf shrinkware can provide 80% of needed functionality; prototyping is facilitated by available tool features and packaging. Outsourcing development and consequent vendor/alliance relationships and management will also be discussed.

There is no sure-fire single strategy to employ. But there are some proven methods, with an identifiable common thread. The basic successful strategy will contain decisions on infrastructure, pilot projects, training, product evaluations, and linkage to business strategy. It is important to develop all strategies around a critical concept—technology integration. All successful client/server solutions have done a good job of integrating the variety of technologies needed. The result is that the user sees seamless functioning. The more elegant the integration effort, the more seamless the solution. Technology elements interoperate with each other, or work together, fluidly. A good job of integration also implies scalability: not only do the parts work well together, but parts of a different size—larger or smaller—can be substituted over time without upsetting the other parts. All successful solutions are well-integrated solutions.

1.7.1 Getting started

There are several scenarios for getting started, depending upon the current business strategy and installed technology base. You will be able to tell where you are as we lay down some basics. Proven methods all deal effectively with many types of issues—politics, technology, costs, and measurable benefits.

First steps include building the requisite infrastructure. The importance of this was discussed earlier. Train the people who will be the developers in the methodologies and the tools, to prepare them. Training is necessary in a number of areas—network technology and protocols, new application development techniques and methodologies, and distributed system management. Tools training is straightforward. More critical is methodology training. This is not simply a matter of learning a new language; the process of developing new applications for the client/server environment is different. By analogy, a user trained to be adept with a word processor will not necessarily write interesting stories. So too, an application developer trained to be adept with development tools will not necessarily produce good applications. The developer must learn new skills in effective methodologies, or get out of the business. Most developer experience suggests that it takes from six to nine months to train a mainframe-based developer adequately to perform effectively in the client/server environment. For this reason, it is critical to plan adequately for training, and not promise that first application too soon.

Infrastructure and training contribute to the start-up cost spike of client/server computing, but if one does not provide for them, the longer-term costs due to lack of training will be more costly. Buy the tools and enablers. Build a team. Prove the concept. Cost/benefit considerations are important as they help set expectations for success.

The right design can remove the IT organization as a pacing item in the implementation cycle.

Increasingly, successful application development and programming teams are adding a human interface designer at the beginning of the cycle. Applications programmers are tightly focused on new tools and methods, and the flow of screens frequently just gets in the way. Without proper attention to the human interface and flow, the success of the application can be affected. Those who recognize this have started filling the gap on the team with a specialist whose job it is to focus exclusively on this interface, and to work closely with the clients to get it right.

1.7.2 Strategies

A common phenomenon in the migration into client/server computing is to progress through a series of implementation strategies. Where you start in this progression depends on your degree of caution or risk aversion, and your confidence in new technologies and methodologies. The most conservative approach barely borders on something that qualifies as client/server computing, but it is a step in the right direction. This approach ties PC clients to mainframe applications using combinations of terminal emulation and *screen-scraping* application front-ends on the PCs. The mainframe application remains unchanged from its role of merely connecting terminal screens to its information and processing power. The PC's processing power is dedicated to receiving screens of information from the mainframe and sending the equivalent of keyboarded requests and commands. The front-end logic on the PC "scrapes" the needed information from received screens and feeds it to the pseudo-client/server application front-end environment in the PC. This environment can consist of regular PC applications, such as word processors and spreadsheets, or custom-built applications integrating information from multiple mainframe sources into one presentation to the user. This approach means lower risk since it leaves the mainframe applications untouched. This approach was popular in the mid-to-late 1980s, but has, by and large, disappeared.

The next approach involves creating data extracts from the mainframe environment and placing these extracts on servers around the network for read-only access by clients. Data updating remains the province of the mainframe. This approach is particularly well suited for decision support applications.

Another approach involves moving all of the application logic to client workstations and allowing them to manipulate data stored on departmental relational database servers.

Then there is the distributed application approach, where logic is distributed among networked servers and clients. These processes communicate with one another using RPCs, interprocess communications, or messaging APIs.

If one is currently in a principally-mainframe computing environment and evolving to client/server computing, one is downsizing, probably to a smaller computer. The principal options for downsizing legacy applications to client/server computing include replacing, rewriting, transferring, emulating, converting, and integrating. Buying a new application on a smaller computer to replace the legacy functions can require customization, data conversion and restructuring, and retraining of users and perhaps operators. Rewriting the legacy application for the smaller computer can take a lot of time for requirements definition, design, coding, testing, and installation, and can require data conversion and restructuring, and retraining of users. Moving or transferring the application to the smaller computer is possible with minimal or no code changes if the application vendor offers this. Transferring an application can be achieved in a relatively short time, with little or no user retraining and straightforward data conversion, but can require a careful analysis of system calls and operating parameters and controls. Some applications can be moved to a smaller computer without change and run using a product that emulates the old environment. Little or no code changes are needed—nor is user retraining. New development continues with existing tools, and data probably need conversion to new structures. Converting an application to a smaller computer by changing system calls requires almost no user retraining, but does require data conversion to new structures, new development using new tools, and operation and control changes. Integration involves implementing one or more functions of the application on a smaller computer with a new front-end that tightly integrates with the old application, surrounding it with a new appearance. Integration requires user retraining, application design, coding and testing, and changes to operating parameters and controls. Some data conversion to new structures may also be needed.

Policy decisions precede technology decisions. An architecture consisting of standards and rules, formulated in the policy-setting stage, is used to filter technology decisions and the transition to a client/server computing solution.

Most start their technology decisions and implementation strategy at the bottom—network, database, tools. Others feel that one should start with the application, at the top, then work on the tool selection. In this order, the right selection of tools to do the application resulting in portability makes the lower selections of database and network easy and interchangeable.

Start with architecture—tool selections (window painters, code generators, and database management systems), corporate data model, development methodology, system utilities, operating and control procedures, and support. Then there are standards (protocols, naming, access security, administration), and training.

A development methodology is nothing more than an organized and specific schedule with checkpoints, deliverables, and measurable results. You can choose to do this in a number of ways. This is referred to as *information engineering*, a process that has distinct waterfall life-cycle phases emphasizing the definition of types of information important to the business and how they relate to each other. Another methodology is iterative development, or rapid prototyping. Rather than focusing on information, this methodology focuses on business processes, or how people actually do work. In a continually spiraling fashion, one repetitively analyzes, designs, codes, tests, and critiques with the user community. Developing in an iterative fashion and prototyping along the way helps to ensure that user needs are met by getting critical feedback during the stages of development. Alterations are easier and cheaper this way. This helps users figure out exactly what they want, without requiring as much of their time in the process. It can efficiently help to generate quick support for the new application.

1.7.3 Mainframe legacy

Companies with mainframe legacy environments have extensive amounts of information stored there that needs to be accessed. This information cannot just be moved to alternative environments overnight. This process takes time. For some transition period, the information in the legacy environment will need to be accessed from the new client/server environment. Some companies will choose to extend this transition period indefinitely, and not move the information. Many will rely on one of numerous middleware providers to bridge these environments. There are several dozen such companies, many of which are database providers.

There are many other factors inhibiting a complete abandonment of the mainframe. High-speed printing remains a strong requirement. Often, legacy applications that are used for the day-to-day operation of the business are available only in the mainframe environment. Many years of systems management software that is reliable and usable resides there. Most measures of availability and response times continue to give an edge to mainframe processing. Recent advances in mainframe parallel processing power and Complementary Metal Oxide Semiconductor (CMOS) chip technology are narrowing the price/performance gap favoring client/server platforms.

The mainframe is not dead or extinct. Many businesses are using the mainframe as a huge server, and integrating it with their client/server architectures as just another platform. Mainframe vendors will continue to improve and facilitate this integration process. Their future viability depends on doing so successfully.

1.7.4 Business process selection

Employ a risk/reward model to determine the degree of risk the organization can afford to take. Apply this assessment to the candidate business process or application. Determine the value that the improvement is going to provide to the business. Its quantifiable value should be greater than its risk. This textbook business case analysis and process is no different for client/server computing.

Decision support systems can be down for an hour or so. Manufacturing or online teleprocessing applications are very sensitive to outages. In practice, most businesses start with an application that is used by a small population (say, tens of people, as in a departmental setting), and move into applications used by a larger population (say, hundreds of people in an enterprise setting) after valuable experience and success have been achieved. Some experts suggest starting with a business process that is not mission-critical, learning it, and then tackling the mission-critical applications. This gives the planner time to work on the design details, learn the ins and outs of GUI creation, and develop good testing procedures.

Look for candidate functions that increase user satisfaction, are good training opportunities for teaching new computing skills, and promote higher levels of information and systems integration across the business. Keep these objectives in mind as you sort through and analyze the possibilities.

1.7.5 Needs assessment

Typically, needs change faster than the application customization and development cycles. Studying them to death, or trying to keep up with the changes will only delay one's implementation schedule. Focus on the strategic needs, rather than detailed functional needs. The latter is particularly susceptible to regular change. Handle this phenomenon carefully. Changing needs should be recorded and factored in as a next phase. However, the planner should not risk success by constantly aiming at a moving target: sometimes planners fail to reach closure by either studying the problem to death, or with an analysis/paralysis mindset; moreover, they may be overwhelmed by the rapidity of change in the business requirements or the available technology. The best possible assessment should be made with the available information, and then a decision should be reached. The product (set of requirements, a network, an application, a rollout, etc.) could be labeled *Phase 1*, with an immediate statement that additional functions will be available in *Phase 2* and *Phase 3*.

1.7.6 *Component evaluation and selection*

There are two camps on how best to select components. Both have proven successful. One is to select the best possible component for each function involved, including analysis, design, and generation. Then integration and implementation experts are called on to create the solution. The other camp prefers to select the best fully integrated solution. This section will address the first of these camps.

It is better to evaluate and select components on the basis of architecture and strategic fit. Measuring against specific functions can be dangerous: functional support in advancing versions of components makes it difficult to keep up. It is common to witness a phenomenon known as *leap-frogging* among competing products. Functional capabilities can change before the selection gets implemented. Do not struggle with component selections, because these selections are tactical and subject to future shake-out.

Avoid stored procedures: they limit flexibility by locking one in, and can become more expensive later.

1.7.7 *Vertical applications*

Choosing a fully integrated solution is another approach. This applies to industries such as banking, insurance, and pharmaceuticals. Examples abound that show utility for many if not all client/server applications.

1.7.8 Integration

You may be fortunate enough that a vertical application, already fully integrated and self-contained, will completely fill your needs. In all likelihood however, this will not be the case. A new application may need to work together with another, or draw from or feed an existing system or database. A mainframe application may need to be modified to work with the new application. At the desktop, the new application will likely need to run with other software applications. All of these require integration work. Integration is perhaps the toughest step in the entire process of building successful client/server applications. It is also the key to their success.

1.7.9 Outsourcing

A decision to incorporate outsourcing in the client/server strategy can be motivated by a number of factors, including complete lack of experience, reduction of risk, speed, the need to keep overhead low, and overwhelming technology changes, choices, and integration challenges. Outsourcing is one way to avoid a serious pitfall—not having at least one experienced person on the development team.

Partnering with trained, experienced providers is important. They will keep the planner from stubbing his or her toes in common places and save the planner from relearning what he or she already knows. This approach can help to minimize the risks involved. The type of partnership suggested here is more than just hiring subcontractors. One wants the help of experienced vendors or integrators in an alliance where they share costs and opportunities. For example, if the application being developed will be useful to other businesses besides the organization, you might work out the details with the integrator to allow them to sell it to others and pay the organization some royalties. This is a win-win arrangement for multiple parties.

Of course, incorporating outsourcing in an organization's strategy requires that you clearly detail the requirements, technical specifications, and end-user functionality definitions. In reality, these specifications should be spelled out regardless of any outsourcing intentions. Outsourcing simply makes this mandatory. Know what you want, and stick to it. Providers who want the organization's business will comply and satisfy the requirements.

Outside help is also available to do all of the needed integration work discussed previously. Many providers have previous experience getting many of the parts to work together.

See reference [1] for a more extensive treatment of this topic.

1.8 Information Technology department role

This section describes the challenges that the IT department faces with client/server and related issues. Every IT organization considering client/server computing will have some preexisting, or legacy, environment. Avoid "mainframe/terminal" hierarchical mindset. Throw away the old tools, the architectures and standards—desktop computers, servers, GUI, skills acquisition, etc. Set standards based on requirements. Stay focused on changing requirements, and adjust standards accordingly. Employ seamless integration, and transparency. Remove the mystery. Rightsizing demands skill reset or replacement and personality changes. The importance of training and education cannot be overemphasized. The planner should be watchful of malicious obedience—a real resource waste. This section also discusses system and network management aspects, ongoing maintenance, and multivendor support.

By and large, the majority of IT organizations in the business world today are operating at a disadvantage. The role they play in client/server computing is affected by this. IT organizations operate in a context of shrinking budgets. The lucky ones are seeing level or slightly larger budgets. Businesses are even restricting investment to areas that touch customers. Favored business processes for technology investments include such areas as customer service and order processing.

The IT organization is often perceived by the rest of the business as a *black hole* for resources, energy and dollars, and as contributing little value in return. IT leaders need to recognize this, and face it head-on when discussing client/server initiatives with the leaders of other parts of the business. Part of the reason for this perception is that the IT organization has almost no handle on the asset value of the information systems already in place. Many business leaders outside of the IT organization do not realize that maintaining old applications, particularly mainframe-based, can consume up to 80% of available IT resources. Client/server computing represents an opportunity for the IT organization to change this situation. They need to keep client/server initiatives and discussions fully in the context of business value, and track future changes in that asset value. They need to convince the rest of the business to free up legacy application maintenance resources and allow new flexible client/server applications to replace them. Only then will that black hole perception change.

Migrating computing from mainframes to client/server is perhaps the most daunting task facing IT organizations. Many are embarking on the journey, even if they are not fully prepared for it. Many are operating so lean and mean from past downsizing efforts and budget cuts that they lack the time and resources to document proper migration plans that orchestrate the move systematically and pilot the varied steps. They are saddled by simultaneously tackling infrastructure construction, technology evaluations, staff training, and lobbying for the necessary funding. In addition, customers are requesting entirely new capabilities, e.g. intranet and Web page access to internal corporate data. IT must also work closely with the business departments to define and understand their needs. There are some successful role models out there, but who has time to find them? The IT department's role in this is to dedicate the needed time to do all of this. They must, if the business initiative for client/server computing is to be successful. In addition, IT departments must learn about new networking technologies, ATM in particular, since one cannot open a trade press journal or go to a trade show without being bombarded by references to new broadband services. The development of intranets also requires the kind of high speed, particularly in the corporate backbone, made available by ATM technology.

IT organizations are facing an unending and ever-growing backlog of new applications. Further, they are overworked maintaining legacy, but essential, applications. They cannot dump responsibilities for the old stuff, and they have to take time to properly introduce the new stuff. And they probably have fewer people and budget dollars around to do all of this.

CIOs are recasting the skill sets of their people, learning and teaching what *business* and *customer* mean, teaming their people with outside contractors, reducing staff size while increasing service to their internal customers and dependence on their internal customers, whom they do not manage, to fill resource voids in software development efforts. They are even hiring contract labor to maintain their mainframe legacy systems so their people can learn the new ways. They are offering technology awareness briefings to their internal customers so they see what it does now and might do in the future. They are changing their people measurement and reward systems, and their job descriptions to emphasize performance as consultants to their internal customers. They are colocating their staffs with user departments. This provides the opportunity to see and participate in their day-to-day business duties. They are letting go mainframe bigots. They are emphasizing the integration of technology and existing software packages, rather than developing their own software from scratch. The majority of IT organizations are recognizing the need for and changing their mission to focus on technology integration. It may not be far into the future when the very department name is affected by this trend. Instead of the IT (Information Technology) department, they will reverse the letters and be known as the TI (Technology Integration) department.

As companies successfully implement client/server computing, many are finding that the composition of their IT staff needs to change dramatically. Once information is readily available directly to the business departments through their new client/server applications, the IT department may no longer need the services of many people, including some not generally thought about initially. The population of applications coders using languages such as Cobol immediately comes to mind here as being increasingly expendable. But this same trend is now extending to former business analysts, business liaisons, and even the information resource center that used to provide and support computing tools. These people in the middle between business clients and business information are no longer needed in many cases. The new client/server applications give the business clients direct access to their data. Those in now expendable jobs face a tough choice: adapt to the new way of computing and learn new skills, or find someplace else to apply their old skills. Some adapt willingly, eager to improve their skills, and others are reluctant. Those who refuse to adapt face a dwindling supply of commercial positions using the technology familiar to them.

Other IT positions on the chopping block include anyone specializing in charge-back systems, due to the considerable difference in cost between client/server equipment and centralized processing on mainframes. This drastically reduces the need for application usage tracking for chargeback purposes. Additional likely targets are those specializing in translating data for higher levels of management. With direct access to the data at all levels of management, these intermediaries or conduits are no longer needed. Other specialists in jeopardy include equipment operators (consoles, printers, etc.) and those who know only a single function, platform, application, language, or tool. The best advice here is to become a generalist well versed in many technologies, or risk losing your job.

Many IT chiefs recognize this job-threatening situation and turn it into a career opportunity by offering training opportunities to avoid losing valuable people. When they see that the supply of fully trained client/server computing capable replacements waiting on the streets is rather small, and even nonexistent in some areas, they realize that training is an attractive option. The responsibility to make a prudent decision to change still rests in the hands of the employees. They need to take charge of their own marketabilities, upgrade their skills, and control their own destinies. There are many alternative specializations to choose from that enjoy a high level of demand. The progressive IT department interested in positioning itself for the future should consider nurturing these alternative talents. All of those people in jobs becoming increasingly expendable should consider these alternatives also.

One of the most obvious specialists in demand is the person who is experienced with client/server application development tools; in addition, intranet/Internet and security experts are in demand. We have already mentioned the importance of becoming a generalist, with skills in many platforms and technologies. The roles of LAN and WAN experts are becoming increasingly critical to businesses implementing client/

server computing in network-centric environments. As we have said in an earlier section, the network is becoming the system. Almost as hot are specialists in desktop hardware, applications, operating systems, and integration. All of these client/server technologies come together on the client's desktop computer. The integrator who can make all of these technologies fit together and function smoothly in that computer is a key person in the success of client/server computing implementations. Those who have a thorough knowledge of how their business operates are key to successful client/server application development, especially those who can step in and who are able to codevelop that application with IT and business department people.

IT application development staffs are increasingly demonstrating a willingness and eagerness to collaborate with user departments, given management support for motivation, training, user integration, and evaluation. They are getting a freer hand when it comes to justifying a plan. They like working on high profile projects. They like learning new technology. Some are getting the time they need to learn and schedule leniency to complete projects. They are learning how to integrate and work with their less computer-literate internal customers.

The rest of the CIO's organization, usually consisting of telecommunications, operations, and technical services, are focused on core technology and infrastructure for the whole business.

Application developers who have spent twenty years building menu-based applications using dumb terminals are in for real culture shock in the client/server world. Even the very simple context of Microsoft Windows and GUIs is a major shift. But for those attempting the transition, the difficult part is not learning how to use the screen-painting tool. The biggest challenge is designing a really good human interface, without retaining the look and feel of a character-based interface. Serious developers face an even larger challenge. Competency also requires a working knowledge of perhaps Visual Basic, PowerBuilder, and an SQL database manager. Then there is the mindset shift required while applying these new tools. The shift needed is from building menu-based applications to ones that are event-based. This means no more functional decomposition using structured analysis and design. Now developers must be able to express themselves in object-oriented ways, using encapsulation, inheritance and polymorphism (see Chapter 3). Instead of Cobol procedures and data definitions, they need to understand object linking and broker architectures with C++ or SmallTalk.

There are a few more dimensions to this new world of applications development requiring shifting skill sets. Moving from a proprietary mainframe-based environment to an open systems environment means that knowledge of one hardware box or operating system is nowhere near enough. Working in the open environment means knowing many different hardware platforms, operating systems, and middleware pieces. Now developers will need to know about UNIX, Windows, NT, DOS, OS/2, Oracle, Sybase, broadband communications, etc.

Another significant difference is the shift of staff and control from central to departments. Developers are now likely to have been redeployed and find themselves reporting to end-user department managers, not to IT department managers. This contributes to an environment best described as collaborative with some centralized control. Central establishment of global computing standards and a global infrastructure that departmental IT groups maintain are often the basis for this collaboration. Redeployment of staff allows the central IT group to become smaller. Application development and deployment teams are rooted in the business departments. These teams identify the department initiatives and technology solutions that meet central standards and overall business objectives. Exceptions to standards can certainly be granted, but must be looked on as a temporary cost of doing business, and not as a permanent addition to overhead that will likely loom large in support costs later. Any exceptions should be fully funded and supported by the department requiring them. This practice helps to minimize their number and lifespan.

1.8.1 Loss of control

Many IT managers are faced with a dilemma. They try to maintain control over enterprise-wide information systems and data to ensure integrity. Modern technologies, such as select implementations of object-oriented technology, make this difficult, as business users can "do their own thing." Many must assume this risk in order to support a more flexible and adaptable business. They can be torn between these two forces. The truly innovative IS department can turn this to an advantage. Making everyone in the business a programmer can improve the deployment of applications. It's a balancing act that can be employed without creating chaos. IT staff need to stay in touch with users, and not at each others' throats.

1.8.2 Resistance to change

It is not uncommon to experience a potentially debilitating phenomenon when putting IT departments through the changes required for successful client/server computing implementations. Not everyone likes to change, or wants to change in the ways required or planned. Resistance can appear in many shapes and forms. It can be critical to recognize them and deal with them quickly and effectively. The risks and exposure by not doing so are great. At best, one will waste time and energy, impacting schedules and workload. Your efforts could lose important forward momentum while you spin in circles, dealing with resistance later on. It will sidetrack others working on the project; eliminate it as quickly as possible.

As discussed earlier, standards and consistency are critical foundation elements in successful implementations. These elements often require technical support although, unfortunately, some capable technical support people might not agree with specific component or standard selections. One may see half-hearted or selective support behavior from these people.

Resistance to change is a people phenomenon. Evidence increasingly supports the belief that change on a larger scale, as represented in business process reengineering projects, is met with enough people resistance to stand out as the major cause for failure. A small percentage of resistance is malicious. Some cases of sabotage are possible. But the vast majority are seldom overt. They are often hard to detect, and even harder to fix. To successfully counter this trend, it is essential to get people involved. Assure that the business culture is adjusted to embrace constant change. Tell everyone what is going on, in as much detail as possible, as often as possible. Offer training sessions and workshops. Cajole with rewards and recognition. Tell them everything again. You will find that you need to constantly sell the project to gain universal acceptance.

1.9 Business department role

This section presents perspectives on the importance of client/server computing to a corporation. It is important to business process reengineering; to the alignment of business and IT goals, objectives and visions; to the delivery of coherent information access across the entire enterprise. Successful implementation requires coordination and collaboration across business department boundaries. Proper training is important to successful implementations. End-users are finding their own short-term client/server solutions, fostering isolation, chaos, and uncontrolled decentralization. This raises costs company-wide and lowers the degree of system integration and accessibility.

The clients in the business department are getting involved in the systems development process in order to get the systems they really need. They are overcoming their reluctance to get involved with something that is beyond their scope of knowledge. Some still find it uncomfortable and confusing. And some want to own the development process, since it is their responsibility if it fails. They cannot afford to waste time and money on a bad system. They are helping to define system requirements, processes that can be automated, the vision for the system, and prototypes. They are fostering the development of systems with a business focus, rather than a technology focus. The people who will be using the new system are now developing and testing it.

1.9.1 "Do your own thing" implications

A business department can "do their own thing" with object-oriented technologies. The appeal of limiting the role of the IT department comes from foreseen short decision cycles and freedom of choice.

Doing so can jeopardize the integrity of business data and related information systems. Hidden costs can quickly surface when it is time to connect to the rest of the business. Typical problems that arise with isolated development efforts include interoperability failure, security problems, and inadequate testing, and operational procedures.

1.9.2 Juggling control

Two factors are showing an influence and affecting the balance of controls between business departments and the IT department. Business departments are finding the need to devote more time to application development and custom queries and reports, either as the developers themselves, or as active participants in the process. Business departments have also discovered that the multivendor and multiproduct network environments (that they have, in some cases, created themselves), are more and more difficult to maintain and integrate with new applications and technologies. They want to get out of the network management business, and are increasingly giving control of this facet of client/server computing to the IT department. This provides the business departments with the needed time for application development.

As distributed processing puts more and more computing power and data in the hands of the user, the user assumes added responsibilities for activities more traditionally performed by the IT department—backup and security.

1.10 Impact on organization structure

The very structure of the IT organization and business departments will need to change to accommodate and facilitate client/server implementations. One needs to take into account the organizational considerations driving department reengineering to accommodate client/server computing, both during the development phase and during the ongoing support phase. The importance of core business and infrastructure focus is explored in this section. Continued emphasis on alignment with business goals during restructuring is important. Distributed support and alliances can influence organization structure.

Client/server computing even has an impact on the organization structure of the IT department. Even the commonly used names for these organizations reflects a shift in emphasis. *Management Informations Systems* (MIS) was popular years ago. Then the focus shifted to variations, including IS and IT, where the emphasis was on the applications systems and the underlying technology respectively. Now, *Information Management* is commonly heard, where the emphasis is purely on information and the proper management of it, most frequently implying its availability (access and delivery of it).

1.10.1 Organization restructuring motivations and definitions

Decentralization of the IT organization introduces new challenges to stay in tune with the core IT functions that cannot be decentralized. Many IT organizations are currently divided into functional areas—application development, network support, operations, etc. Almost all such organizations find that implementation and support of client/server solutions require close coordination of efforts and teamwork among people across all of these functional areas. The difficulty, and therefore the pressure to change these organizations, arises because these people are not generally accustomed to working this closely with each other. They do not generally do so effectively or accurately.

The most common organizational impact of client/server computing is the distribution of application development personnel from the IT department out to the business departments. Distributed systems and applications create pressure for distributed personnel. Likewise, technology operations personnel are beginning to follow. A centralized operations staff may be appropriate for situations where servers are located centrally, but when the servers are spread all over the business departments, it is common to find distributed operators running them.

Traditional application development and support hierarchical structures are yielding to polarization of people around business processes, including product development, manufacturing, customer acquisition, customer service, order fulfillment, dealer operations, etc. The goal is to get closer to the customer. This also helps reduce the number of layers in the hierarchy. This naturally brings IS department people together with their internal customers, the clients, to work jointly. This increases the demand for training in teamwork concepts and processes.

1.10.2 Organization structure suggestions

There are a growing number of creative ways to structure an organization to function more effectively in a client/server environment. Some companies develop and train technology experts in databases, graphical user interfaces, etc. They are put on the team to assist the business process analysts and the end-users for each application development project. The users exert a strong influence on the design, the analysts keep the focus on process reengineering, and the technology experts guide and shape the appropriate technology aspects and tools. Companies transitioning to client/server computing also quickly discover the need for transition in the organizational structure from a functional and hierarchical structure to one that is very flat and process-oriented. This means really getting close to the customers in the business departments to understand their processes.

1.11 A virtual future

What does the future hold? Success with client/server applications will depend upon how closely one can match the concepts and theories of the corporation of the future, as proposed by William H. Davidow and Michael S. Malone in *The Virtual Corporation*.* With future evolution of development tools and the maturation of distributed object libraries, it will be possible to achieve a level of virtual client/server applications. These applications will be customized for each client or customer. It will be possible to make near instant adjustments to applications, achieving extremely short development cycle times. The trends in object technology and tools will make it possible to accelerate successes in client/server applications. As Davidow and Malone point out, the key to quick response in a virtual corporation is trust.† With the right technology infrastructure, tools, and training in place, the clients can be trusted to make their own adjustments. They will become coproducers of client/server applications. Information linkage

---

* William H. Davidow and Michael S. Malone, *The Virtual Corporation* (New York: HarperCollins, 1992), Chapter 10: A Virtual Future.

† Ibid., p. 58.

is a key to becoming a virtual corporation.* Information linkage and flow are achieved with client/server applications.

Workgroups and collaborating teams hold the key to future productivity improvements achievable with client/server computing solutions. Different groups of people across organizational boundaries will be working closely together using team-based applications. Standards across business units will allow highly distributed technology planning and implementation. Workgroup computing will replace personal computing, but not PCs, as the standard method of employing computing technology and applications in the workplace.

1.12 Conclusion

This chapter provided a business perspective of the client/server issue. It focused on the practical, application-level perspective of this field, in order to stress the obvious: organizations are increasingly relying on client/server technology to support more and more business functions. The chapters that follow in Part 1 will provide more technical considerations. These technical considerations will be critical to the viability, performance, and gain of using ATM and related broadband technology to support second-generation client/server environments, as discussed in Part 3.

1.13 References

1 D. Minoli, *Analyzing Outsourcing*, New York, NY: McGraw-Hill, 1994.
2 D. Minoli, *Internet and Intranet Engineering*, New York, NY: McGraw-Hill, 1997.

---

* William H. Davidow and Michael S. Malone, *The Virtual Corporation*, p. 64.

chapter 2

Present mode of operation: Computing client/server environments now in place

The previous chapter discussed in a broad manner the business imperatives driving corporations to the use of client/server systems or intranet-based systems. This chapter discusses the kind of first-generation client/server systems now being deployed in many organizations, from a more technical perspective than covered in Chapter 1. Many of these issues have to be taken into consideration when designing second-generation systems which use ATM as the network transport technology, discussed in the third part of this book. Additionally, these issues apply to intranets.

As we venture into this topic, we note that some may take the view that one does not really need ATM as much with client/server outside the server farm, because LAN technologies are very effective with client/server. These authors view this as being a myopic perspective. The amount of information being transacted across networks continues to increase, particularly as end-users become reliant on GUI-, graphics-, and Virtual Reality-based interfaces. Microprocessors operating at 50 million instructions per second are common today, and soon processors with capabilities of hundreds of MIPS will be a commodity item. (Applications requiring 1000 MIPS are already here). According to *Amdahl's Law*, a megabit of I/O capacity is needed for every MIPS of processor performance. Some computing applications already require 1000 MIPS. This implies that the I/O needs to be 50–1000 Mbps at this time, and higher by the end of the decade. Although the network throughput tends to lag the I/O throughput by a few years, these kinds of speeds will be needed in a matter of a few seasons. Ethernet provides only a fraction of a Mbps per user (for a typically loaded network), or at most 7 Mbps for a switched system; 100-Mbps Ethernet provides only a few Mbps per user (for a typically loaded network), or at most 70 Mbps for a switched system (this based both on protocol and hub/bridge/router throughput considerations.) The same is true for FDDI. ATM, on the other hand, provides 155 Mbps *per user*. This is not to imply that FDDI in the local area and services such as Frame Relay in the wide area are not viable at this juncture. But if the planner in thinking strategically (in terms of what we call a few seasons), then ATM is likely the answer. In fact, many corporations have already deployed ATM in the server farm at this time. Furthermore, ATM is a platform to support wide area service such as frame relay, as well as legacy LAN services such as Ethernet—hence, ATM will play a significant role in client/server system one way or another. If ATM is not employed natively, it likely will be employed to support LANE or MPOA systems.

2.1 Background*

As discussed in the previous chapter, starting in the late 1980s and continuing through the 1990s, many organizations have transformed their mission-critical computing infrastructures by implementing LAN-based architectures. PCs and workstations are now almost universally connected to LANs. In turn, local or departmental LANs are connected across the corporate enterprise by multiprotocol routers; such tight connectivity is sought whether the organization is clustered in a building, or spread out over a campus, metropolitan area, state, nation, or several nations or continents.

Companies continue to use automation in general, and IT in particular, to improve productivity of core business functions. Automation and IT have been employed by companies to reengineer the way corporate work is done. For example, in a traditional corporate environment, middle managers relayed filtered information from the production floor to the executive level, and in turn, dispensed directives from the executives to the workers. Now databases and telecommunication networks collect and distribute that information in a more effective and unbiased manner [3].

For Fortune 5000 companies' the recent annual return for their investment in IT has been high [3]. This type of return has fueled the continued introduction of this technology; however, such introduction carries its own cost, which companies are now trying to control. Therefore, IT is itself now being reengineered. Many companies are now introducing client/server architectures, and sometimes take the opportunity not only of reengineering the IT environment, but also to accomplish (some degree of) outsourcing at the same time [12], [13], [20].

The focus on business accountability has caused departments and workgroups in recent years to introduce workstation technology to solve problems with which the traditional central IT organization was either slow or unable to deal. This, however, resulted in islands of automation that prevented effective communication of information and access to processes and applications developed in another area. Reengineered IT organizations recognize this reality and the value of personal computers; such IT organizations see their new role as the establishment of enterprise standards to facilitate application and infrastructure interoperability [10].

This chapter serves as a short technical primer in this area: The advantages and challenges of client/server computing are addressed. Additionally, a short synopsis of local and remote communication technologies is provided. Communication is critical to client/server systems, and therefore this material serves as a primer for Parts 2 and 3.

---

* Portions of this chapter are synthesized from a number of sources previously published by Mr. Minoli on this topic, including [11], [14], and [20].

2.2 Client/server systems: Practical definition

2.2.1 Key client/server concepts

The basics of client/server computing involve dividing the work between two computer systems. One is the system on the desktop, which is generally, but not always, referred to as client. The other is somewhere on the network, along with perhaps other servers. Clients initiate requests for some service, for example database lookup/update, read from/write to a remote mass storage, dialing out on one of a pool of modems, or printing a report or document; the server accomplishes the task on behalf of the client [10].

In the client/server arrangement, the client is the consumer of the services provided by the server or servers. The concept behind the client/server architecture is to support a clear separation of functions: the server acts as a service provider responding to work requests from the various clients. Note that the same piece of equipment can be used as either a client or a server; what makes the difference is the software that is loaded onto it. In fact, the same piece of equipment can act as a client and as a server in different instances. Table 2.1 provides, as a working tool, a glossary of key client/server terms and concepts that can be utilized to facilitate the reading of the early chapters of this book.

Table 2.1 Glossary of key client/server terms and concepts (list not exhaustive)

API	The Application Programming Interface is a set of call programs and functions that enables clients and servers to communicate
Back-end	The database engine. Back-end functions include storing, dispensing, and manipulating the information.
Client	A (networked) information requester that can query databases and/or other information from a server. At the physical device level, the client is a PC or workstation.
Common ORB Architecture (CORBA)	An ORB standard endorsed by the Object Management Group (OMB).
Distributed Computing Environment (DCE)	A set of integrated software modules that provides an environment for creating, using, and maintaining client/server applications on a network. It includes capabilities such as security, directory, synchronization, file sharing, RPCs, and multithreading.
Distributed database	A client/server database system based on a network supporting many clients and servers.
Distributed Relational Database Architecture (DRDA)	An IBM enhancement that allows information to be distributed among SQL/DS and DB2 databases.

Table 2.1 Glossary of key client/server terms and concepts (list not exhaustive) (continued)

Dynamic Data Exchange (DDE)	A message-based protocol used in the context of Microsoft Windows which allows applications to automatically request and exchange information, thereby supporting interprocess communication. The protocol allows an application running in one window to query an application running in another window.
Front-end	A client application working in cooperation with a backend engine that manipulates, presents and displays data.
Object	A named entity that combines a data structure with an associated operation. Expressed more formally: Object={Unique identifier} U {data} U {operations}
Object Linking and Embedding (OLE)	A client/server capability (protocol) in the context of Microsoft Windows that enables the creation of compound documents. It is an extension of DDE's capabilities. A document (e.g., a spreadsheet, a database entry, a video clip, etc.) can be embedded within or linked to another document. When an embedded element is referenced, the application that created it must be loaded and activated; if, for example, the object is edited, these edits pertain only to the document that contains the object and not the more general instance of the object. If the object is linked, it points to an original file external to the document; if, for example, the object is edited, these edits are automatically loaded onto the original document.
Object Request Broker (ORB)	Software that handles the communication tasks for messages used between objects in a distributed, multiplatform environment.
Object-oriented language	Linguistic support for objects. Objects can be dynamically generated and passed as operation parameters. *Pure* languages offer no other facilities but those related to classes and objects. *Hybrid* languages superimpose object-oriented concepts on an alternative programming paradigm.
Open Software Foundation (OSF)	A not-for-profit organization aiming at delivering an open computing environment based on industry standards. It works with members to set technical directions and licenses software. Also see DCE.
OSF/1	OSF's multiprocessing operating system.
Relational Database	A database where information access is limited to the selection of rows that satisfy all search criteria.
Server	A computer that stores information required by networked clients. It can be a PC, workstation, minicomputer, or mainframe.
Windows Open Services Architecture (WOSA)	A single system-level interface for connecting front-end applications with back-end services for Windows-based applications. Using WOSA, application developers and users do not need to be concerned about conversing with numerous services which may employ parochial protocols and interfaces; these details are handled by the operating systems and not by the applications themselves. WOSA provides an extensible framework where applications seamlessly access information and network resources in a distributed environment. It uses Dynamic-Link Library (DLL) methods to enable software components to be linked at run-time.

(Table based partially on [13], [21], [22]).

As discussed in Chapter 1, the term *client/server* is only loosely defined at the practical level: the term is used to refer to a variety of systems, from simple remote-access file system to complex database engines. Many people hold that the terms *client/server* and *network database* are synonymous; in fact the database server technology used in systems developed by Microsoft, Sybase, Oracle, and others, fits most definitions of client/server computing. Some view client/server as the culmination of the trend toward downsizing applications from the minicomputer and the mainframe, to the desktop [13].

The following general definition has been advanced: *client/server computing is any application in which the requester of actions or information is on one system and the supplier of action or information is on another* [4]. Most client/server systems have a many-to-one design: more than one client typically makes requests of the server. Many enterprise systems fit this definition.

Even a classical Systems Network Architecture (SNA) fits this definition. The program in the 3270 terminal takes data entered by a user and submits them (through a cluster controller) to a server application on a mainframe; the server processes the requests and the resulting data are sent back to the terminal. However, when most people talk about client/server they have something else in mind.* Closer to the contemporary use of the word are file servers systems such as Novell's NetWare or Banyan's VINES, which respond to client requests by supplying data in various logical aggregations, typically files. Even more complex examples of client/server systems are database engines that support sophisticated data structures. (Examples of these systems include those developed and marketed by Sybase, Oracle Corp., and Microsoft Corp.) These database systems respond to queries from clients, perform activities based on those queries, and return discrete responses to the clients. In some sophisticated cases, a client/server application can take a complex calculation submitted by a client and partition the calculation into a number of smaller components. These stand-alone calculations are then submitted to a series of calculation servers in a *CPU farm* that can perform them simultaneously. Once each server has responded with its subresult, the client/server application consolidates the calculation components and is able to rapidly calculate the desired final answer.

In the 1960s and 1970s, companies looked to their central ITs organizations to satisfy evolving market and economic demands. Host-based systems provided adequate support by automating back-room tasks, such as customer information, accounting, and other batch processing jobs. Host-based systems also facilitated control functions and data integrity. As discussed in the previous chapter, the 1980s proved that host-based

---

* Keeping a database on a mainframe can be considered consistent with client/server computing principles if the application itself that uses the database runs on a PC or workstation.

systems could not keep pace with the growing computing demand imposed on the organization by market and economic forces. Market and economic demands forced departments and divisions to turn to personal computers, workstations, and LANs to achieve the responsiveness they needed to run on-line mission-critical business applications. End-users worked together to achieve competitive advantage and solve their departmental mandates [12].

The PC, workstation, and LAN deployments of the late 1980s and 1990s helped give birth to client/server computing, which efficiently integrates data, applications, and computer services. End-users now respond to business demands faster using their desktop and portable computers linked to resources located throughout the network. At the same time, many IT organizations are discovering that they can lower their computing costs by off loading processing from the mainframe to more affordable, smaller machines that have become available [12]. While the mainframe provides a level of control over data, the cost savings that organizations can experience are often perceived to be large enough to justify the migration of applications off the mainframe. As a result, IT organizations have moved toward a client/server computing architecture for both cost benefits and flexibility. Figure 2.1 depicts two illustrative examples of client/server architectures. The first example shows departmental use of client/server; the second example depicts an enterprise-wide system that also includes mainframes [5], [6]. Note that multiple clients can rely on a single server.

2.2.2 Motivations

Based on the discussion above, a client/server LAN architecture is a computing environment in which software applications are distributed among entities on the LAN. The clients request information from one or more LAN servers that store software applications, data, and network operating systems. The network operating system allows the clients to share the data and applications that are stored in the server, and to share peripherals on the LAN. Figure 2.2 depicts a logical view of a client/server environment.

The client is the entity requesting that work be done; a server is the entity performing a set of tasks on behalf of the client. The client system provides presentation services to the ultimate (human) user. As covered in Chapter 1, there has been almost a universal movement toward GUIs as the effective method for presenting information to people. This windowing environment allows the client system (and the user) to support several simultaneous sessions. Facilities such as Dynamic Data Exchange and Object Level Embedding (see Table 2.1), provide the means to support cut-and-paste operations between such diverse applications as graphics, spreadsheets, and word processing documents.

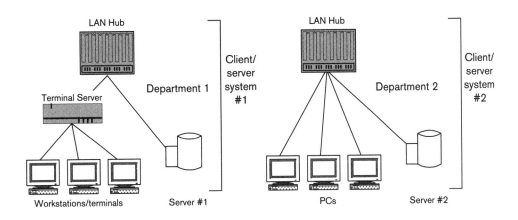

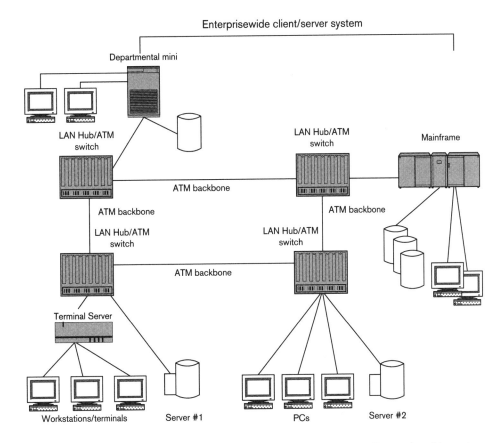

Figure 2.1 Client/server systems. Top: Departmental systems; Bottom: Enterprisewide system

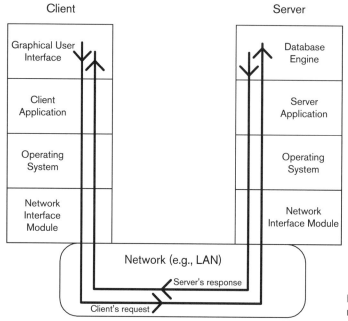

Client

Server

Graphical User Interface	Database Engine
Client Application	Server Application
Operating System	Operating System
Network Interface Module	Network Interface Module

Network (e.g., LAN)

Server's response

Client's request

Figure 2.2 Client/server model, logical view

There are three basic functions supporting computing: data management; processing; and presentation (to user). Client/server systems allow the distribution of these functions among appropriate devices as shown in Figure 2.3. Table 2.2 depicts some of the features associated with client/server "implementation" variations [7],[8].

The user's processor controls the user interface and issues commands to direct the activity of the server across the LAN. This is done through the use of Remote Procedure Calls. RPCs are software programs with distributed capabilities. Applications that are implemented on the LAN can call these procedures by ordering messages, translating different codes, and maintaining the integrity of the protocol. Not all applications in a client/server architecture are stored on a server: clients may also be capable of storing applications and data locally. When clients possess individual operating systems the network is referred to as *loosely* coupled.

The goal is to have a client/server platform that operates in an open environment. In an open environment, the requester-service procedures and necessary support messages are based on well-defined standards, allowing multiple platforms (using possibly different hardware and software) to interact seamlessly. RPCs play a role in the quest for openness. One of the key advantages of open environments is that servers may grow as the need arises, without being forced to buy from a single supplier. Additionally, any needed changes to the operating system or hardware can be done without having to

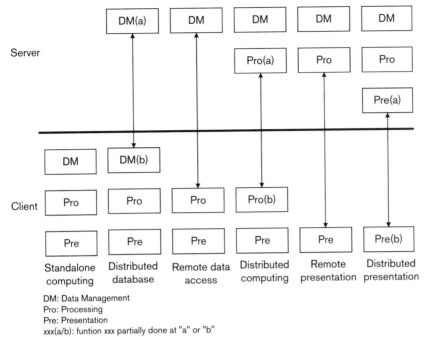

Figure 2.3   Various client/server implementations

modify the client applications. Some of the benefits of using a client/server architecture include [7]:

- Increased productivity
- Control/reduction of costs by sharing resources
- Ease of management through focusing efforts onto a few servers
- Ability to adapt to new needs

Table 2.2   Features associated with client/server "implementation" variations

Variation	Application	Examples	Pluses	Minuses
Distributed Presentation	Existing mainframe-based applications	PCs X-terminals X-servers	No changes to existing applications; improved Human-Machine Interface; inexpensive desktop	Increased system computational load
Remote Presentation	Independent management of user environment; new or existing applications	Workstations PCs DECwindow/Motif	Server is offloaded; can be used for existing applications	Degraded performance for multi-application environments

Table 2.2   Features associated with client/server "implementation" variations (continued)

Variation	Application	Examples	Pluses	Minuses
Distributed Computing	Computing components executed by most appropriate platform (array processors, mainframe, mini, etc.)	Workstations High-end PCs Minicomputers Mainframes Adjunct processors	All resources are optimally used	Cooperative computing is required. (Processing must in some sense be coordinated)
Remote Data Access	Common data with independent applications; Decision Support Systems	Workstations High-end PCs Minicomputers Mainframes SQL access 4th Generations Languages DECquery	Reliable data; computing choices closer to user	Database machine performance affects all users
Distributed Database	Resource sharing for desktop applications	Workstations High-end PCs Minicomputers Mainframes Oracle's Oracle Server IBM's Database Manager Sybases's SQL Server Novell's NetWare SQL Gupta's SQLBase Other 4th Generation Languages	Good utilization of all devices; maximum independence	Difficult to scale up

In the stand-alone computing environment, all the intelligence is placed in the PC. Even when the data resides in a file server, the file server simply stores the file in a functionally equivalent manner as if it were a local hard-disk. For example, to do a sort, the entire file is downloaded to the PC which does all the computing; the file may eventually be reloaded in a sorted form to the server. The server has no ability to manage or control the data. Two problems of this static-server architecture are [9]:

- The number of simultaneous users is rather small, due to performance problems related to the movement of files and indexes.

- Multiple applications usually require replication of the data into multiple databases, often of different file formats. This makes database synchronization difficult.

In a more sophisticated client/server environment, the server has the capability to perform database management. This means that the server (also known as the *back-end* or *database engine*) can run a (relational) database management system using a multitasking operating system (e.g., OS/2 or UNIX). See Table 2.2. A relatively powerful microprocessor is required to run the multitasking Operating System, the database manager, and the concurrent user sessions. Typically this is a Pentium-based system.

In a client/server environment, the workstation (also known as the *front-end*) is responsible for *presentation* functions (i.e., display of data according to specified user interfaces, editing and validating data, and managing the keyboard and mouse). These functions are easy to implement, making the cost of the repetitive module low (N modules for N end-users). This results in the following advantages [9]:

- Support of many concurrent users (a few hundred)
- Reduction in cost, since front-end software is simple
- Availability of software from a variety of vendors, performing a variety of functions and sharing the database
- Data integrity (single database shared by all users)

The four common methods of linking client/server applications are: application program interfaces (APIs), database servers, remote windowing, and RPC software:

1 *APIs*   A commonly used method of sharing information on a client/server network is through the use of *Network APIs*. These are vendor-provided functions that enable application programmers to access network resources in a standardized manner. Network APIs also allow for the connection of various applications running under the same operating system. Vendor-supplied APIs are not easily portable among different operating systems. SPX (Novell NetWare), Named Pipes (Microsoft LAN Manager), and Sockets (Berkeley UNIX) are examples of APIs. A long-term goal is to come up with vendor-independent APIs. (This topic is revisited later.)

2 *Database servers*   A database server is a dedicated server in a client/server network that provides clients with distributed access to database resources. The database servers usually employ the Structured Query Language relational database to communicate between the client and the server. SQL is a de facto standard language supported by many vendors, thereby running on multiple platforms. (A number of vendors have some syntactical differences and extensions meant to improve developer productivity—these extensions should be assessed to determine if the benefit accrued from their use outweighs the incompatibilities that may arise.)

Using SQL, database servers allow a client to download a table, as opposed to downloading the entire database. This feature reduces LAN and WAN traffic, thereby improving performance. SQL database servers extend user processing applications across various network operating systems via RPCs. SQL is a simple conversation-like language relying on English commands such as SELECT, FROM,

WHERE, etc. to perform database inquiries. For example, the user can issue the command:

```
SELECT customer, balance FROM checking-account-list
   WHERE balance ≤ 1,000.
```

3 *Remote windowing*   Remote windowing is an extension of the *windowing* concepts commonly used with PCs. Remote windowing allows for multivendor connectivity through the use of the Universal Terminal Standard. This concept allows the viewing of multiple user processing applications concurrently from remote locations. To properly distinguish Microsoft Windows from the generic concept of *windowing*, the following definition is provided. Windowing is a software feature that offers split-screen capability in which the different partitions of the display form rectangular areas. These rectangular forms, usually are accompanied by GUIs, can be moved or resized on the screen. Microsoft Windows is a specific vendor application providing windowing.

4 *RPCs*   RPCs are based on computer-aided software engineering (CASE) principles. This concept allows conventional procedure calls to be extended across a single- or multi-vendor network. RPCs function across several communication layers. Programmers are shielded from the networking environment, allowing them to concentrate on the functional aspects of the applications under development. The computing industry generally describes two RPC technologies as industry standards. They are Open Network Computing (ONC™) RPC (often called SunRPC), and Network Computing System (NCS™). An international standard RPC based on the Remote Operations Service Element and Abstract Syntax Notation One would be desirable.

Services   Client workstations operate by issuing requests for services (see Table 2.3 for a typical list). The responder to such service may be on the same processor (e.g., a request for a locally stored file), or a remotely networked processor. The critical fact here is that the format of the request must be the same, regardless of where the responder is located. The NOS intercepts the request and if necessary, translates or adds the details required by the intended responder. This NOS service is known as *redirection*. This capability intercepts the client's operating system calls and redirects them to the server operating systems. Requests such as file access, directory inquiries, printing, and application activation, are trapped by the redirection software and redirected over the LAN or WAN to the correct server.

As seen in Table 2.3, application servers provide the same business functionality as was supported in the past by (more expensive) mainframes and minicomputers. These services are invoked in response to a client's request, specifically via RPCs. As already indicated, these requests are issued by the client system to the NOS. The request processing module of the client formats the request into the appropriate RPC and passes that to the application layer of the client's application layer of the communication protocol stack. What now becomes a Protocol Data Unit (PDU) is further passed down the protocol stack, sent over the network, and received by the server through the communication protocol stack. The PDU is reconstituted into the RPC which is delivered to the server's processing logic.

Table 2.3   Typical client/server services

Database services	First-generation database services were actually file server functions with an altered interface, and execute the database engine mostly in the client. More sophisticated systems support database interactions via SQL syntax (e.g., Sybase, IBM's database manager, Oracle, Ingress, etc.).
Fax services	Clients can route requests for faxing, even though the fax system may be busy with another document. Requests are redirected by NOS software and managed in a fax queue. Notification of delivery is often provided. Applications themselves need not provide these capabilities.
Message services	With this service, which supports buffering, scheduling, and arbitration, messages can be sent to and received from the network.
Network services	These services provide support for actual communication protocols such as TCP/IP (over Ethernet, Token Ring, FDDI, etc.), APPN, etc. These services enable LAN and WAN connectivity. The application accesses the network services over the API.
Print services	Clients can route requests for printing, even though the printer may be busy with another document. Requests are redirected by NOS software and managed in a printer queue. Notification of delivery is often provided. Applications themselves need not provide these capabilities.
Remote boot services	Skeleton operating system is contained in the local workstation (e.g., on a X-terminal); additional capabilities are loaded over the network.
Windowing services	This service provides the workstation with the ability to activate, rescale, move, or hide a window. Applications themselves need not support these physical windowing capabilities (the application, using the GUI capability, places data into a virtual screen—the window service handles screen placement and manipulation).
File services	Support access to the virtual directories and files located on both the client's harddisk and in some network server (here through redirection).

RPCs standardize the way programmers write calls (invocations) to procedures (e.g., subroutines) stored somewhere in the network. If an application issues a functional request and this request is embedded in an RPC, the requested function can be located anywhere in the enterprise network (or even outside the company's enterprise); naturally, considerations as to security and access rights have to be taken into account. The RPC facility provides the invocation and execution of requests from processors running on possibly different operating systems and different hardware platforms. Many RPCs also provide data translation services; here the call causes dynamic translation of data between systems with different physical data storage formats. RPC standards are evolving and are being adopted by the industry, to promote open environments [4], [13].

2.2.3 Why client/server applications are being deployed

Organizations, driven by the pressures for IT cost reductions discussed in Chapter 1, properly inquire if a client/server-based solution is the correct approach to their applications development needs. Companies are now deploying client/server systems despite cultural and technical challenges that can include migrating both IT and users off mainframes and onto foreign platforms, tackling new (open) standards and ensuring that client/server data do not degrade a network's performance [6]. As discussed earlier, there are advantages in deploying client/server applications. Client/server systems typically deliver more information to the user; they do this faster and potentially in a more readable format than available with legacy systems [4]. Many client/server applications can be built using off-the-shelf tools that take advantage of GUIs.

Client/server systems enable the users to be more productive through the integration of personal desktop tools and corporate systems. Mechanisms such as OLE, DDE, and CORBA (Table 2.1) support these productivity improvements. Client/server systems leverage the business experience of the user in combination with tools that are usable by noncomputer professionals.

Cost savings   Client/server applications usually result in long-term monetary savings, although these savings can be achieved only if the cost to support distributed applications is low. Studies have shown that when mainframe-based legacy systems are replaced with client/server systems, their combined costs is, in most cases, less than the operating system, application software, hardware, and maintenance costs of the original system. Cost reductions are also realized by more efficient use of the computing resources. In a client/server system, the client only formulates the request for data and then processes the reduced data set returned by the server; this implies that the user requires a less powerful processor than if the client performed all the application tasks locally. In fairness, however, the cost of machine cycles has been coming down, so that these savings alone may not be as important as time goes by.

The implementation of a GUI-based presentation front-end to an application (as implied in Figure 2.3) can also result in savings in terms of a shorter learning time for new users, and perhaps, a shorter time to complete a given production task, particularly when shortcuts are implemented, obviating the need to navigate multilayer menus. The

IT organization can deliver data to end-users faster in the form they want because end-users choose their front-end tools and IT organizations maintain central control over the data with programmable servers and other tools [12].

Additionally, a well-designed client/server query/response process results in fewer data being transacted over the network. This eliminates (or reduces) the cost of having to incrementally upgrade the network components to provide additional bandwidth, particularly in a WAN context where bandwidth costs are still non-trivial (this, however, also applies at the local level, pushing the user to higher speed LANs—e.g., 100 Mbps LANs, FDDI, and ATM LANs). This upgrade also applies to bridges, routers, modem pools, etc. However, the requirement for bandwidth is inevitably on the increase, and ATM will be needed at some point in the next few years in many companies. Network management tools are essential to control traffic in the client/server system. Also, coming changes in networking options make it critical that applications are built using standard protocols to isolate the location of the data and process from the application. Thus, a database or application server may move from the department to the headquarters, as new high-capacity communication services (such as ATM) reduce the communication charges (due to economies of scale and integration) and provide LAN-like performance over the WAN.

Not all client/server systems now being installed, however, aim at replacing legacy systems. IT managers realize that in may cases these applications can be used to enhance the capabilities obtainable with existing systems. One example of this is the intranet.

Many organizations have seen client/server emerge in a grass roots fashion, at the departmental level. In these organizations, success in departmental client/server computing is now driving an enterprise-wide demand for greater access to corporate data for access to applications once in the hands of a few users, and to email services, in order to further satisfy departmental requirements for improving business productivity and remaining competitive. However, client/server computing on a departmental level provides benefits only within specific departments; as a result, data are duplicated on other servers or PCs by rekeying or downloading information from the mainframe. New data may also be created completely outside the mainframe environment on a network server. The desirable solution is to balance end-user responsiveness with IT control by deploying client/server computing across the entire organization. Proponents hold that client/server computing is now proving itself an effective architecture of strategic value for linking all of an organization's computing resources, in the form of *enterprise-wide client/server computing* as shown in Figure 2.1 bottom [12]. In this computing environment end-users, departments, and IT can again join to create one cohesive computing environment. Front and back office end-users anywhere in the organization can access corporate data on their desktop, and central control of data is put back in the hands of the IT department.

Challenges When a technology is as popular as client/server, it seems as if it is the only option: if the organization has a newly developed database, the user probably has to get at it through client/server connections. For many legacy systems, the old way of doing things may be perceived to be so expensive or so hard to integrate with new applications that client/server technology ostensively appears to be an obvious choice [10]. But does this imply that client/server is the universal answer? In reality, there is a complex process for assessing this multidimensional issue, that entails investing the time and effort to develop rigorous models for testing and evaluating client/server technologies and applying them in appropriate areas. [17].

Some see flexibility with client/server computing, but note that there is a price to pay for that flexibility. For example, the IT department may have to buy, say, 200 copies of a licensed software (rather than having it built in-house) and a few months later, when the software is upgraded, need to obtain the upgrade kits: this can be done for one or two updates, but eventually the applications have to be repurchased. Also, the retraining necessary can be a major cost factor. Hence, there are several challenges associated with client/server architectures, including the following:

- There are cost and design considerations that have to be taken into account when considering deployment of client/server systems. Early on, the time and resources needed to develop client/server applications typically exceed what would be needed for a traditional monolithic approach [4]. In part, this is due to the fact that traditional applications have been designed for over 30 years, while client/server systems are relatively new. Also there are many hidden cost factors to take into account.

- Maintenance costs for mission-critical client/server system can be similar to those for mainframes. For example, critical portions of a client/server system need to be located in a secure environment, including backup power, air conditioning, fault tolerance, offsite data vaulting, and real time system management, etc.; these requirements are similar to those for the legacy systems.

- Existing computers need to be upgraded to participate in client/server computing. For example, in some environments legacy systems need to be retained to maintain volumes of data on disk farms that are too large for smaller systems. Intranet data may also be resident there. In these cases, mainframe costs are reduced but not eliminated, with the cost of the newer client/server systems simply being additive.

- Client/server systems rely in an increased measure on communication. Networks may need to be made more robust, more reliable, and have to be carefully optimized for response time. Client/server traffic can degrade a network, particularly when organizations configure client/server networks according to expected usage and not peak usage [6]. The speed of the server is immaterial if the network is the bottleneck; impaired performance (for example, slow response time) can affect an entire department, say twenty or thirty people.

There also are nontechnology challenges: people at all levels have to be trained in the client/server technology, and, as implied in Chapter 1, human resources can represent some of the greatest costs. As thousands of departments and IT organizations deploy client/server computing and information becomes increasingly more "splintered," the corporation runs the risk of losing its information resource as a key strategic asset. In addition, central IT is running the risk of becoming isolated as systems multiply outside the mainframe environment. And while some IT organizations experience success in cutting costs by moving applications off the mainframe, this solution does not address information management as a strategic, enterprise-wide asset [12].

Corporate senior management in many Fortune 1500 companies is forcing the move to a client/server, claiming that such paradigm is significantly less expensive and a more effective approach to computing. But there are IT professionals who remain skeptical, pointing out that there is little hard data to support those benefits and a growing body of evidence that calls them into question. "Fuzzy economic models" may have been used to justify a decision [17]. For some applications or business environments, client/server may not the best answer. In some such situations, client/server could entail more complexity than needed and an investment of resources beyond the value of the benefits that can be derived. An important consideration in assessing the value of client/server computing is related to the way the work is split between client and server.

How should one approach existing (perhaps old) database applications developed before client/server systems entered the scene? Software development is a labor-intensive effort, even when programmers develop 10 debugged lines per hour. Some estimate the US industry to be a $100 billion a year industry. Assuming a 10-year life cycle, this implies an investment of about $1 trillion in software. Such investment cannot be ignored in favor of a complete overhaul, particularly in an age of fiscal conservatism.

2.2.4 Transitioning to client/server computing

Enterprise-wide client/server computing empowers organizations to reengineer business processes, and distribute transactions in order to streamline operations, while providing new and better services to customers. The transition to enterprise-wide client/server computing is an evolutionary effort having three stages. These steps have in fact been used by major organizations that have already made the transition [12]:

1 Deployment of client/server computing for departmental applications

2 Integration of mainframe-based applications with a client/server network

3 Deployment of client/server computing on an enterprise-wide level

(Naturally some progressive companies can go directly to the third step if they so choose; however, the three-phase evolution is more common.)

Deployment of client/server computing for departmental applications As noted earlier, client/server computing first evolved within work groups and departments to cut costs, provide alternatives to host systems, and improve performance and access to information. Client/server computing can provide substantial competitive advantage by enabling departments to work faster and better. Client/server computing can create, when properly implemented, a more effective environment for line-of-business applications.

Integrating mainframe-based applications with a client/server network The successful deployment of client/server systems on a departmental level sets the stage for the next phase: end-users soon seek to access data outside their existing client/server environments. As the integration occurs, the client/server system interoperates with relational and nonrelational database management systems, indexed files, mainframe data, and other services provided by existing legacy applications. This can be accomplished through gateway products and open interfaces. Mainframe vendors, like IBM, have brought out mainframe-LAN software to facilitate the use of mainframes as superservers in client/server networks. Figure 2.4 shows an example [18]. Users are beginning to create server farms in secure rooms and are letting the IT department manage them; a mainframe-based alternative to a multitude of servers may be cost effective in specific situations.

Deployment of client/server computing on an enterprise-wide level With the establishment of successful departmental client/server networks that interoperate with resources outside those networks, organizations are ready to pursue the most strategic stage of client/server development—enterprise-wide client/server computing. This phase goes well beyond departmental client/server and gateway products by providing the total integration of department and corporate IT applications that span the enterprise. This environment enables the organization to leverage both existing central and line-of-business systems. With enterprise-wide client/server applications, the IT organization is able to reestablish control over data while at the same time supporting a truly distributed environment. The IT organization now can maximize the value of information by

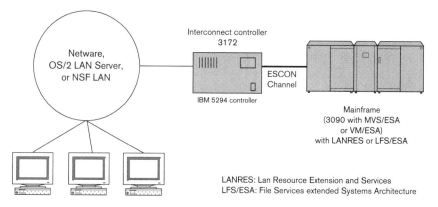

Interconnect controller
3172

Netware,
OS/2 LAN Server,
or NSF LAN

IBM 5294 controller

ESCON
Channel

Mainframe
(3090 with MVS/ESA
or VM/ESA)
with LANRES or LFS/ESA

LANRES: Lan Resource Extension and Services
LFS/ESA: File Services extended Systems Architecture

Figure 2.4   Integrating a mainframe as a superserver

increasing its availability and at the same time maintain central control over data integrity. End-users can access data from anywhere in the enterprise from their desktop.

2.2.5 Using SQL

Structured Query Language is a de facto "standard" language for creating, updating and querying databases, as discussed earlier. Some of the key design aspects of SQL are:

- To provide a data access language that could be proven to manipulate the data correctly and reliably
- To remove the physical storage feel-and-look of the data from the user

SQL is a flat-file implementation with extracted indexes, to provide direct access to the records (rows) of the file (table) being accessed; each field (columns) can be used as part of the search criteria. However, there are subtle differences introduced in each vendor's product. Multiple databases using different dialects of SQL may well exist in client/server network. This forces IT managers to retain in-house SQL-trained programmers to deal with these differences.

APIs, a type of middleware, can bring some stability to this environment. The APIs provide connectivity between applications and databases. One example of an API is Microsoft Corp.'s Open Database Connectivity (ODBC): it allows Windows based clients to access data from multiple relational databases management systems (e.g., IBM Corp.'s DB2 and Digital Equipment Corp.'s Rdb) and from its own SQL Server. ODBC also links to Apple Computer's Data Access Language. The Integrated Database Applications Programming Interface (IDAPI) initiative, was being advanced by

Microsoft competitors (such as Borland International, IBM, Novell, and WorldPerfect Corp.). Other APIs have been advanced [6].

Vendors are now bringing more sophisticated client/server software to the market, particularly in the context of networked databases (that is, distributed database systems). The new software aims at improved performance, while supporting asynchronous communication between clients and servers; in addition, added administrative and diagnostic features are being introduced [16]. Other features being added include *multiprotocol interchange* to handle protocol conversion without having to tax the database system itself.

Object-oriented Database Management Systems Object-oriented Database Management Systems (OODBMS) are an extension of SQL. Records are stored as objects (see Table 2.1); this allows more complex data types to be manipulated with a single or with a few commands. In addition to an object-oriented view of the data, there are, as noted in Table 2.1, object-oriented languages (see Chapter 3). The benefits of such an object-based approach are that the objects can be acquired and assembled to create applications. Conceivably, in the future one may not buy entire applications, but rather, applications may be assembled from a collection of objects built by different "construction" firms.

2.3 Distributed computing environment

DCE is a set of integrated software modules that provides an environment for creating, using, and maintaining client/server applications on a network (see [11] for a more extensive discussion). DCE is sponsored by the Open Software Foundation (OSF), which is a nonprofit organization aiming at delivering an open computing environment based on industry standards. Some see DCE as the most important architecture to be defined for the client/server technology. DCE includes capabilities such as security, directory, synchronization, file sharing, RPCs, and multithreading. One can view DCE as a "black software box"* installed by the major hardware and software vendors that in theory eliminates their technological barriers; such a black software box connects a

---

* More exactly, a prepackaged set of integrated interoperability applications (RPCs, presentation services, naming, security, threads, time services, distributed file services, management, and communications) that enables connection of diverse hardware and software systems, applications, and databases.

variety of operating systems, dissimilar hardware platforms, incompatible communications protocols, application and database systems, in a transparent manner for all concerned (end-users, system managers, and application developers) [13]. Another way of looking at this is as a bridge between the embedded base of applications and future applications and platforms.

2.4 Communication systems in place

Client/server systems rely, by definition, on communication and networks. Client/server computing can be implemented on a number of communication protocol suits, including NetWare IPX/SPX, NetBIOS, TCP/IP RPC, OSI, and SNA LU6.2. IT managers must select the protocol suite that best suits their installed base and applications inventory. One advantage of TCP/IP is that many, if not the majority of, applications support the Internet protocol suite. There in an increased need for multiplatform connectivity, making the problem technically challenging. Early SQL versions often used a considerable portion of the network's bandwidth by pushing nonessential data onto the network; later SQL versions from Oracle, Sybase, and Gupta Technologies, among others, make better use of bandwidth by storing procedures on the server. This reduces the amount of request data required from a server to trigger a transaction [6]. Developing client/server applications across a wide area network is even more challenging.

To make distributed computing a reality, one needs a sophisticated network infrastructure that can support not only client-to-server communication, but also server-to-server communication [16]. Server-to-server interactions are complex and resource-intensive. Some distributed database management systems support data replication, which is the process of copying data, distributing it to remote sites, and retaining synchronization as changes are made to the data in real time. However, without an effective underlying network (that is, a network of adequate bandwidth, reliability, flexibility, etc.), replication is of limited value. The need to establish flexible WAN infrastructures is now recognized by many of the network database vendors [16].

This section examines communication systems at the local and remote level that may be used to support client/server environments. Except for this section, the discussion in the rest of the book focuses on ATM. Readers who are familiar with these topics may choose to skip over the synopsis provided herewith.

2.4.1 Local connectivity

Local connectivity for traditional client/servers systems or intranet-based systems is physically achieved using LANs. Strategically, higher speed LANs will be required; however, in the short term any number of technologies will probably be adequate to various degrees. LAN technology has encompassed three generations. *First-generation* technology spanned the period covering the mid 1970s to late 1980s. Many corporations have or are still deploying these LANs based on coaxial cable or twisted-pair cable media. *Second-generation* technology emerged in the late 1980s to early 1990s, and is based on shared fiber optic cable media or high data-rate copper; this includes FDDI and 100 Mbps Ethernet. *Third-generation* LANs (e.g. based on ATM) are now beginning to become commercially available, and will see major deployment in the late 1990s to support new high-bandwidth applications such as multimedia, video, desk-to-desk video-conferencing and high-throughput client/server systems. The transmission speed achievable with LANs varies from 4 to 16 Mbps for first-generations; 100 Mbps for second-generation LANs; to Gbps rates for third-generation LANs. The need to interconnect collocated or remotely located LANs has emerged as a key need of the 1990s. The trend is toward enterprise-wide networking where all departments of a company are interconnected with a seamless (backbone) network, allowing company-wide access of all information and hardware resources. Enterprise-wide client/server systems, as well as intranets, rely on these enterprise-wide networks. The following depicts some key premises systems in support of client/server and other evolving business applications:

- Traditional LANs with microsegmentation
- Switched hubs: dedicated 10 Mbps ethernet to each desktop over twisted-pair cable
- High-speed token ring
- Fiber Distributed Data Interface(FDDI)/ Copper Distributed Data Interface (CDDI)
- FDDI II
- Fast Ethernet based on CSMA/CD (100 Mbps LAN)
- Fast Ethernet not based on CSMA/CD (100 Mbps LAN)
- Evolving gigabit LANs
- Local ATM LAN at 25 Mbps
- Local ATM LAN at 100 Mbps: FDDI PHY
- Local ATM at LAN 155 Mbps: 8B/10B Fiber Channel Standard PHY
- Local ATM LAN at 155 Mbps: SONET PHY
- LAN Emulation (LANE)

LAN technologies   *First-generation* LANs were developed in the early 1970s to provide what was then considered high-speed local connectivity among user devices. The contention-based Ethernet LAN technology was brought to the market by a joint effort among Xerox, Intel, and Digital Equipment Corp. Ethernet initially employed coaxial cable arranged in a logical bus and operating at 10 Mbps; now, thin coaxial and twisted-pair cable are used, usually in conjunction with wiring hubs and physical star arrangements. Extensive standardization work has been done by the Institute of Electrical and Electronic Engineers (IEEE) in the past fifteen years, leading to well-known standards such as the IEEE 802.2, 802.3, 802.4, and 802.5.

In the early 1980s, a token bus and a token ring technology were also developed, operating at 4 Mbps (a 16 Mbps system is also available). The token medium-sharing discipline is a variant of the polling method common in traditional data networks; however, instead of centrally controlled polling, the token is passed from station to station in an equitable manner. Only the LAN station possessing the token can transmit. Token ring systems took the approach of using shielded twisted-pair wires as the underlying medium, mainly because such a medium is cheaper and simpler to install than coaxial cable (however, unshielded twisted-pair (UTP) is expected to become the dominant LAN medium for traditional LANs). Over the past decade, the cost of connecting a user to a LAN decreased from about $1,000 to less than $50.

Higher network performance is required in order to support the applications now being put online by organizations that go beyond the movement of just data, including imaging, multimedia, and videoconferencing applications. One way of increasing the bandwidth available to applications is to replace the existing network with one based on FDDI. Efforts on *second-generation* LANs started in the early 1980s; products began to enter the market in the late 1980s. This token-based backbone/campus technology extends LAN features in terms of the geographic radius, covering a campus, as well as in the speed, reaching 100 Mbps. Implementors initially settled on multimode fiber as the underlying medium, although support for singlemode fiber was added in the late 1980s. One factor that has slowed the deployment of FDDI systems has been the cost of the interface cards. The cost of connecting a user to a FDDI LAN started out at about $8,000 and is now around $500– 1200. Efforts to facilitate the use of twisted-pair copper wires for FDDI have been underway, to bring the station access cost down (copper based interfaces cost in the $500– 700 range). While standards work in this arena has been slow in picking up speed, progress has been made in the recent past. 100-Mbps Ethernet technology now being deployed, as well as higher speed token ring technology, are candidates for second-generation systems.

Starting in the early 1990s, efforts have been under way to develop *third-generation* LANs supporting gigabit-per-second speeds (0.2–0.6 Gbps) over UTP or fiber facilities

[15]. These efforts are based on ATM mechanisms. ATM mechanisms were first developed in the context of wide area networking; the same technology is being applied in the premises networking context using ATM-based hubs and switches. Work along these lines is sponsored by industry vendors under the auspices of the ATM Forum. ATM switches to support high-end workstations have been available commercially since 1993. Workstation manufacturers are developing interface cards to connect their equipment to ATM switches. Initial costs were around $4,000 per port, but these costs should come down considerably (to $700) in the next couple of years as chipsets emerge. (Currently the cost for a desktop connection is as low as $700 for 25-Mbps LANs and $1,000 for 155-Mbps LANs.)

Table 2.4 summarizes some of the features of these three generations of LAN technology. Given the preceding discussion, one should not assume that traditional LANs will disappear from the business landscape. There will be a continued need for text-based business functions. However, as companies move to image-based operations, multimedia and desktop videoconferencing, the higher speed systems will be required.

LAN topologies   There are three major physical first-generation LAN topologies: star, ring, and bus. A *star* network is joined at a single point, generally with central control (such as a wiring hub). In a *ring* network the nodes are linked into a continuous circle on a common cable, and signals are passed unidirectionally around the circle from node to node, with signal regeneration at each node. A *bus* network is a single line of cable to which the nodes are connected directly by taps. It is normally employed with distributed control, but it can also be based on central control. Unlike the ring, however, a bus is passive, which means that the signals are not regenerated and retransmitted at each node.

Other configuration variations are available, particularly when looking at the LAN from a physical perspective; these are the *star-shaped ring* and the *star-shaped bus*. The first variation represents a wiring methodology to facilitate physical management: at the logical level the network is a ring; at the physical level it is a star centralized at some convenient point. Similarly, the second variation provides a logical bus, but wired in a star configuration using wiring hubs. Table 2.5 summarizes the use of these topologies in the three generations of LANs.

Medium-sharing disciplines   As discussed above, in traditional LANs there are two common ways of ensuring that nodes gain orderly access to the network, and that no more than one node at a time gains control of the shared LAN channel. The first is by the contention method; the second is by the token variant of polling.

Table 2.4 Typical features of LANs

Generation	Speed (Mbps)	Equipment	WAN Interconnection speed/services	Applications
First	4–16 (Ethernet, Token Ring)	Terminals PCs Workstations	9.6 kbps 56kbps T1 Frame relay SMDS	Office automation; decision support business functions as accounting (spread-sheets) and project management; mainframe access; manufacturing; some image applications
Second	100 (FDDI)	PCs High-end workstations High-end servers (CD-ROM and WORM image servers)	Fractional T1 T1 T3 SMDS	Backbone interconnection of LANs; CAD/CAM graphics; imaging;
Third	150–622* (ATM) 200–800 (gigibit LANs)	High-end workstations Video equipment High-end servers (CD-ROMs, WORM jukeboxes)	SONET B-ISDN/cell relay	Multimedia; desk-to-desk multimedia; conferencing; multimedia messaging CAD/CAM; visualization; animation; imaging; Digital Video (distance learning); LAN-based training; supercomputer/scientific application

*More in the future.

Table 2.5 LAN Topologies

LAN	Early	Recent
1st generation, Broadband	Bus	Bus
1st generation, Ethernet	Bus	Star-shaped bus
1st generation, Token-RIng	Ring	Star-shaped ring
2nd generation	Fiber Double Ring	Star-shaped double ring
3rd generation	Star-based access	—

The contention method is known as *carrier sense multiple access with collision detection* (CSMA/CD). If a node has a message to send, it checks the shared-medium network until it senses that it is traffic free and then it transmits. However, since all the nodes in the network have the right to contend for access, the node keeps monitoring the network to determine if a competing signal has been transmitted simultaneously with its own. If a second node is indeed transmitting, the two signals will collide. Both nodes detect the collision, stop transmitting, and wait for a random time before attempting to regain access.

Token-based LANs avoid the collisions inherent in Ethernet by requiring each node to defer transmission until it receives a token. The token is a control packet that is circulated around the network from node to node, in a preestablished sequence, when no transmission is otherwise taking place. The token signifies exclusive right to transmission, and no node can send data without it. Each node constantly monitors the network to detect any data frame addressed to it. When the token is received by a node, and it has nothing to send, it passes the token along to the next node in the sequence. If the token is accepted, it is passed on after the node has completed transmitting the data it has in its buffer. The token must be surrendered to the successor node within a specific time, so that no node can monopolize the network resources. Each node knows the address of its predecessor and successor. Note that ATM-based networks are not subject to this kind of contention.

Lower layer LAN protocols   In a LAN environment, layer 1 and 2 functions of the OSI Reference Model (OSIRM) have been defined by the IEEE 802 standards for first-generation LANs, by ANSI X3T9.5 for second-generation LANs, and by industry groups such as the ATM Forum, Alliance for Telecommunication Industry Solutions, and International Telecommunication Union (the last two bodies having standardized the supporting ATM functions) for third-generation LANs.

Using internetworking protocols defined at Layer 3 (such as IP—Internet Protocol), and connection-oriented transport-layer protocols (such as TCP—Transmission Control Protocol), one can build the LAN protocol suite up to layer 7 to support functions like email, file transfer, and directories. The use of TCP/IP has become commercially common.

Because LANs are based on a shared medium, the link layer is split into two sublayers. These sublayers are the Medium Access Control (MAC) sublayer, and the Logical Link Control (LLC) sublayer. The LLC sublayer provides a media independent interface to higher layers; these days that is done via the Subnetwork Access Protocol (SNAP). The MAC procedure is part of the protocol that governs access to the transmission medium. This is done independently of the physical characteristics of the medium, but taking into account the topological aspects of the subnetwork. Different IEEE 802 MAC standards represent different protocols used for sharing the medium (IEEE 802.3 is the contention-based Ethernet and IEEE 802.5 is the token-based system). See Table 2.6.

Table 2.6 Functions at specified protocol levels

LLC/ SNAP	Reliable transfer of frames Connection to higher layers
MAC	Addressing Frame construction Token/collision handling
PHY	Encoding/decoding Clocking
PMD	Cable parameters (optical/electrical) Connectors

PHY = Physical Layer Protocol-explicit only in more recent standards such as FDDI, Local ATM
PMD = Physical Medium Dependent-explicit only in more recent standards such as FDDI, SONET, ATM

Connectionless versus connection-oriented communication   Two basic forms of communication (service) are possible for both LANs and WANs: *Connection-oriented mode* and *connectionless mode*.

A connection-oriented service involves a connection establishment phase, an information transfer phase, and a connection termination phase. This implies that a logical connection is set up between end-systems prior to exchanging data. These phases define the sequence of events ensuring successful data transmission. Sequencing of data, flow control, and transparent error handling are some of the capabilities inherent with this service mode. One disadvantage of this approach is the delay experienced in setting up the connection. Traditional carrier services, including circuit switching, X.25 packet switching, and early Frame Relay service (discussed later) are examples of connection-oriented transmission; LLC 2 is also a connection-oriented protocol.

In a connectionless service, each data unit is independently routed to the destination. No connection-establishment tasks are required, since each data unit is independent of the previous or subsequent ones. Hence, a connectionless mode service provides for transfer of data units (cells, frames, or packets) without regard to the establishment or maintenance of connections. The basic MAC/LLC (i.e., LLC 1) transfer mechanism of a LAN is connectionless. In this connectionless mode transmission delivery is uncertain, due to the possibility of errors. Connectionless communication shifts the responsibility for the integrity to a higher layer, where the integrity check is done only once, instead of being done at every lower layer. Connectionless communication can occur at any Layer of the protocol model. At the Network Layer, a well-known connectionless protocol is IP.

TCP/IP protocol suite The basic TCP/IP protocol suite is shown in Table 2.7 for both LAN and WAN environments (there are about one hundred protocols in the Internet suite). A TCP/IP LAN application involves: a user connection over a standard LAN system (IEEE 802.3,.4,.5 over LLC); software in the PC and/or server implementing the IP, TCP and related protocols, and programs running on the PCs or servers to provide the needed application. (The application may use other higher layer protocols for file transfer, network management, and so on.)

Table 2.7   TCP/IP-based communication; key protocols

	LAN environment	WAN environment
Layer 7–Layer 5	Application specific protocols such as TELNET (terminal sessions), FTP and SFTP (file transfer), SMTP (email), SNMP (management), DNS (directory), and HTTP (Web)	
Layer 4	TCP, UDP, EGP/IGP (routing)	TCP, UDP
Layer 3	IP, ICMP, ARP/ RARP (address)	IP, ICMP X.25 PLP
Layer 2	LLC CSMA/CD, Token ring, Token bus	LAP-B, LAP-D, ATM
Layer 1	IEEE 802.3, .4, .5 (PMD portions)	Physical channels

SFTP = Simple File Transfer Protocol
SMTP = Simple Mail Transfer Protocol
DNS = Domain Name Service
ICMP = Internet Control Message Protocol
RARP = Reverse Address Resolution Protocol
IGP = Internal Gateway Protocol

FTP = File Transfer Protocol
SNMP = Simple Network Management Protocol
UDP = User Datagram Protocol
ARP = Address Resolution Protocol
EGP = External Gateway Protocol
PMD = Physicial Medium Dependent

IP protocol In a TCP/IP environment, IP provides the underlying mechanism to move data from one end system (say, the client) on one LAN to another end system (say, the server) on the same or different LAN. IP makes the underlying network transparent to the upper layers, TCP in particular. It is a connectionless packet delivery protocol, where each IP packet is treated independently. (In this context, packets are also called *datagrams*.) IP provides two basic services: addressing and fragmentation or reassembly of long packets. IP adds no guarantees of delivery, reliability, flow control, or error recovery to the underlying network other than what the Data Link layer mechanism already provides. IP expects the higher layers to handle such functions. IP may lose packets, deliver them out of order, or duplicate them; IP defers these contingencies to the higher layers (TCP, in particular). Another way of saying this is that IP delivers on a "best-effort basis." There are no connections, physical or virtual, maintained by IP.

Transmission Control Protocol (TCP)   Since IP is an "unreliable," best-effort con-nectionless network layer protocol, TCP (a transport layer protocol) must provide reli-ability, flow control, and error recovery. TCP is a connection-oriented, end-to-end reliable protocol providing logical connections between pairs of processes. Some TCP features are:

- *Data transfer*   From the applications viewpoint, TCP transfers a contiguous stream of octets through the interconnected network. The application does not have to segment the data into blocks or packets since TCP does this by grouping the octets in *TCP segments* that are then passed to IP for transmission to the desti-nation. TCP determines how to segment the data and it forwards the data at its own convenience.

- *Reliability*   TCP assigns a sequence number to each TCP segment transmitted, and expects a positive acknowledgment from the receiving peer TCP. If the acknowledgment is not received within a specified timeout interval, the segment is retransmitted. The receiving TCP uses the sequence numbers to rearrange the seg-ments if they arrive out of order, and to discard duplicate segments.

- *Flow control*   The receiving TCP signals to the sender the number of octets it can receive beyond the last received TCP segment, without causing an overflow in its internal buffers. This indication is sent in the acknowledgment in the form of the highest sequence number it can receive without problems. (This approach is also known as a window mechanism.)

- *Logical connections*   To achieve reliability and flow control, TCP must maintain certain status information for each data stream. The combination of this status, including sockets, sequence numbers and window sizes, is called a logical connec-tion (also known as a virtual circuit).

- *Multiplexing*   this is achieved through the use of a ports mechanism.

- *Duplex communication*   TCP provides for concurrent data streams in both directions.

  (Naturally, protocols other than TCP can be used.)

FDDI   The FDDI is a set of standards that defines a shared medium LAN utilizing fiber (singlemode and multimode), and now, twisted-pair cabling. The aggregate band-width supported by FDDI is 100 Mbps. It uses a token-based discipline to manage mul-tiple access. FDDI was developed with data communication in mind (rather than, for example, video or multimedia), particularly for backbone LAN interconnection in a campus or building floor riser environment. FDDI networks are now used both as a backbone (*back-end*) technology to connect departmental LANs, and as a *front-end* technology to directly connect workstations. As noted earlier, FDDI has experienced slow penetration because the cost of the device attachment has remained high.

Even for the traditional applications, there is a recognized potential for network bottlenecks in the near future, not only because of the increased number of users and the introduction of client/server systems (where data are not locally located at the PC but must be obtained across a distance), but also because of the increasing deployment of a new graphics-intensive or image-intensive applications. Therefore, even systems providing an aggregate throughput of 100 Mbps, such as FDDI, may be inadequate for high throughput applications. ATM is a scalable technology that can meet evolving requirements.

100-Mbps Ethernet systems   In 1993, about a dozen companies announced that they were investigating the possibility of developing Ethernet systems operating at 100 Mbps using voice-grade unshielded twisted-pair cable. These systems are also called *Fast Ethernet*. The goal is to deliver 100 Mbps to the desktop cheaper than would be the case with FDDI-based adapters. Some companies are exploring the same signaling scheme used in copper-based FDDI, while other companies are looking at other schemes.

The issues associated with this endeavor have been: Does one keep the same CSMA/CD MAC as the 10-Mbps system, or does one move to a MAC that is more isochronous in nature? Does one aim for voice-grade unshielded wiring (Type 3), use data-grade unshielded wiring (Type 5), or shielded wiring (Type 1)? Can one retain two-pair wiring or will four-pair system be needed/preferred? In the opinion of a majority of interested parties, one wants to keep the existing wiring and replace the PC/workstation and hub cards for no more than a fifty dollars. The target is to deliver 100 Mbps (aggregate shared bandwidth) to the desktop for no more that twice the cost of a 10Base-T system. A number of proposals where made to the IEEE 802.3 Committee, in addition to other variants. The goals of the effort, as adopted by the IEEE Committee are shown in the following list:

- 100 Mbps
- 100 meters to the hub
- 802.3 MAC frame format
- EIA 568 wiring specification (Category 3)
- 802-equivalent error rates
- Consistency with FCC and European radiation emission standards
- Simultaneous support of 10 and 100 Mbps

- Media-independent interfaces
- Support of multiple hubs
- Use of RJ-45 connector for UTP

In some proposals, the frame would remain the same as the ethernet frame, but the signaling (how the frame is transmitted over the medium, as specified in the Physical and Physical Medium Dependent (PMD) sublayers) would be changed. Because of these changes, new workstation/PC network interface cards and new hubs would be required. (Note that LLC, TCP/IP, and the applications themselves do not require any modifications.) In addition, because of propagation time issues, the diameter of the network (maximum end-to-end cable length) would have to be reduced by an order of magnitude, from the current 2,500 meters to 250 meters. If the ethernets in questions are interconnected over an FDDI backbone (i.e., hubs interface to an FDDI network), then the distance reduction would likely not be a problem; however, if the network hubs are connected over twisted-pair cable supporting a single logical network, then the diameter restriction will likely be a problem. A way around this problem is to utilize bridges between hubs.

The ability to operate at higher speeds without having to modify major portions of the MAC protocols has been demonstrated for some time, in both the Ethernet and token ring context. (Sixty-four Mbps token ring systems have been prototyped; however, new network interface cards for the PMD would be required in both cases.) There has been broad vendor support for this proposal. Dual speed (10/100 Mbps) adapters and dual speed hub ports have emerged. Bridging between the two systems is relatively easy (as long as the effective speed/throughput is consistent across both networks).

In other proposals the MAC protocol is also replaced, eliminating the contention scheme (which is in fact the culprit for variable delays and throughput in the network), and replacing with a Demand Priority Protocol using a scheme called Quartet Signaling. Four pairs are required with this approach.

Two alternatives have emerged, in the final analysis, as standards: 100Base-T (IEEE 802.3u) and Demand Priority 100VG-AnyLAN (IEEE 802.12). Extensions have been made over the years to IEEE 802.3 Ethernet, since it was originally standardized in 1983. These extensions include Ethernet switching, full-duplex Ethernet, and most recently, Fast Ethernet (IEEE 802.3u.) In particular, Ethernet switching has been fairly successful at the commercial level.* Ethernet-based technologies (Ethernet switching,

---

* Switching is a hub-centric form of Ethernet that takes advantage of the star topology now prevalent in LANs. It effectively eliminates Ethernet collisions by placing each workstation on its own segment (the only collisions occurring when the hub and the workstation both try to transmit information simultaneously).

full-duplex Ethernet, and Fast Ethernet, along with hubs, routers and adapters) tend to interwork with some degree of cohesion. Therefore, some see a continued, firmly rooted opportunity for this technology. Others see ATM as the next corporate LAN technology. It is worth noting that all the new protocols support UTP wiring, thereby eliminating a potential first hurdle related to possible deployment in the corporate landscape. However, there are significant technology, embedded base, internetting, and management issues impacting the actual deployment prognosis.

2.4.2 Wide area connectivity

There are several factors that characterize wide area services that are of particular relevance to client/server environments. Table 2.8 highlights some of these characteristics; however, not every possible combination shown in this table corresponds to a service which can be secured from a carrier. Figure 2.5 shows some of the more common combinations. Connection-oriented communication highlighted in both the table and the figure is similar to the traditional dedicated line or circuit-switched environment where the user goes through a connectivity setup phase, an information transfer phase, and a connectivity teardown phase. (For a circuit-switched call, this is done in real time; for a dedicated line service, the setup is done at service initiation time and the teardown is done at service cancellation time.) In a connectionless service, each data unit is treated independently of the previous one, and no connectivity setup/teardown is required, much the same way as an information frame is transferred in a LAN.

Strategically, higher speed WANs will be required; however, in the short term any number of technologies will probably be adequate to various degrees. Table 2.9 depicts

Table 2.8 Key factors for wide area connectivity

Characteristic	Typical ranges
Speed (bandwidth)	$n \times 64$ kbps, T1/DS1/E1 (1.544–2.048 Mbps), T2/DS2 (6.312 Mbps), T3/DS3 (44.736 Mbps), STS-1 (51.84 Mbps), STS-3c (155.250 Mbps), STS-12c (622.08 Mbps)
Bearer Mode	Connection-oriented or Connectionless
Switching type	None (dedicated line), Circuit switched, Packet-switched (frame relay, cell relay)
Symmetry	Bidirectional symmetric bandwidth, Bidirectional asymmetric bandwidth, Unidirectional
Connection type supported (signaling support)	Point-to-point, Point-to-multipoint, Multipoint-to-multipoint
Geographic scope of coverage	IntraLATA, InterLATA, International

Table 2.9 High-speed service and related terms

Cell relay service	A method to multiplex, switch, and transport a variety of high-capacity signals, using short, fixed-length data units known as cells. The Asynchronous Transfer Mode is the accepted international standard for the cell structure. 155- or 622-Mbps public switched WAN service is available (service is also possible over a private switch), where the user's cells are delivered at high-speed to a remote destination (or destinations). Both a Permanent Virtual Circuit (PVC) service and a Switched Virtual Circuits (SVC) service are evolving.
Fractional T1	A point-to-point dedicated service supporting $n \times 64$ kbps connectivity (typically, $n = 2, 4, 6, 12$).
Frame relay, private	A multiplexed service obtained over a private high-speed backbone equipped with appropriate nodal processors (fast packet switches). Used to interconnect LANs at $n \times 64$ kbps or 1.544 Mbps.
Frame relay, public	A multiplexed service provided by a carrier. The user has a single access line into the network and can deliver frames to remote users without having to provide dedicated communication links or switches. Used to interconnect LANs at $n \times 64$ kbps or 1.544 Mbps.
ISDN H0	A switched service providing physical connectivity at 384 kbps, using the ISDN call setup mechanism.
ISDN H11	A switched service providing physical connectivity at 1.536 kbps, using the ISDN call setup mechanism.
SMDS	Switched Multimegabit Data Service, a public switched service supporting connection-less cell-based communication at 1.544 and 45 Mbps access speed, targeted for LAN interconnection. Importance to diminish in future.
SONET	Synchronous Optical Network (known as Synchronous Digital Hierarchy outside the US), is a specification for digital hierarchy levels at multiple of 52 Mbps. Also, a point-to-point dedicated service supporting $n \times 52$-Mbps connectivity over fiber-based facilities.
Switched T1	A switched service providing physical connectivity at 1.536 Mbps.
T1 (DS1)	A point-to-point dedicated service supporting 1.544-Mbps aggregate connectivity.
T3 (DS3)	A point-to-point dedicated service supporting 44.736-Mbps aggregate connectivity or 28 DS1 subchannels.

some of the key telecommunication services now becoming available in support of distributed computing. Table 2.10 groups these services into four types, namely dedicated/switched and low speed/high speed. Figure 2.6 shows the applicability of some of the key interoffice/long distance high speed services plotted against the burstiness requirement of the application. (Burstiness is the ratio of the instantaneous traffic to the average traffic. [14]). Figure 2.7 shows an example of a client/server system implemented across a WAN.

Cell relay service   Asynchronous Transfer Mode is a high bandwidth, low delay switching and multiplexing communication technology supporting wide area communications; as noted, the same technology is now also being applied to the development of next-generation LANs. (To be exact, ATM refers to the network platform while cell relay service refers to the actual service obtainable over an ATM platform.) The general

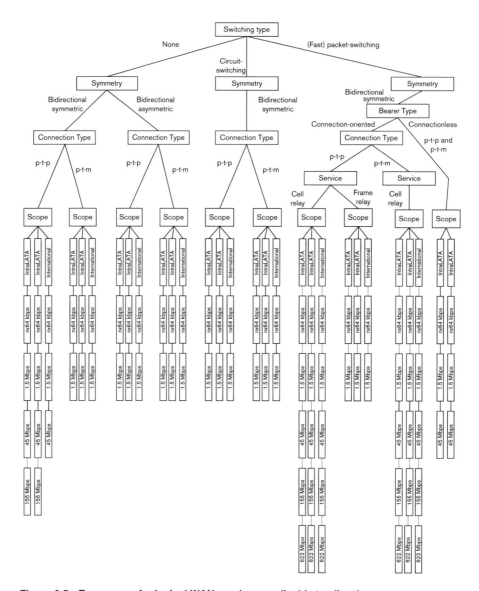

Figure 2.5   Taxonomy of principal WAN services applicable to client/server

industry consensus is that ATM is the WAN service of choice for applications requiring high throughput. It is connectivity-oriented technology supporting a number of categories of statistical multiplexing. For readers familiar with the operation of a protocol stack, it is simply a matter of realizing what functional partitioning has been instituted by the designers of ATM, and what the peer entities are in the user's equipment and in the network. The cell relay protocols equate approximately to the functionality of the

Table 2.10 Classification of key WAN services in support of client/server systems

	Nonswitched	Switched
Low speed	Analog private line DDS private line Fractional T1 private line T1 private line Frame relay (Permanent Virtual Circuit)	Dialup with modem ISDN Packet switched network Frame relay (Switched Virtual Circuit)
High speed	T3 private line SONET private line ATM/Cell Relay Service (Permanent Virtual Circuit)	Switched Multi-megabit Data Service (SMDS) ATM/Cell Relay Service (Switched Virtual Circuit)

MAC/LLC layers of a traditional LAN, but with the following differences: random access is not utilized, channel sharing is done differently, and the underlying media may be different [19].

Two remotely located user devices (say a client and a server) needing to communicate over an ATM network can establish one or more bidirectional virtual (i.e., not hard-wired or dedicated) connections between them to transmit cells (fixed length packets 53 bytes long). This connection is identified by each user by an appropriate identifier, similar in some respects to how virtual channels are identified in a packet switched network. Once such a basic connection is set up, user devices can utilize the virtual connection-oriented channel for specific communication tasks. Each active channel has an

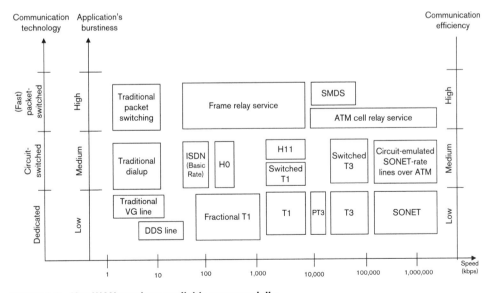

Figure 2.6 Key WAN services available commercially

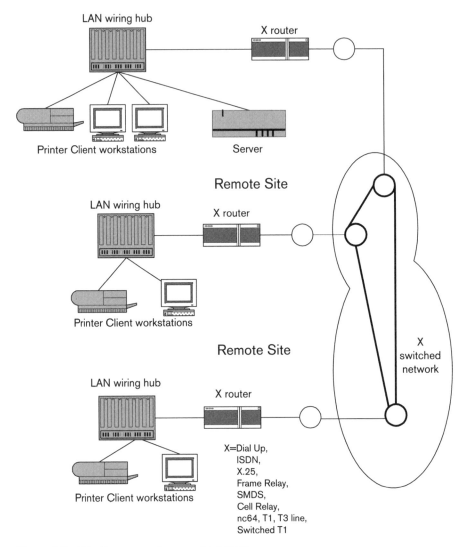

Figure 2.7   Client/server system across a WAN

associated bandwidth negotiated with the network at connection setup time. The transfer capacities at the User Network Interface (UNI) are 155.52 Mbps and 44.736 Mbps.

Connections in an ATM network support both circuit mode and packet mode services of a single media or mixed media and multimedia. ATM carries several types of traffic including Constant Bit Rate (CBR) and Variable Bit Rate (VBR). For example, video transmission generates CBR traffic, while data applications (say, router traffic for a traditional LAN) generate VBR traffic. CBR transfer rate parameters for on-demand services are negotiated at call setup time. (CBR transfer rate parameters for permanent services are agreed upon with the carrier from which the user obtains service.) VBR services are described by a number of traffic-related parameters, peak rate, sustained rate, maximum burst length, etc., that are also negotiated at call setup time.

For wide area communication, cell relay entails the following aspects:

- Specification of the network interface configuration, i.e., the required protocols and procedures that the user needs to implement in his/her equipment in order to obtain the high speed high-quality cell relay service. The user equipment can be comprised of a variety of elements (workstations, routers, servers, multiplexers, etc.). The access speed and other Quality of Service (QoS) factors can be specified by the user. The interface covers both the information flow and the call control flow (that is, the user has a "transmit" channel and a "signaling" channel).

- A high-speed, typically fiber-based, local loop to enable the user's information stream originating at a user's location to reach the broadband switch at the Serving Central Office or some other hub location, where it is appropriately handled.

- A high-speed broadband switch that is able to interconnect users at the required bandwidth rates.

- A Call Control capability (at the broadband switch or other location) to accept the user's service requests and to allocate network resources to satisfy these requests. The call control capability supports point-to-point, point-to-multipoint, and multipoint-to-multipoint connectivity.

- A network capability to maintain the requested bandwidth, connectivity, and QoS.

- An interoffice high-speed network infrastructure supporting wide area connectivity.

- An interoffice (overlay) signaling network to carry the users' service requests (i.e., signaling information) to the appropriate destination.

The access protocol in the user equipment consists of a Physical Layer at the lowest level and an ATM layer over it that provides information transfer for all services. Above the ATM layer, the ATM Adaptation Layer (AAL) provides service-dependent functions to the layer above the AAL. (The layers above the AAL are somewhat similar to TCP/IP in a traditional LAN; in fact, TCP/IP may continue to be used by users' PCs and hosts—note that AALs usually only go as high as the Data Link Layer.) The AAL protocols are implemented in the user's equipment. The Service Data Units reaching the AAL consist of user information coming down the protocol stack, e.g., from a TCP/IP stack or from a video codec; the information is segmented/cellularized by AAL into the 53-octet cells, so that they can be efficiently shipped through the network. The AAL enhances the services provided by the ATM layer to support the functions required by the next higher layer. The AAL-specific information is nested in the information field of the ATM cell. To minimize the number of AAL protocols, a service classification has been defined based on the following three parameters: timing relation between source and destination (required or not required); bit rate (constant or variable); and connection mode (connection-oriented or connectionless). Five classes of applications are then defined, as follows:

- *Class A*   Timing required, bit rate constant, Connection-oriented
- *Class B*   Timing required, bit rate variable, Connection-oriented
- *Class C*   Timing not required, bit rate variable, Connection-oriented
- *Class D*   Timing not required, bit rate variable, Connectionless
- *Class X*   Unrestricted (bit rate variable, Connection-oriented or Connectionless).

Wide area networks providing Cell Relay Services started to appear in 1994, with more widespread penetration soon thereafter. There is keen interest in ATM and Cell Relay Service on the part of local exchange carriers, interexchange carriers, and international carriers. Cell Relay Service provides both a Permanent Virtual Circuit and a Switched Virtual Circuit service. A PVC implementation establishes a fixed path through the network for each source-destination pair, which remains defined for a long period of time (weeks, months, or years). In SVC, resources are put in place only for the duration of the actual session (minutes or hours). Early carrier offerings supported only PVC service (SVC service is expected to appear in 1997–98). Cell Relay Service is expected to be used in large companies.

This topic will be treated in more detail in Chapter 4.

Frame Relay Service   Frame Relay Service (FRS) is a connection-oriented service operating at $n \times 64$ kbps or 1.544 Mbps (2.048 Mbps in Europe). It is offered by a variety of carriers, including the Alternate Access Providers (AAPs), Regional Bell Operating Companies, and interexchange carriers. It began to be available in early 1991 and by press time it was available in most US and in many European cities. FRS is positioned for LAN interconnection. Given the relatively low speed, it is marginally useful for high speed applications. Compared to X.25-based service, FRS aims at reducing network delays, providing more efficient bandwidth utilization and decreasing communication equipment cost. The increase in efficiency and reduction in delay is achieved by performing error correction on an end-to-end basis rather than on a link-by-link basis, as is the case, for example, in traditional packet switching. This makes the protocol much simpler. Communication links are now carried in an increasing number on fiber optic facilities, making them cleaner, as measured by the Bit Error Rate. Because the circuits are much cleaner, it is more effective to perform error management on an end-to-end basis. Most of the applications to date have been for wide area LAN interconnection where the LANs support traditional data-only applications. Some experimentation in support of video-conferencing and voice has been reported, but with limited success.

A frame relay interface can support multiple sessions over a single physical access line. Equipment implementing frame relay interfaces have been implemented on such products as LAN bridges and routers, as well as on T1 multiplexers. Frame relay provides both a PVC and SVC service. In practice, all user implementations and all carrier offerings initially only supported PVCs (SVC service may appear in 1997–98, although this is unlikely.) Frame Relay Service is expected to be used in medium to large companies.

Digital dedicated line services   In spite of the emergence of other digital services, high speed dedicated digital lines operating at $n \times 64$ kbps ($n = 1, 2, 6, 12$), 1.544 Mbps (also known as T1) and 45 Mbps (also known as T3) still represent a common way to interconnect remote LANs. A dedicated line implies that the entire bandwidth can be applied to the interconnection task (unless a portion of the bandwidth is allocated to another application). Since the bandwidth is not generally shared, there is no delay variation, and there is no frame discard over the WAN, dedicated lines are somewhat better suited for high performance applications compared, for example, with FRS. This approach, however, does have at least three drawbacks:

1 Relatively high cost

2 Multitude of lines, growing as 0.5 times the square of the number of locations to be connected, implying high communication and network management cost

3 Inflexibility to reach off-net locations, typically providing connectivity between only two or a few sites

Use of high speed dedicated services are expected in medium-to large companies.

Other Technologies   For a thorough description of the other technologies identified in Table 2.10, the reader may consult [23].

2.5 *References*

3   T. E. Bell," Jobs at Risk," *IEEE Spectrum*, August 1993, page 26.

4   R. Moskowitz, "What are Clients and Servers Anyway?," *Network Computing*, Client/server Supplement: May 1993.

5   "Data Communication," *Sharing the Load: Client/server Computing*, March 21, 1989, pages 19–29.

6   J. C. Panettieri, "How to Break Through the Logjam," *Network Computing*, Client/server Supplement, May 1993.

7   L. Berg, "Implementing Client/Server Computing," Washington, DC: COMNET 92, Jan. 1992.

8   K. Myhre, "Please Explain Client/Server?," Washington, DC: COMNET 92, Jan. 1992.

9   D. Ferris, "Client/server Database Models are Emerging," *Network World*, May 11, 1992.

10 S. Morse, "Client/Servers is Not Always the Best Solution," *Network Computing*, Client/server Supplement, May 1993.

11 D. Minoli, *First, Second, and Next Generation LANs*, New York, NY: McGraw-Hill, 1993.

12 Promotional Material, *Network Computing*, Client/Server Supplement, May 1993.

13 P. Smith, *Client/Server Computing*, Carmel, IN: Sams Publishing, 1992.

14 D. Minoli, *Imaging in Corporate Environments*, New York, NY: McGraw-Hill, 1994.

15 D. Minoli, Third Generation LANs, *Proceedings of TEXPO 1993*, San Francisco, CA: April 6–8, 1993.

16 J. Cox, "Oracle to Cast SQL*Net at Distributed Apps," *Communications Week*, August 2, 1993, page 1.

17 J. Cox, "Users Urge: See Client/Server Clearly," *Communications Week*, June 21, 1993, page 11.

18 T. Wilson, "IBM Continues Client/Server Shift," *Communications Week*, June 21, 1993, page 4.

19 D. Minoli, ATM Makes its Entrance, WAN Connections-Supplement of August 1993 *Network Computing Magazine,* page 22.

20 D. Minoli, *Analyzing Outsourcing*, New York, NY: McGraw-Hill, 1994.

21 A. Freedman, *Electronic Computer Glossary*, The Computer Language Co., 1993.

22 H. Newton, *Newton's Telecom Dictionary*, 1993.

23 D. Minoli, *Enterprise Networking, From Fractional T1 to SONET, from Frame Relay to BISDN,* Norwoord, MA: Artech House, 1993.

chapter 3

Multidistributed databases: Client/server systems and more

3.1 Introduction and background

The purpose of this chapter is to discuss databases and distributed database technology with an eye on client/server systems. In addition, aspects of object-oriented programming (OOP) are covered; these are included because many client/server applications now use OOP methods. This chapter further discusses requirements found in PMO client/server systems; these requirements will have to be supported by future mode of operation client/server systems based on ATM transport.

A distributed database is one that customers or users see as a single, coherent collection of information from their locations, but that is actually formed by one or more databases at numerous locations within a network. The data exist in one or more places in the network and customers who need the data can get to them as if they were within their own computers. The means by which the data are retrieved and the location of the data are transparent to the customers. The users see only a menu, for example, and select an item. They have no idea that the inquiry might be going to a computer in another site. The trend toward distributed databases allows for greater empowerment of the business units to develop and maintain their own systems. The World Wide Web is an excellent example of a distributed system, although it is not a distributed database in the technical sense of the word. Distributed databases are predicated on the availability of ubiquitous (company-wide) high-speed and reliable networks [42], [49–60].

As already discussed, today, businesses must respond to rapidly changing market conditions, continuously reduce operational costs, and reevaluate their business strategies. Corporations are focusing on decentralization, downsizing, and quality management. They must be able to react quickly to the constant changes in technology to maintain competitiveness. This predicament necessitates information systems that are flexible, scalable, maintainable, and cost-effective. Yet, many businesses find that the traditional information system architectures (mainframes) do not easily support these objectives. The client/server computing approach and intranets have become a natural outgrowth of the popularity of the PC and the widespread use of LANs and high-speed WANs. The client/server approach has become a popular and effective method of designing modular information systems that facilitate data access, provide user-friendly work environments, and also promote reductions in cost and systems maintenance [39].

As companies juggle for control of profits and losses, one is faced with new management strategies: business process reengineering, downsizing, rightsizing, and outsourcing [43]. Business process reengineering (BPR) is an approach where companies reengineer their processes. In downsizing and rightsizing, computers are replaced with smaller computers of equal capabilities. Corporations are moving to client/server computing to reduce expenditures. These savings take form in hardware, software, and labor. In replacing mainframes with smaller workstations or PCs, businesses have shifted the emphasis off programmers and onto end users. Traditionally, mainframes were supported by large information systems staff; now, fewer people are required to maintain the smaller computers. Applications that fully exploit the benefits of GUIs, foster computer literacy among nonprogramming staff [39].

The past has seen a host-centric environment for transaction processing. Technology is changing so rapidly that IT departments and business units have to work together to make strategic planning decisions for the corporation. The IT culture is continuously changing, and distributed processing and client/server technologies are currently in the forefront of application development. The mainframe systems, known as legacy systems, are still widely used and will be for some time. The manufacturers of mainframe systems are now developing and introducing *open* systems which allow these new technologies to interact [49–60].

The introduction of intranets in the corporate landscape is another milestone in the evolution of the corporate repository of information. Both the Internet and the corporate intranet are premier examples of highly distributed information repositories. Planners should be sure to track both of these developments in this context since they will likely be asked to support this technology, which in turn, has client/server and ATM undertones.

3.2 Evolution of the database

3.2.1 What is a database?

A database is an organized collection of data, for example, the telephone directory, canceled checks, or a daily appointment book. Consider the telephone directory and the information contained in it—a listing of people by last name (the white pages) including their address and telephone number. If we focus on a specific person, John Smith, in database terminology, we would consider his entry in the directory a *record*. This record is made up of *fields*—name, address, and telephone number; each is a piece of the information that is given about John Smith. [39], [45–48].

A *computer* database, such as a personal spreadsheet containing addresses, telephone numbers, and birthdays, is different from the previous example because it is run on a computer and stored on a computer disk. There are several advantages to a computer database. One is the relative ease involved in searching for particular information. All database software tools enable a user to search for specific data. Depending on the software, these searches may be simple, such as locating an address, or may be more complex, such as finding all customer names whose accounts are delinquent. Another advantage is that it is simpler to perform a calculation (on a few columns on a computer spreadsheet) to estimate a monthly budget than to manually add and subtract totals on weekly payroll stubs.

Databases have become a fast growing industry over the past quarter century. The success of databases is due largely as a result of the transition of the information industry from paper-based services to computer-based services. Read-only databases are now available in CD-ROM format and may be publicly accessible via the Internet or online services. The growth of the database industry can be measured in terms of an increase of the number of database records, online searches, database producers, database vendors, and databases themselves. This is depicted in Figure 3.1.* Over the period from 1975 to 1992, there was a steady increase of both database entries and databases. Highly distributed databases are the next step in the evolution.

3.2.2 Architectures

Databases are usually categorized by the way they maintain data relationships.† The data contained within databases are usually held together and accessed through the use of basic data structures. These structures—linked lists, tree structures and hashing algorithms—have evolved along with the database. See Table 3.1 [39] [45–48].

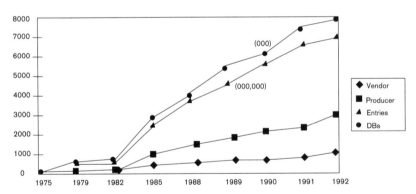

Figure 3.1 Growth in number of database vendors, database producers, database entries, and databases

---

* Kathleen Young Marracaccio, *Gale Directory of Databases, Volume 1: On-line Databases,* January 1993, Gale Research Inc., 1993.

† Don Burleson, "More Than 'Just Pretend'," *Database Programming & Design,* October 1995, pp. 52ff.

Table 3.1 Evolution of database architecture

Decade	Database architecture	Features
1960s	Flat files	Simple data storage
1970s	Hierarchical/network	Data storage Data relationships
1980s	Relational	Data storage Data relationship Easy access
1990s	Object-oriented	Data storage Data relationships Behavior storage

Flat files   A flat file is a file that contains records of information that are typically delimited by a comma or a tab; the data may also be contained in one long line, making it difficult to extract specific data. Typically, flat files are found in existing mainframe or highly dedicated minicomputer applications. For example, a process control application software may output process data into flat files: *unique time and date, value1, value2, value3, value4,* etc. These files may be used to create entries in a more conventional database. While flat files may be useful, they carry overhead in terms of generating the file and then processing and parsing it into a database.

Hierarchical databases   In hierarchical databases, parent-child relationships are defined for database records. One-to-one and one-to-many relationships between records and their subordinate records may be established; however, the many-to-many relationship is not supported. This type of database model was prevalent in mainframe applications. Data within a hierarchical database could be accessed via a program. End-users could not easily retrieve desired information without the help of a database programmer [39].

Relational databases   The relational database was developed in 1969 by E. F. Codd, and is based on relational calculus.* Relational databases organize data into two-dimensional "tables." Relationships are established between tables based on common information within the tables' rows and columns. These relationships encourage less data repetition, faster data access (queries), and a simpler (normalized) data storage. The most important aspect of relational databases is the method of access to the data stored within the database: a simple SQL query. This allows nonprogrammers and end-users unassisted access to information within the database.

---

* Karen Watterson, *Client/Server Technology for Managers.* Addison Wesley, 1995. Chapter 4.

Object-oriented databases   An object-oriented database (OOD) treats data as objects. These objects hold nontraditional data such as entire documents, scanned images (pictures), and multimedia files. An offshoot of object-oriented programming (discussed later), these databases accommodate the rising demand for complex data storage marrying the object concepts of inheritance, polymorphism, and encapsulation. However, this architecture is still relatively new in traditional relational databases. (Movement of these kinds of objects requires a lot of bandwidth, e.g., as provided by ATM.)

3.2.3   Practical applications for databases

There are many practical uses for databases. For example, there are business, consumer interest-oriented, health/life science-related, law, academic, science and engineering, and governmental databases. These databases may contain data in the form of words, numbers, images, or sounds. Electronic information services such as bulletin boards, electronic mail, and electronic conferencing contain data that is transient.* Several commercial online services such as America Online make software databases available. CompuHelp provides online help for visually impaired computer users.

An example of a distributed database is a collection of inventory information accessed and kept up-to-date by point-of-sale applications running in a retail store's LAN. With this example, the terminals located at cashier stations and information desks would all be able to access an updated copy of inventory databases. The LAN connections eliminate the need to store data in each workstation that needs it. It provides a single source of data and can help ensure that the inventory information is current and consistent. There is only one version of inventory at a given point which is seen by all the workstations on the LAN. This type of setup will save on data storage costs, especially if the only alternative is to duplicate the data on all workstations [42].

Another example of a distributed database is the reverse of our first example of a single source of data with multiple locations accessing it. A company with headquarters in one city may have sales offices in other cities. Each sales office can maintain a database of its own transactions. The corporate office can access each of the sales office's databases as if it were a single cohesive database. If the corporate office needs a monthly or weekly sales summary report, it can run an application that accesses the distributed databases as if all the data were located at the corporate headquarters. Headquarters can

---

* Kathleen Young Maracaccio, *Gale Directory of Databases, Volume 1: On-line Databases,* January 1993, Gale Research Inc., 1993.

get the reports it needs without having to duplicate the sales office databases. This also allows the sales offices to keep the data at their locations for quick access, and it eliminates a single point of failure for all the sales offices combined: if all the data were located at headquarters and there was a problem, then all the sales offices would be affected. With the databases distributed only the sales office with the problem would be affected. There is no duplication of data in any location so only one version of data is seen by any location [42].

A third example is a combination of the first two. Consider an insurance company with multiple distributed databases that are available to other locations. In this example, the collection of databases at all locations constitutes a distributed database. Any customer within the network will see the data as one entity in their computer. When a customer calls an agent in regards to a claim, the agent can retrieve the customer's data from a workstation. The information can be within the workstation, on the LAN, at some regional office, at headquarters, or scattered across several locations. It looks the same to the agent no matter where the data are truly located. Each location can access and make reports on the data as if they were right along side them [42].

A fourth example of a distributed database environment is a food distributor. In this example, there is one headquarters and several warehouse locations, each with its own database, and all the field salesman have laptops. In this scenario, each salesman's laptop dials into the appropriate warehouse location to get a complete listing of inventory and prices for processing the next day's transactions. In this case, the laptops would upload that day's orders and the warehouse computer would be updated accordingly so as to download the proper data for the sales force. Then headquarters could run reports against the warehouse location databases and get updated data [42].

To give a sense of the size of some databases, particularly centralized databases, some recent survey information follows. Of interest are the total number of users, total number of records, and total size. The greatest number of users is TRW Information Systems, which serves about 50,000 users. The greatest number of records is, again, TRW Information Systems. This database, running DB2 and Oracle, holds 5,274,000,000 records. The largest database is US Customs which has a 2-TB database on an IBM-compatible mainframe. The US Customs' border enforcement database has 4,500,000,000 records and serves 20,000 users. This database handles 100 million updates per day, and is up and running 160–168 hours per week. Tables 3.2–3.4 havemore examples.*

---

* David Stoder, "The Big Get Bigger," *Database Programming & Design*, October 1995, pages 7 ff.

Table 3.2 Highest number of users

Rank	Organization	Hardware platform	DBMS	Number of users
1	TRW	IBM-compatible mainframe, AT&T GIS Server	DB2/MVS Oracle	50,000
2	Federal Express	IBM-compatible mainframe	IMS	25,000
3	Ford Motor Co.	IBM-compatible mainframe	IMS/DB2	20,000

Table 3.3 Most number of records

Rank	Organization	Hardware platform	DBMS	Records (in millions)
1	TRW	IBM-compatible mainframe, AT&T GIS Server	DB2/MVS Oracle	5,724
2	US Customs	IBM-compatible mainframe	CA-Datacom	4,500
3	Bell Sygma	IBM-compatible mainframe	DB2/MVS	3,500

Table 3.4 Largest database

Rank	Organization	Hardware platform	DBMS	Gigabytes
1	TRW	IBM-compatible mainframe, AT&T GIS Server	CA-Datacom	2,000
2	TRW	IBM-compatible mainframe, AT&T GIS Server	DB2/MVS Oracle	1,500
3	Equitable Life	IBM-compatible mainframe	DB2/MVS	953

3.3 Client/server: A distributed computing environment

3.3.1 Understanding traditional computing

As discussed in previous chapters, during the 1960s and 1970s, mainframe computers emerged as an important business tool. At the time, they typically had one powerful processor with several *dumb terminals* connected to it. See Figure 3.2. These terminals, such as the DEC VT100 or the IBM 3270, relied on the host computer (mainframe) to run the application program; they looked much like today's computer screens, except they displayed only characters. A typical scenario would involve a roomful of data entry operators, each sitting at a terminal and entering data. In this approach, the investment was not in the numerous dumb terminals, but in the processor that was needed to drive all of them. It is for this reason that the terminals were capable only of text and not graphics: the resources required to drive graphics terminals would have been too great and too expensive [39].

Large mainframe systems were also usually supported by an entire department comprised of programmers and mainframe experts. It was upon this department that the life and well-being of the mainframe system and the company depended. There was very little (if any) power at the hands of the user to change an existing application or to simply modify a report generated by the system. This was largely based on the complicated programming and expertise that mainframe upkeep entailed. Mainframe systems were built with very little end-user interaction in mind.

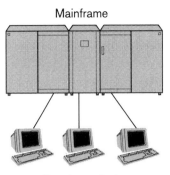

Mainframe

Dumb terminals

Figure 3.2 Traditional computing architecture

In the 1980s PCs, Macintoshes, and UNIX workstations began to displace mainframes and minicomputers. This new generation of computers had their own processors, with terminals that were capable of graphics. They were *more affordable* than mainframes and were capable of more diverse tasks than the dedicated mainframes. They also offered the user more flexibility. For instance, a user could more readily customize his or her own command prompt (among other things). Table 3.5* describes some of the strengths and weaknesses of mainframes.

Table 3.5 Mainframe strengths and weaknesses

Mainframe strengths	Mainframe weaknesses
Secure	Inflexible
Reliable	Expensive
Good for high-volume transaction	Not designed for interactive decision support and ad hoc queries
Program (including operating system) development according to rigorous methodologies	Programs can take years to be delivered
Availability of specialized tools for network and database management	Proprietary

* Karen Watterson, *Client/Server Technology for Managers,* Addison Wesley, 1995. Chapter 1.

3.3.2 The appearance of client/server

Moving into the 1990s, one finds a computer in most private homes and on every desk in most major corporations. We also find that most of these computers are linked to other computers or have the capability to do so via network adapter or modem. Capitalizing on this idea, client/server is an architecture that distributes workloads, such as printing, file retrieval, and maintaining databases, between two or more computers [39]. There are benefits to be obtained from moving to a client/server architecture. Recent studies suggest that the greatest benefits from client/server computing will be in the following areas:*

- Greater use of packaged software

- Lower operations costs by effective use of office automation

- Lower hardware and software costs by avoiding extravagant start-up costs

Today, new business requirements are transforming corporate information systems. The client/server architecture takes advantage of the technologically advanced desktop computer's GUIs, high performance networks, including ATM, and the processing power of servers. Businesses are demanding more and more from *all* of their employees. With increased productivity in mind, easy-to-use GUIs and shorter application development cycles are shifting more power and information to nontechnical end-users. Previously, in the traditional model, the IS or IT department system analysts and programmers had designed and implemented applications that they believed would suit the business' needs. This approach created rigid and inflexible systems that sometimes fell short of user's expectations and needs. Table 3.6 compares the two architectures.

Client/server computing allows for numerous operating systems for server platforms, such as Netware, OS/2, Window NT, MVS, VMS, and UNIX. The OSF, founded in 1988, has set a goal to build distributed computing environment compatibility into its distributed computing architecture. The important technologies defined for OSF include RPC services, data sharing services, email naming, security services, time services, parallel programming support, data sharing, and print services. UNIX is a desirable server platform due to the range of platform sizes and the sizable base of application and development software available. The IEEE established a group to develop a standard portable operating system called POSIX (POSIX is UNIX-like but not identical to UNIX.) Most vendors comply with the POSIX standard today, such as DEC's OPENMVS operating system.

---

* David Simpson, "CUT COSTS with Client/Server Computing? HERE'S HOW!," *Datamation*, October 1, 1995, pages 42ff.

Table 3.6 Mainframe versus client/server architecture

Mainframe architecture	Client/server architecture
Occupy one or more rooms	Can be a small desk top or portable laptop computer
High maintenance, usually with major vendor	Maintenance can be done over the telephone or at a local computer store
Huge capital investment	Hardware upgrades require a nominal fee
Software programming in languages like COBOL	Software programming in languages like C++ and SQL
TB of disk storage is common	PC-based servers can offer only a few dozen GB

When utilizing SQL, the customers can access data from anywhere in the network. SQL is an industry standard for data access. The data can be on a LAN, WAN, local PC, or mainframe, but customers do not have to know about it. Data do not have to reside in one place, they can be distributed throughout an enterprise. A network may be based on OSI, TCP/IP, or SNA protocols, and SQL can still be utilized.

3.3.3 The three components

A client can be defined as a single-customer workstation that provides presentation services and the appropriate computing, connectivity, and database services relevant to the business need. A server is one or more multiuser processors providing computer services and connectivity to solve the business' needs. The client requests services from the server and the server processes the request and returns a result. Client/server is a software model of computing, not a hardware definition. Typically, the platforms and operating systems are not homogenous, so the communication mechanism may be extended through APIs and RPCs. Effective client/server computing will be platform-independent. Changes in platform and underlying technology should be transparent to the customer. There are three parts to the architecture: the client, the server, and the network.

The client   The *client*, usually a desktop PC or workstation, is the end-user interface. It has two responsibilities: presentation management and application logic. The client PC can achieve what mainframe dumb terminals could not: it can support graphical user interfaces. Dumb terminals did not have the capacity for the point-and-click GUIs of client/server. They were strictly character (text) based and left little to the presentation. Today's PCs can afford the graphical representations of applications (icons), smart (pull down) menus, toolbars, online help, dialog boxes, step-by-step pop-up windows,

"Are you sure" message windows, undo buttons, drag and drop, cut and paste, 24-bit colors, Star Trek screen savers, and scanned-in photo background displays.

The second, more behind-the-screens function of the client computer is the application logic. The fact that each client has its own CPU, allows it to do its own processing. Clients are capable of multitasking, running the client software and other applications at the same time. Clients also have local disk storage and expandable memory. It is possible to tailor a client to suit the exact needs of each employee. This reduces cost and optimizes a user's productivity. Clients may also be software. For example, a spreadsheet that accesses data from an external source qualifies as a client. Since client/server applications may be commercial or customized, it depends on the individual application on whether the client is hardware or software.

The server   Like *client*, *servers* can refer to hardware and software. Servers are sometimes referred to as applications servers, and may be mainframes, UNIX workstations, or high-end PCs. In a client/server system, the server applications, such as a database management system (DBMS), provide data to the clients. As related to hardware, the important features of a server are scalability, fault tolerance, reliability, and performance. On the data side, the important features are security, version control, application management, standards, code reusability, and interoperability.

When discussing client/server applications, certain concepts come into play: data mart, data warehouse, data dictionary, and repository. Data marts and data warehouses are methods of data storage. A data warehouse centralizes data while a distributed data mart puts data where they are needed. In data warehouses we usually find copies of the data, rather than the original data. It may be that the data are arranged into subsets for faster user access. Figure 3.3* illustrates the differences between the data storage approaches. Data dictionaries and repositories are methods of managing a DBMS. A data dictionary manages database definitions and serves as a passive tool. It typically contains data about the database. A repository is an active management tool. It encompasses version control, dependency management, standards management, impact analysis, and project management.

There are many different kinds of servers: database, email, fax, communication, print servers, and file servers. Regardless of the server's function, the most important characteristic of a DBMS, whether the data is distributed or warehoused, is that users may access it at any time, in a reliable fashion.

---

* Shaku Atre and Peter Storer, "Data Distribution and Warehousing," *DBMS Database & Client/Server Solutions*, October 1995, pages ff.

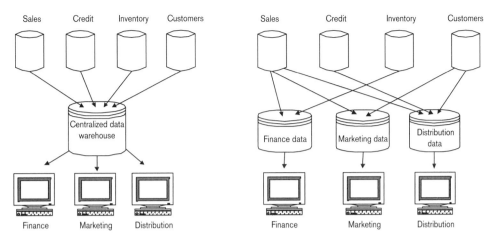

Figure 3.3   Data warehousing and distributed data

The network   This book emphasizes the importance of the communications network that ties the host and the clients together. Without a communications network, the client/server architecture would regress to simple computers acting as independent workstations. The network serves as the infrastructure for client/server applications. Whether the network is Ethernet or Token Ring, or if it is a local area network, wide area network, or metropolitan area network, the important thing is that it provides the communications between the clients and the servers. Technologies such as Ethernet, Token Ring, Fiber Distributed Data Interface, and ATM are important. Upper layer protocols, particularly TCP/IP, also come into the discussion. The use of ATM in both the LAN and WAN areas enables client/server systems to move data more expeditiously.

An appropriate description of client/server computing is that the network is the computer. Customers want to feel that somewhere on the network are the services they need. Interoperability is important. The Open Systems Interconnection (OSI) Reference Model provides an industry standard framework for network and system interoperability. The OSI model defines seven protocol layers:

- Application (support)
- Presentation
- Session
- Transport
- Network

- Data Link
- Physical

The Physical layer is the lowest level of the OSI model and defines the physical and electrical characteristics of the connections. The Data Link layer defines the basic units (e.g., cells) of data travels over a simple link. The Network layer is responsible for multiplexing and routing messages to the correct destinations. The Transport layer is responsible for ensuring end-to-end error free transmissions. The Session layer coordinates communication between applications running on two processors. The Presentation layer translates data from machine form from one processor to another. The Application layer is where the application processor directly talks.

The advantages obtained via interconnected PCs are:

- Graphical and more intuitive user interfaces
- Scalability
- Flexibility
- More knowledgeable users
- End-user involvement
- Cost savings and improved performance

LAN based PCs also match the capabilities of traditional mainframe computing such as data security, integrity, reliability, and performance, while contributing additional improvements such as unassisted access to data, ability to customize and print reports on demand, and the most important feature in this highly competitive realm of technology, interoperability (discussed later) with other hardware platforms and application software. Users do not require years of programming experience to maintain or customize their applications [39].

3.3.4 Plethora of architectures

There are different varieties of client/server models based on the varying architectures or on their functionality. Figure 3.4 illustrates the partitioning of application functions. This model serves as a guideline to developing client/server applications and logically distributing the burden of processing.*

---

* Paul Reed and Steve Jackson, "Separation ANXIETY," *Database Programming & Design*, October 1995, pages 42ff.

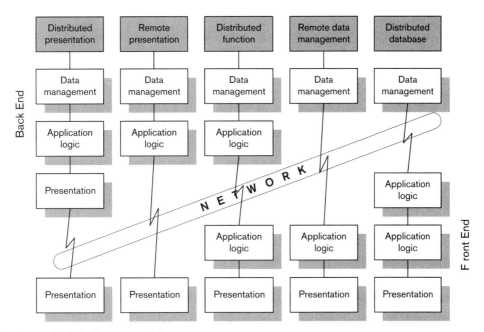

Figure 3.4   Client/server model

OLTP and decision support systems   The client/server model supports both OLTP (On Line Transaction Processing) and decision support systems.* OLTP applications are sometimes referred to as *mission-critical applications* because companies depend on these applications for business. They tend to be concerned with getting data into a computer. A transaction is a set of two or more database updates that must be completed in an "all-or-nothing" fashion. Transaction processing involves updating all of the involved database for one or all transactions. If all of these database updates are not completed then they must be ignored. An example of this all-or-nothing concept: if an update were made to a company's accounts receivable database and not updated in the customer order database, then not only would a customer not be billed from an item, there would be inconsistencies in the company's end-of-quarter reports. Early client/server applications were viewed as nonessential from an operations standpoint; these types of applications are sometimes referred to as decision support systems. They tend to involve retrieving large amounts of information, but on an irregular basis. See Figure 3.5 [39].

Multi-tier   In another client/server architecture, consideration is given to network loading and direct access to data (located directly in a mainframe or process information

---

*   Karen Watterson, *Client/Server Technology for Managers,* Addison Wesley, 1995. Chapter 1.

coming directly from plant instruments). See Figure 3.6. There are one-tier, two-tier, and three-tier systems. In a one-tier system (a laptop computer or a desktop used for telecommuting applications), the PC may be configured as both the client and the server. (This is mentioned for the sake of thoroughness and is best thought of as a telecommuting tool or remote access for traveling employees.) A two-tier system directly links client computers (desktops) to host data. In a three-tier system, an intermediate server is layered between the host server and the clients.

Multiple servers   In most organizations, information is distributed or stored in several hosts, as shown in Figure 3.7. This distribution of data may (and usually does) involve different computer platforms, eg., an IBM MVS mainframe, a DEC Alpha running VMS, or a Pentium computer running Windows NT. In this case, client/server applications would involve different hosts running different applications. The hosts would be networked together enabling a user or users to access data from any or all of the hosts.

Reengineered environments   Another client/server approach is the reengineered application. Of course, building a new client/server application from the ground up is not a trivial task, but redesigning an existing mainframe to benefit from its capabilities and adding newer technologies to facilitate access by more users and

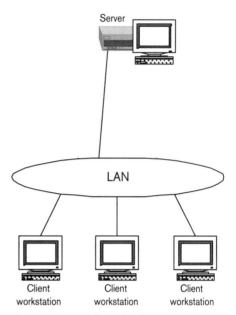

Figure 3.5   Simple early client/server architecture

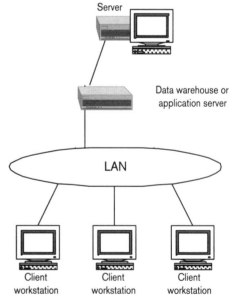

Figure 3.6   Multi-tier client/server architecture

improved applications is also challenging. Mainframe systems were solely maintained by a group of in-house programmers who tailored and groomed the systems over the years. Reengineering involves working through a mainframe application and perhaps modularizing and rewriting portions of it to create a *seamless* interconnection with the new system. Reengineering and client/server are often side-by-side, because new information systems are easily redesigned not only by rethinking the processes but by replacing the computer architecture as well [44–48].

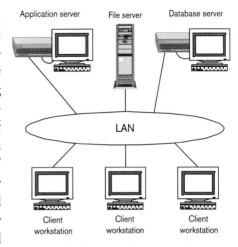

Figure 3.7   Multiple client/server architectures

3.4 Mainframes' role

In a client/server environment, it is possible for a mainframe system to still exist. In fact, it is most probable that in many organizations client/server systems live in harmony with mainframes. Mainframes still exist in industry not only due to their intrinsic capabilities, but also because companies have too much invested in them to replace them. In a press-time survey of IT managers, 64% planned to incorporate mainframes into client/server applications, 25% planned to phase out mainframes, and 11% planned to downsize applications to client/server.*†

IBM's System/360 architecture has continuously advanced since its first introduction in the 1960s. Around 1970, it was enhanced to support virtual storage and was renamed System/370; in the 1980s it was again enhanced to increase the amount of addressable memory from 16 MB to 2 GB. It was renamed eXtended Architecture, or XA; in the 1990s is was enhanced to support several new features, including a new subsystem called Enterprise Systems Architecture (ESA).‡

---

* "Not Your Father's Mainframe," A table based on problem client/server areas based on a survey of 100 IS managers.

† "Not Your Father's Mainframe," Results of *What Are Your Mainframe Plans?* Chart.

‡ Doug Lowe, *Client/Server Computing for Dummies,* IDG Books, 1995. Chapter 19.

Mainframes computers are not only bigger than PCs in a physical sense but also in an operational sense. They have more computational power (in terms of instructions per second), they have more memory (several hundred MB of RAM), they have more disk storage capacity (terabytes), and have high efficiency in transaction processing (mostly due to the internal hardware—channels, controllers, etc.). There is a movement to combine the mainframe and client/server to get the best of both worlds. Mainframe vendors such as IBM, Amdahl, and Hitachi Data Systems are recognizing this trend and creating an environment that facilitates the integration of their systems with client/servers.* Companies want an affordable and flexible approach, and yet do not want to sacrifice the dependability and computational power afforded by mainframes. In this hybrid approach, mainframes act as reliable servers to PCs or workstations which act as an inexpensive client/server solution.

3.5 Middleware

Middleware is the "go-between" that sits in the middle of the client and the server. It refers to the variety of methods for establishing communications between the host server and the client applications. It can be hardware, software, and both. It serves almost as a communications protocol between the various layers of client/server applications.

There are different categories of middleware. Some middleware routes messages between different platforms; this is called *network* or *messaging middleware*. This includes RPCs and interprocess communications that shield programmers from network details. Another category of middleware is *database middleware*, which comes in the form of APIs and gateways. This kind of middleware shields clients from database server details. It translates incoming data requests into database commands. APIs contain defined functions that can be used to further customize database functionality as required. Some popular APIs include Microsoft's Open Database Connectivity (ODBC) and IBM's Distributed Relational Database Architecture (DRDA). Gateways, such as Oracle's SQL*Connect and Sybase's Open Server are more DBMS-specific. The third category of middleware is the *copy management/replications server middleware*. This type of middleware can be programmed to replicate copies of data at fixed intervals, or on demand; this function is more important with a distributed database environment. A good replication server keeps network traffic at a minimum and ensures that each component of a distributed database will have data as close to real time as possible [39].

---

* "Not Your Father's Mainframe."

One challenge for major corporations is to be able to interface from legacy systems to these new client/server setups. Client/server technologies such as relational databases and GUIs offer benefits to the developers of mission critical applications; it is estimated, however, that 80% of all corporate data still reside in proprietary, nonrelational database environments. As client/server moves further into mission-critical roles, the demand for access to the legacy systems will increase. Total replacement of the legacy systems is not always practical or possible. The costs involved may be high, and the time it would take may be prohibitive. The option is then to integrate legacy systems with new client/server applications [42], [49–60].

Integration allows developers to concentrate on new applications that will add value to the corporation, rather than recreating existing functions, as discussed in Chapter 1. Most of the integration has been limited to small applications that spice up or change the feel of a cumbersome mainframe application. Many organizations are turning to middleware to address the complexities of building distributed applications. The emerging class of middleware offers a better solution to legacy systems integration. These products support a broad set of connectivity options and also offer performance and manageability required for mission-critical client/server applications. Middleware allows the creation of open interface services. The services act as agents on behalf of the client application and respond to requests and managing the necessary interaction with legacy systems. This allows for smooth cooperation between legacy systems and client/server applications [42], [49–60].

A number of varieties of middleware exist. One common form is OLTP. Such products as IBM's CICS, NCR's Top End, DEC's ACMS, Novell's Tuxedo, and Transarc's Encina are examples of OLTPs. These all provide many middleware benefits.

Middleware hides the complexities which are intrinsic with heterogeneous, multi-protocol networks including TCP/IP, SNA, Bisync and other proprietary protocols. Middleware products provide many features that simplify development and maintenance of interface services. Developers are insulated from low level communications details which will allow them more time to concentrate on business solutions at hand. Graphical programming tools and simple communications APIs reduce the complexity of distributed systems development. Interface services developed with these tools are published on the network and subsequently made available to any authorized client. Many applications share the same interface services, reducing duplication of effort and simplifying maintenance. Middleware tools are designed to enable interoperability between tools from many vendors [42], [49–60].

Middleware allows distributed and client/server applications to run smoothly on legacy systems, and also increases connectivity, performance and manageability. It saves customers time by navigating information through the legacy system. It benefits customer by enabling them to select the most sophisticated equipment from any vendor and allow them to adapt to it [42], [49–60].

Systems management is a challenging task. First-generation client/server tools enhanced developer productivity but fell short on manageability. Middleware products address systems manageability through graphical systems monitors and open management interfaces which support performance, fault, and configuration management.

Performance management is accomplished through gathering and reporting of key performance and utilization statistics. Administrators use this information to tune a system for optimized performance and capacity planning. Finding and resolving problems in a large distributed database environment can be difficult. Middleware integrates the distributed components of an application and provides tools for fault management. Alarms and alerts are reported to online system monitors where graphical tools allow system administrators to view them and resolve the problem [42], [49–60].

Configuration management is simplified with graphical tools for maintaining system resources. These resources are managed in a centralized database that is dynamically replicated to all sites. Most companies have invested heavily in their legacy systems, so the need for middleware will continue into the future. Middleware will ensure integration capabilities between new and existing environments.

Middleware suits both aspects of systems management. It allows network users to connect clients to servers by using database networking middleware. It also allows application developers to fulfill their needs through database language middleware that handles a variety of database management systems and SQLs. Without middleware's ability to smooth over the incompatibilities among computers and to accommodate the changing networks, client/server computing might not develop at all.

Middleware programs can help insulate companies from network failures by ensuring that important messages do not get lost. This is important in banking where there are transactions including cash-machine withdrawals. One would want to assure that a transaction gets sent once and only once. There are numerous middleware programs being developed with this in mind, including IBM's MQ Series Software. The MQ Series creates a sort of postal system to move messages and tasks among many incompatible computers [42], [49–60]. The MQ Series is a family of products from IBM which provides advanced messaging functions with guaranteed delivery across such platforms as IBM's OS/2, DOS, OS/400, AIX, VSE/ESA, MVS/ESA, DEC's VMS, Tandem Stratum, Sun, HP, and UNIX. Through the MQ Series API the application access the communications services. That facility protects the message when on the queue and ensures delivery to the recipient's system with proper notification.

Messaging middleware most often conforms to one of two models—*process-to-process messaging* or *message queuing*. The process-to-process model requires both sending and receiving processes to be available at the same time. This does not allow for much flexibility. Message queuing is more flexible; when a sender wants to send a message it is placed on a queue and when the receiver is ready, it takes it from the queue. Since message queuing does not require the sender and receiver to be up at the same time it allows for more flexibility; it eases time constraints and consumes fewer resources [42], [49–60].

Message queuing utilizes a queue manager, which is a software program that is responsible for the message-queuing services used by applications. It can take care of one or many queues. Messaging middleware supports asynchronous communications which ensure that a process is never blocked once it has sent or received a message. This allows multiple requests to be processed concurrently, thereby utilizing the network more effectively.

There are three types of message-queuing middleware—*nonpersistent*, *persistent* and *transactional*. Nonpersistent message queuing relies on memory-based queues. Messages do not persist during failures. It is obvious that this type of queuing would not be suitable for many business needs. Persistent message queuing is similar, but the queues are disk-based and not memory-based, so that they can be saved and retrieved after failures that may arise. Transactional message queuing enables messages to survive during failures and to exhibit transactional characteristics. (They know the state of the message if a process fails, and can determine if the message was successful.) [42], [49–60]

As an example, IBM MQ Series allows application developers to choose between nonpersistent and persistent queues. It also supports triggering, which means a process can be launched when a message is placed in a queue. The MQ Series is responsible for the integrity and security of its resource and for optimizing the performance and availability of that resource. One drawback to the MQ Series is that it is not totally aware of the resource managers around it. The MQ Series can ensure a message once it is placed on a queue but it cannot ensure that the message makes it to the queue in the first place. If a problem occurs that inhibits the message from reaching the queue the MQ Series remains ignorant of that fact. The flexibility of the middleware described above should make it a viable solution in the future of distributed computing [42], [49–60].

3.6 *Distributed databases*

We now return to the more general topic being discussed in this chapter. A distributed database is one in which data is distributed between two or more databases that are connected by a communications network. These databases may be located within the same building or at different geographical locations. The fact that the data are separated over more than one database is transparent to the user: users of distributed databases should be able to perform the same functions as they would on a single database [39].

PC (client) applications are not released from any data presentation or processing requirements. They may simply request the desired data from the database (or unknowingly, several databases) and focus on analyzing or presenting them to their advantage. The client applications may be designed with no dependence on the physical location of the database. If the data is moved or if the databases are upgraded, this will have little impact on the user. Users may tailor their applications to manipulate the data and present it graphically, in charts, or may automate data queries. For example, if a user has to modify inventory accounts for some customers, there may be certain data that would be queried for each. It would be useful to streamline this query by presenting it to the user in an organized fashion and also by allowing the user to easily modify and save the changes to the database. This process would not only be less time consuming, but easier to learn for a new employee.

This distributed approach frees each PC from maintaining a local copy of the database (which may be significantly large) and places that duty upon several database servers (or one central database server). Large quantities of data may be stored within any database. In distributed databases, this information is stored within two or more databases and made available to any number of users, preferably in a location closest to the heavy users. For example, parts and inventory data might be stored in an inventory database and located on a server near the (distribution) shipping and receiving department. This enables faster query responses from the database, hence minimizing delays.

In the distributed approach, the various databases may be on different hardware platforms. It is typical to find the data on a mainframe, a UNIX server, or a VAX station. Thus, in the case where phasing out a mainframe and phasing in a new server is the strategy, a distributed approach becomes a likely candidate for the job. It would enable access to mainframe data while slowly migrating to the new hardware application [39]. Advantages of distributed databases include the following [42], [49–60]:

- Distributed databases allow the enterprise to place programs and data where they make business sense, usually mirroring the same structure as the corporation. This gives the corporation a lot more flexibility, for instance, if a branch moves. It allows for moving the data with the branch or combining them with some other operation.

- Distributed databases empower the business units in the enterprise to control their own processing and data. This also allows each business unit to secure the data and keep the data integrity at whatever level they feel appropriate.

- Distributed databases allow for better business continuation planning. There is no longer a single point of failure, as with all the data residing on one mainframe computer. If one site or database gets hit with a disaster, this limits the extent of the downtime to only one piece of the database and not all the data. This is important since if all of the data are located in a central data center the business is subject to that center's uptime and disaster continuation plans. It is best to have a mix of databases where one failure will not halt business altogether.

- Distributed databases allow an enterprise to move program and data from one site to another more readily.

3.6.1 Data replication/partitioning

There are three requirements to distributed databases: users must be able to access data on multiple processors without knowing where the data are located; data tables must be able to be stored on many processors at one time; and copies of tables distributed on multiple processors must be synchronized at all times. Maintaining a distributed database is not limited to PC maintenance and user-friendly query applications. Each database in a distributed system is managed by a local DBMS. This way, each DBMS maintains independence in operation and administration, while being able to share and access data with other databases in the group of logical databases.

There are three approaches to distributed databases: *partitioning*, *replication*, or a *combination of the two*. In any case, the DBMS must maintain data consistency among all of the databases. Partitioning involves dividing and distributing the data by department or geographic location. Replication involves a central database that maintains a master copy of the data while full or partial copies of the data are sent to be cached at remote locations. This is also a space conservation method, but it may tend to be stressful on the network.

The critical concern in distributed database is the reliability issue that arises from the fact that the network connecting the various databases may fail. ATM and SONET technology can help here. This possibility is increased by the complex queries that may be made. For this reason, there is data replication. As stated above, replication creates a replica or a copy of data and sends it to remote locations. Replication offers:

- Improved performance by distributing the work load among servers
- Reliability and availability by serving as a backup to a failed server or network

(This same approach is used in the Internet, and can also be employed in intranets.)

One of the challenges faced by replication is a distributed system in which databases are geographically distant. If a change is made to a database in New York, how certain is it that it will be updated in Los Angeles? Can it be possible that two users may make the same query and get different results—that one user may access the new data while the other may access the old and not yet updated data?

There are two approaches to data replication: *strongly consistent replication* and *weakly consistent replication.* In strongly consistent replication, a database may become unavailable while it is updating new information. In this situation it is possible for a user to access the new data in from one database server and another user to wait for data from another database server, until the update has been completed. This synchronous replication involves overhead and may appear slow to users. The approach is valuable in decision-support replication where current data is imperative to business. Weakly consistent replication, asynchronous updates, may be used in situations where data is not urgent in nature. It is possible that data are updated only once daily. This might be used in an application where information such as a customer address or an item description field is to be updated—cases where data are usually unchanging and fairly constant. Experts offer the following rules for distributed databases;* these rules offer guidelines for designing distributed databases—they also highlight some of the current advantages and disadvantages.

Rule 1 *Local autonomy*   Each server within a distributed database system should have control over the database.

Rule 2 *No reliance on a central site*   A distributed database should be independent from a central site of command.

Rule 3 *Continuous operation*   A distributed database should maintain continuous operation. It should not have to be shut down for routine maintenance.

Rule 4 *Location transparency and location independence*   A user should not be concerned with the location of desired data or ever need to know on which server the data are located.

Rule 5 *Fragmentation independence*   If a data table is fragmented across several servers, the DBMS should reconstruct the data without any user interaction.

Rule 6 *Replication independence*   Users should not be aware that data has been replicated, that replicas exist, or where the copies are kept.

Rule 7 *Distributed query processing*   Queries should be handled in the most efficient manner.

Rule 8 *Distributed transaction processing*   A distributed database system should handle transactions that span more than one server in the network.

Rule 9 *Hardware independence*   Hardware platforms should not hinder the performance or the usages of the data.

---

* Doug Lowe, *Client/Server Computing for Dummies*, IDG Books, 1995 Chapter 14.

Rule 10 *Operating system independence*   Operating systems should not hinder the performance or the usage of the data.

Rule 11 *Network independence*   Networks and network protocols should be transparent to the users.

Rule 12 *DBMS independence*   It must be possible to mix various different DBMS systems with no impact on the performance or usage of the system.

Client/server and distributed database strive for open systems. In an open system environment, computers, and applications are vendor-independent. For example, hardware platform *A* running operating system *a* can communicate with hardware platform *B* running a slightly different version of the operating system *a*, as if they were both on the same hardware platform and running the same operating system. One obstacle in the road to client/server and open systems is the issue of interoperability.* The revolution against centralized control has created users that purchase hardware and software based on their needs, with little regard to interoperability. Interoperability is important in linking multivendor systems, networks, and applications to provide improved information access. It streamlines data retrieval by enabling users to seamlessly access other applications on other computers in other departments via the LAN. It will foster the growth of electronic commerce and business partners by linking organizations that are geographically distant. Table 3.7 outlines some of the advantages and disadvantages to distributed databases [39], [44–48].

The major disadvantage in dealing with distributed databases and client/server technologies is the administration of such environments. In the past, application programmers had to know how to log on and run their programs. Today they have to be able to administer each platform within their distributed databases. There is a significant learning curve that has to be addressed by corporations. There are numerous platforms that personnel have to be responsible for. For example, it is estimated that a programmer with a PC spends 25–40% of his/her time on administrative PC duties.

The cost of educating and training personnel on these duties and platforms has certainly increased. The manageability of these technologies is an issue. Instead of having an IT department in charge of performance management and response time issues on the mainframe, those issues are brought down into each individual business unit and its personnel. Other issues including backup, availability, and security are also now the business unit's responsibility.

The synchronization of data has to be an issue with these technologies. If numerous remote customers are accessing data on different platforms they have to be guaranteed

---

* Bob Violino, "Bringing Harmony to Business," *Information Week*, October 2, 1995, pp. 34ff.

Table 3.7 Client/server advantages and disadvantages

Pros	Cons
Users need good GUIs. The current DBMS tools and GUIs are better than in the past. It is possible for a user to customize his or her own interface without the help of a programmer. This fosters increased productivity, more experienced workers, and a sense of pride in accomplishment for the worker.	When users need to query data at multiple sites, response times are slow. Updates of multiple sites usually require all sites to be up and running in order to complete a distributed transaction.
Users have access to data stored in any database in the system, they increase local processing efficiency that in turn increases network efficiency, and they also allow connectivity to mainframe data. This translates into a cost savings in terms of salvageability of an existing mainframe system and access to legacy data.	Distributed databases are restricted by the volume of traffic over expensive wide-area networks.
Platform independence allows access to any hardware platform or operating system. This translates in freedom from hardware and software (including DBMS) standardization.	With distributed databases, a large concern is the integrity of data. How can a user be certain that the data he or she is viewing are the most recent data? As systems get larger and more widespread, this issue of ensuring real time data becomes increasingly prominent.
With distributed databases, if one server suffers from loss of power (or worse) a replica of data may ease the recovery of the unavailable system.	Standards. There are many different standards that apply to client/server, networks, distributed computing, etc. While SQL is the de facto database query language, it comes in many different dialects. Each database vendor has adopted his or her own dialect of structured query language. This is not a major issue if each database within the distributed system is from the same database vendor. However, when various databases are involved, the data queries may get complex
Rapid application deployment. This model of software development focuses on prototyping and iterative development.	Security. Easy access leads to major security issues. One method of security is controlling access at the database level and by restricting user read and write privileges to data. Another layer of security may be placed at the network layer. These measures are not foolproof, but are useful in protecting data.
Joint application development. This method of application development involves the end user input during all phases of development.	
Distributed database systems allow room to grow. This architecture is not limited to the number of users or servers in the network. It may be customized in size and speed as desired.	

the correct copy of the data. This is also an issue on a mainframe but is more complicated in the distributed environment.

3.6.2 Distributed database planning

There are five basic steps that should be taken in order to plan a distributed database; these steps are as follows [42–60]:

1 Identify and assess the organization's goals and expectations

2 Design the database

3 Network and communications considerations

4 Management strategy

5 Transition to distributed data

The first step is to identify goals and expectations. One should have a clear vision of the business needs and be able to identify what data are necessary to fulfill the vision. Data modeling is necessary. One should also decide whether a decentralized approach is the right direction in which to head: a specific application solution might be better served by a centralized approach [42].

The next step is to design the database. The data modeling done in the previous step should help here. One of the questions, regarding the design of the database, is where to put the data relative to the customers and applications that will utilize it. To decide this one should look at the performance necessary, security, and currency along with availability of data across locations, the amount of data being retrieved, and the processing environment (i.e., mainframe or workstations) [42], [49–60].

Performance is important. Customers require the fastest access to data that is possible. In general, the closer one puts data to the customer the faster they can access them (all other things constant). The data should be placed closest to the customers who will be utilizing them. For example, on a LAN if one customer needs a certain program or data and the rest do not, then it should be kept in his or her computer and not the LAN server [42].

Data should also reside in the location with the most activity, if feasible. In particular, data should be placed on the same LAN segment or IP subnet as the majority of the intended users, to the extent possible. One should also code so that the least amount of data as possible are sent to remote locations. An application that only occasionally needs to access data in a remote location is most likely the best candidate for a distributed database. Good table design and enough network capacity are also issues when dealing with performance [42], [49–60]. ATM technology should alleviate capacity limitations intrinsic with legacy networks.

Security and availability should also be looked at for placement of the data for the best design. Data should be placed where they can be fully secured and available.

Business continuation plans should be addressed. Distributed copies of the data might be necessary at times both for backup and ad hoc queries [42].

The network and communications should be considered in great detail. This can make or break a good distributed database design. With companies increasingly distributing data across multiple platforms, database administrators now, more than ever, have to understand networking components affected. Again, ATM technology (including LANE and MPOA) should prove useful in this context.

3.6.3 Optimizing performance of distributed databases

Performance can usually be defined as a combination of throughput and response time. Throughput can be defined as the amount of work processed in a certain unit of time. Each component of a distributed environment has to be considered so as not to have a weak link. A throughput chain can be viewed as all the components necessary to complete a transaction. A performance individual should spend his time optimizing throughput on the weak links of the chain.

Performance has always been an issue in the traditional mainframe host-centric environments. Most large corporations with large data centers and IT departments already have people dedicated to monitoring mainframes and even network resources. With so much development in the distributed database environment, the systems people within business units should also be aware of performance issues and how to optimize the performance of their databases. Failure to recognize and respond to signs of performance degradation within the distributed environment, can be detrimental [42]. ATM can improve overall performance; however, one cannot ignore server issues.

Overall system performance is usually increased when designed for performance from the outset. Overtuning and microtuning should be avoided. Microtuning is when one tunes the client/server environment without considering the surrounding environment. An example of this is a well-tuned standalone program that runs smoothly until introduced to a network environment. Overtuning is possible also; this can divert resources away from areas in greater need of those resources [42], [49–60].

Customers are mainly concerned with response time. This is the amount of time it takes for a predefined set of work or transaction to process. Response time is usually easier to assess, due to the fact that the customers will notify you when problems arise. A proactive approach should be utilized when dealing with performance and response time, so that a problem can be discovered and corrected prior to notification by a customer [42], [49–60].

The major influences on performance within client/server applications are hardware and concurrent access requirements, and the underlying network technology. The processing speed of the hardware involved has a significant influence on throughput. The entire spectrum of hardware should be considered, including workstations, hard drives, mainframes, network communication services, and network access technology (e.g., Ethernet NICs, ATM NICs, etc.). The pieces that impact client /server performance are processing speed of a client workstation, speed of workstation hard drives, size and MIPS supported by mainframe, type and speed of disk drives and controllers being used on mainframe, and the network physically being utilized.

Contention is also a consideration when viewing performance. This arises when the demand for a resource is high. When multiple processes or customers try to utilize a resource at the same time, degradation of performance can occur. If the transactions are not coded such that they can bypass the resource and come back for it at a later time, then degradation most certainly will occur. Coding should include the bypass or work around of an unavailable resource [42], [49–60].

Performance of a server is determined by the performance of the DBMS being utilized. Dataset placement strategy, memory allocation pools and cache have to all be tuned; efficient SQL and access paths have to be utilized.

Distributed database and client/server programs should be designed to be flexible enough to deal with where data is stored, and how best to access it. It should also deal with how the work should be prioritized, and which location houses the data necessary. Performance monitoring and tuning is difficult to maintain in any environment and is complicated even more in the client/server arena [42], [49–60].

3.7 Client/server in the Internet and in intranets

The WWW (also called *the Web*) is a global user-read-only distributed information system. Any node on the Internet with its own IP address may act as a WWW server. To access the Web, each server site must run a Web server program, such as the httpd daemon for UNIX (free copies of httpd may be obtained on many Web sites). It runs on port 80 of TCP. Each server site must also provide a home page; this is the starting line for browsing any site. Most home pages are hypertext documents that contain information about that site and possibly links to other Web sites. On the client side there are programs that are called *browsers*, such as Mosaic, Navigator, or Explorer. (Mosaic may also be obtained for free.) A browser allows users to perform simple word searches or complex searches of phrases or objects. These Internet browsers reflect the required characteristics of distributed database. Any user may request any data at any location within the network regardless of the physical location of the data. Browsers provide excellent interfaces to network databases. Table 3.8 lists some of the popular client/server applications that are found on the Internet [40], [44].* Some of these applications, e.g., Web browsing and FTP, are now appearing in corporate intranets.

Table 3.8   Internet/intranet client/server applications

Application	Function
archie	User requests a list of all publicly accessible files on a particular topic. In this case a user does not need a login account in order to access files from an anonymous FTP side.
finger	User requests information on a particular user at a particular site. The information returned about the user can include the date and time that the user last logged in. In addition, *Finger* can return any specific information that a user wants to convey to other users—similar to a *.profile* in UNIX.
FTP (File Transfer Protocol)	Allows users to login remotely to a server machine. Once logged in, users can transfer files between the local and remote systems. *FTP* is widely used on LANs that do not have distributed file systems.
gopher	Using a simple graphical user interface, users can access data and services from a server node. Users may browse and retrieve multimedia information. *Gopher* is a step above FTP in terms of ease of use, but a step below WWW.
telnet	Allows users to log in remotely to a server machine. Once logged in, users can run programs on the remote CPU.
veronica (very easy rodent-oriented netwide index to computerized archives)	Similar to archie, except that *veronica* searches though publicly accessible gopher sites, whereas archie searches anonymous FTP sites.
WAIS (Wide Area Information Server)	Client asks server to do key word or key phrase search though vast databases maintained by the Wide Area Information Service. If a site has a very large amount of data such as an online encyclopedia or dictionary, this is a good way to serve that data to clients.
WWW (World Wide Web)	Clients ask for data, the server returns data, client determines how to invoke the served data. Users may browse hypermedia information. *WWW* is the current superstar of Internet client/server applications.

---

* Johnson M. Hart and Barry Rosenberg, *Client/Server Computing for Technical Professionals,* Addison Wesley, 1995, Chapter 8.

A prime requirement of network databases is that the component data files be in a standardized format. Many Internet databases are in the *tagged field format* referring to files in which each data record contains tags—keywords or codes, to indicate fields. The Standard Generalized Markup Language (SGML) provides a systematic approach to tagging data. HyperText Markup Language (HTML), used in WWW documents is an SGML application. HyperText Transfer Protocol (HTTP) is the protocol that WWW servers and clients use to transfer. It runs over TCP/IP at port 80. This topic is revisited in Chapter 7.

3.8 Object-oriented programming

This section deals with the principles of object-oriented programming and how these technologies will effect the future of all programming languages. Many of the client/server and distributed database applications are written using OOP.

3.8.1 The need for a new software development technique

As early as 1986, it was recognized that the software industry was lagging behind the hardware industry in implementing reusability to reduce the development effort [24]. The approaches advocated at that time still remain the driving principles behind the search for a way to improve programming. Analysis shows that the hardware industry was able to introduce large reusable components which exponentially increased hardware cost-effectiveness. However, the software industry still has not learned how to do it as routinely. Over the twenty years the hardware industry was doubling its output year by year, and the software industry was just gaining productivity with arithmetic growth. The software industry progressed from assembly language to FORTRAN, to C, to Lisp, effectively changing its tools to increase productivity, but never changing its unit of modularity.

The principle of modularity dictates that if any part of a system depends on the internals of another part, then the complexity increases as the square of the size of the system [25]. Figure 3.8 shows a number of parts of a system represented graphically by the circles; the lines represent the interactions between them. The more interactions you have between the systems, the more lines you will accumulate. With each system depending on the others, you end up with a maze of interactions. As the size of your program increases, it becomes more complex and harder to build, and it becomes harder to understand, and harder to maintain [25].

Graham [26] cites a survey of 1970's Defense Projects that showed their fate according to US government statistics. Figure 3.9 [26] shown below, illustrates that a very small percentage of the projects was ever used. Graham states that this provided the impetus

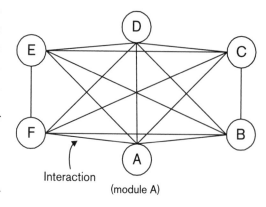

Figure 3.8   Complex interactions

toward structured methods based on the realization that many systems were either not finished, not used, or were delivered with major errors. He also states that these systems were mainly mainframe systems written in COBOL, so it is impossible to make comparisons to systems developed with modern tools in the 1990s. However, it is obvious that the development techniques were less than effective and that something needed to be done to increase the speed and reliability of development procedures. Otherwise, software would never be able to keep up with the advances in hardware. New software development methods were needed so developers would be able to produce error free software quickly.

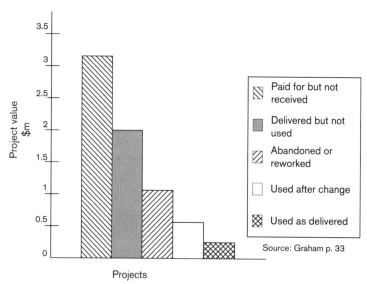

Figure 3.9   Disposition of software projects

3.8.2 Evolution of object-oriented programming

Object-Oriented Programming was the next step in the evolution of programming languages. In Table 3.9, the processes, and the types of data they used, show the progression from machine instructions using simple memory cells to structured programming using abstract data types [41].

Table 3.9   Processes involved in the evolution of programming lanquages

Process	Data
Machine instructions	Memory cells
Formulas	Variables
Procedures	Data structures
Structured Programming	Abstract Data Types

With an abstract data type, one bundles the data with the procedures that work on them and hides the information inside an object. This eliminates the possibility of the data being corrupted by other parts of the system. This was a major change from procedural programming that had global variables and data. It is one of the major concepts behind object-oriented programming [25].

3.8.3 Applicability of object-oriented programming to client/server

Object-oriented development is being looked at as one of the key technologies to be used to move mainframe-based legacy systems to client/server environments. Object-oriented development essentially translates into one basic thing: reusable software that simplifies the software development process. It also offers the advantage of being less prone to errors [27]. Object-oriented programming is looked at as a solution to complexity. One of the main advantages of object-oriented programming is that within its analysis and synthesis lie simplicity and generality. Its analysis is simplified by a small number of independent parts and its synthesis is facilitated by the fact that it is productive, maintainable, and easy to learn [25].

The key benefits of OOP are reusability and extensibility. That is, object-oriented systems can be assembled from prewritten components with minimal effort, and the assembled system will be easy to extend without any need to tinker with the reused components. Other technologies do not offer this capability. To add on to an existing program, one has to be careful not to corrupt the existing code. This is not the case in an object-oriented technology. However, one of the most important aspects of OOP is a design technique that is driven by delegation of responsibilities. This technique is called responsibility-driven design [26], [28].

Cuts development time   Objects are to software what integrated circuits are to hardware [29]. Significant development time is saved and greater functionality is achieved when embedded-system software uses object-oriented languages and methods. That is why today's software is becoming increasingly modular, composed of object-oriented software building blocks. When a function is required for which no off-the-shelf module exists, a similar module is found with well-defined specifications that greatly simplify the required design and development tasks. With an object-oriented approach, much project development is reduced to selecting and configuring one or more off-the-shelf modules. This results in big savings of development time and money. Also, with a building-block approach, more functionality can be incorporated into the product than might otherwise have been practical. What is more, a greater share of the development budget is available to be invested in developing product-specific software. A product that is based on modular software can easily be offered in multiple versions, having varied performance and features, simply by substituting different modules [29].

In an object-oriented system, the modules are treated as black boxes, which are fully specified by their external functional specifications. Consequently, different modules having different internal makeup, but similar external characteristics, can be substituted [29]. Early adopters of the technology have reported development time improvements of 80%. Fortune 1000 companies need to be able to effectively manage their systems, and along with that they need verifiably high quality. This has led approximately one-third of the Fortune 1000 companies to initiate object-oriented applications by the end of 1994 [29], [30].

Time-to-market is probably the most important factor a company faces when developing new products. The company that can establish itself first as the solution provider will gain the market share necessary to ensure its success. If it is first to market, it can begin to improve on its existing product with the revenues it generates while the other companies are still working on their original releases [41].

Code reuse   Essentially, objects are pieces of software—small, reusable, interoperable application components—for building things such as compound documents, user interfaces, database-access systems and network-management systems [27]. By eliminating dependencies between software modules, code eliminates the need to build from scratch everytime. The ability to rapidly produce applications with reusable software objects will knock down the technical barriers, allowing entrance into various markets [27], [28]. Over time, it is expected that a viable market will emerge for software parts or components. Users and others will be able to use these parts or components to build custom applications; however, the successful ones will do much more than just assemble components [27].

A survey was recently done to analyze the reasons for maintenance requests for nearly 500 major projects. Table 3.10 shows their results [26]. The results showed that the major portion of maintenance requests are for changes in user requirements. This showed that most change requests are unavoidable, assuming that the original specifications were correct. The change in user requirements could be a result of inadequate specifications, but it definitely shows how dynamic modern business is and the need for adaptability. Therefore, by having adaptable software systems one will be able to keep up in a changing market. In object-oriented programming, encapsulation offers the greatest promise as a technique for making systems resilient to changes in implementation [41].

Table 3.10   Efforts related to software maintenance

Changes in user requirements	41.8%
Changes in data formats	17.4%
Emergency fixes	12.4%
Routine debugging	9.0%
Hardware changes	6.2%
Documentation	5.5%
Efficiency Improvements	4.0%
Other	3.7%

3.8.4 Technical principles

Abstract data types   The notions of object-oriented programming build on the ideas of abstract data types and add to them important innovations in code sharing and reusability [28]. Foremost is the idea of message passing. In message passing emphasis is placed on the *value,* not on the *operations* to be performed. Implicit in message passing is the idea that the interpretation of the message can vary with different objects. Inheritance allows different data types to share the same code, leading to a reduction in code size and an increase in functionality [28].

Objects Objects are the most significant components of the many key components. An object is a software package that combines data and the related procedures that act upon it. Procedures or methods are associated with the object to describe all the things the object can do. Objects interact with the rest of the system through the use of messages, which are composed of the object's name followed by the name of a method the object can execute [31].

Objects are organized into classes with common features. This refers to the object procedures or methods. These objects should be, as far as possible, based on the real-world entities and concepts of the application or domain. Objects can be either classes or instances of a class, although some use the term *object* synonymously with *instance*. The OMG (Object Management Group) standard is to call the description of classes, *object types*, and to use the term *class* to refer to their implementation [26], [41].

Messages and methods Action is initiated when a message is sent to an agent responsible for the action. The message encodes the request for action and is accompanied by any additional information needed to carry out the request. The receiver is the agent to whom the message was sent. If the message is accepted by the receiver, then it accepts responsibility to carry out the indicated action. In response to a message, a receiver will perform some method to satisfy the request [28]. As stated before, objects, classes, and their instances communicate by message passing. This eliminates data duplication and ensures that changes to data structures encapsulated within objects do not affect other parts of the system with their changes. Messages are often implemented as function calls [26]. The description or signature of a method is called an *operation*. Operations define which messages an object is able to process successfully

Classes and instances A class is a collection of objects which share common attributes and methods. Or it can be thought of as a template that defines the methods and variables included in a particular type of object. Objects that are part of the class contain only their particular values for the variables. An object is called one instance of a particular class [26], [31]. When classes are nested and lower levels inherit the methods and variable definitions of the higher levels you have class hierarchy. Subclasses are defined which are a special case of a class. Subclasses may define their own methods and variables and override any inherited characteristics [31]. Figure 3.10 shows an example of different subclasses under the class Material Object. Each subclass has most, if not all of the attributes of the class above it.

The method invoked by an object in response to a message is determined by the class of the receiver. All objects of a given class use the same method in response to similar messages. When the principal knowledge of a more general category is applicable

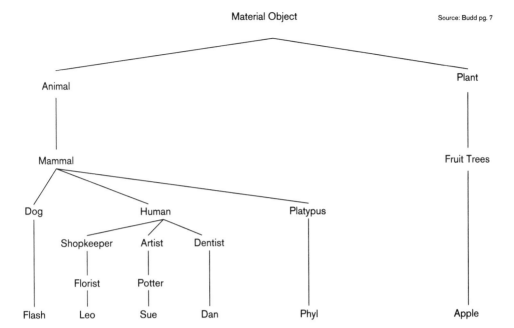

Material Object

Source: Budd pg. 7

Figure 3.10 Subclasses

also to the more specific category it is called inheritance [28]. Classes have different types of responsibilities, therefore there are different types of classes. Some of the different types are listed below:

- *Data managers, data, or state classes*   Maintain data of state information of one sort or another. Data managers are usually the fundamental building blocks of a design.

- *Data sinks or data sources*   Either generate data or accept data and process it further. One example is outputting to a disk. Unlike a data manager they do not hold onto the information, it generates it or processes it.

- *View or observer class*   Class used to display information or an output. Usually a separate view from model because it simplifies the model and it can have multiple views.

- *Facilitator or helper*   Classes that maintain little or no state information but assist in execution of complex tasks. Can be things like drawing lines and text [28].

When trying to determine if a new class should be formed or if the object should remain in the class, the *is-a* and *has-a* relationships are used. The *is-a* relationship relates to class and subclass, the *has-a* relationship defines data maintained within a class. From

Figure 3.10 one can say that a dog is a mammal, so one knows that it should form a subclass [28].

Inheritance   Inheritance is specified as a mechanism that defines a class of objects as a special case of a more general class, automatically including the methods and variables of the general class [31]. Classes can be organized into a hierarchical inheritance structure as shown previously. A subclass inherits attributes from a superclass higher in the tree. An abstract superclass is a class that is used only to create subclasses, for which there are no direct instances [28].

By inheritance, one means the property that instances of a child class (or subclass) can access both data and behavior (methods) associated with a parent class (or superclass). Inheritance is always transitive, so an object can inherit features from superclasses many levels away. If the method is not defined within the receiving object's class, the superclass will be searched for the method [32].

Essentially, the subclasses have an extension of the data and behavior associated with the parent classes. They have all the properties of parent and some additional ones. Because the child is an expansion of the parent it is also a contraction because it is more specialized and has limited use [32]. However, objects usually inherit all and only the features of the classes they belong to but it is also possible in an object-oriented system to allow classes to inherit features from more general superclasses. In this case, inherited features can be overridden and extra features added to deal with exceptions. Inheritance is only one of the conceptual structures with which we organize the world [26]. One common situation occurs where a subclass represents a combination of features from two or more parent classes. The ability of a class to inherit from two or more parent classes is known as multiple inheritance [41].

When a subclass redefines the method of a superclass, it is said to override the parent class. Figure 3.10 showed the platypus being a subclass of mammal. Since a platypus does not have all the characteristics of a mammal, that class would have to override some of the parent class features. When a message is sent to an object, the method is looked for in the immediate class first, then up the chain until it is found. If a method is redefined in a child, it is said to override the parent. This can be used to replace the method of the parent or to refine it in order to preserve the method of the parent class and augment it [28].

The benefits of inheritance include [33]:

- *Software reusability*   You do not have to rewrite code to do simple functions, just create subclasses to do more specific actions with general action predefined. By reusing general code, there is a greater chance of finding errors not previously found; this will create very reliable reusable code.

- *Code sharing*   People can share classes, or subclasses can use the same parent class. It will be written only once and will contribute only once to the size of the program, making it a smaller overall program.

- *Consistency of interface*   Multiple subclasses inherit from the same superclass. They all get the same behavior. So one knows the interfaces to similar objects are similar, there is no confusion that occurs when things are slightly different for each interface.

- *Software components*   One will construct reusable software components that will be available in libraries.

- *Rapid prototyping*   By being able to quickly develop a generic software system based on reusable components, one can concentrate on the new portion of the system and spend development time there. One can rapidly release prototypes of the system and test it to tailor it to exact needs by tuning the specialized parts. This is important for projects where the requirements of the system are not clearly defined.

- *Polymorphism*   This is the ability to reuse a higher level component without being tied to lower level components on which it was built. One can reuse higher level components by changing the lower level components.

- *Information hiding*   The lack of information given decreases interconnectedness of software systems. This decreases complexity and promotes code reuse. One only knows what basic function it performs.

Inheritance does not always work out to the user's advantage. It does have some costs and those costs include [33], [41]:

- *Execution speed*   Inherited methods, which must deal with arbitrary subclasses cannot outperform hand-crafted systems. However, the difference is often small. Also, due to the fact that programmers usually do not know how execution time is being used in their programs, it is better to build it quickly and fine tune the performance of the system once it is built. This prevents worrying about performance issues at the beginning of the development process and delaying the actual development of the system.

- *Program size*   By using generic software components, the software may contain functionality that will not be used by the system. This causes an increase in the size of an inherited system over a custom-built system. However, as memory costs decrease, the size of programs is becoming less of an issue. It is more important to be able to produce quality error-free code rapidly. This will hold down development costs which is becoming far more important than program size.

- *Program complexity*   Overuse of inheritance can in turn create its own form of complexity, even though the aim of object-oriented programming is to reduce overall complexity. Understanding the control flow can be difficult with an inherited program.
- *Message-passing overhead*   Message passing is more costly than simple procedure invocation. One ends up with 2 or 3 additional assembly language instructions, and the total time penalty may amount to 10%. This figure varies across programming languages. The increased cost must be accompanied with the benefits of the object-oriented technique.

Method binding   As mentioned earlier, the search to find a method to invoke in response to a given message begins with the class of the receiver. If no appropriate method is found, the search is conducted in the superclass of this class. The search continues up through the superclass until a method is found or the chain of superclasses ends. If a method is found, it is executed, otherwise an error message is generated. Information in a subclass must be able to override methods defined in a superclass in the case of exceptions. Usually the same name for the method is used to show that they will execute differently. One form of polymorphism is that two objects will respond to a message by performing two different methods [32], [41].

Abstraction and encapsulation   Encapsulation is one of the principal advantages of OOP over other programming styles. The user sees a description of legal operations: only the implementor needs to know the actual data structures, the concrete details are encapsulated within a more abstract framework. Therefore, the data structures and implementation details of an object are hidden from other objects in the system. The only way to access an object's state is to send a message that causes one of the methods to execute. This makes objects basically equivalent to abstract data types in programming [26], [27].

Abstraction represents the essential features of something without including background or essential detail. Abstractions should be complete in that they should encapsulate all the essential properties of an object. In programming terms, this means that objects should abstract and encapsulate both data and process. Things are known by their properties and also through their behavior. The basic idea is that an object is defined by its list of abstract attributes, (often divided into instance variables and class variables), i.e., size, position, color, and a list of procedures it can perform on these attributes. A method is defined as a procedure or function that changes the state of an object or causes it to send a message, i.e., return values [26].

Polymorphism   The ability to use the same expression to denote different operations is referred to as polymorphism. A simple case is when + is used to signify real or integer addition. When the same message, *add 1*, is sent to a bank account and to a list of reminder notes, this message should produce quite different results. Hence, polymorphism allows this shared code to be tailored to fit the specific circumstances of each individual data type. The emphasis on the independence of individual components permits an incremental development process, in which individual software units are designed, programmed and tested before being combined into a large system [26], [28].

The ability to form polymorphic functions is one of the most powerful techniques in object-oriented programming. It permits code to be written once, at a high level of abstraction, and to be tailored as necessary to fit a variety of situations [26]. Polymorphism does introduce an inefficiency into the program due to a lack of complete information the function has. A function with more complete information will have a higher efficiency but, as will be shown later, the inefficiency is not significant [32].

ORB   There are numerous programming languages that claim to object-oriented, but fall short of the claim. For example, there are many people who claim to have distributed object-oriented technology, but their system actually consists of object-oriented clients and servers that utilize standard SQL and RPC techniques for internodal communications. The objects themselves must be distributed across the network and must communicate internodally to have truly distributed objects. The objects communicate through the use of an Object Request Broker (ORB) used as middleware for transporting messages [34].

3.8.5 Standards

A consortium of key vendors formed what is known as the Object Management Group (OMG). The OMG has facilitated the use of object-oriented technologies by arriving at a standard for the ORB, called CORBA (Common Object Request Broker Architecture). If all vendors adhere to CORBA, their products and objects will be able to intercommunicate transparently. This was critical to the advancement of the technology and the use of object libraries [34]. However, standards were being looked at as a possible problem in early rounds. The problem was not a lack of standards but an overabundance. A company looking to implement object-oriented technology could stand to lose a considerable investment if it were to go with the wrong set of standards. This obviously acted as an impediment to the spread of a technology that was long overdue [30].

3.8.6 Performance issues

Performance is hindered in object-oriented programming by the fact that time may be wasted searching a class hierarchy to locate a method or variable. An object-oriented program may run slower than a conventional program, just as an interpreted program will most likely run slower than a compiled one [34].

If the search has to go across a network, there will be a more significant effect. However, by using databases and storing structures directly as composite objects, you can access the information faster than in conventional programming where it is stored in relational form. There can be such a measure of difference that a distributed object network can actually run faster than non object-oriented client/server implementations [34].

The issue of slower performance is not looked at a major factor in the future of object-oriented technology. The reason being that the efficiency of hardware will always improve on speed, so you might as well start out with the best type of programming and work from there [25].

The more fundamental problem is that companies try to implement an object-oriented environment using procedural methods. Companies are slowly learning how to implement the architecture in the most efficient ways. Examples exist of companies misusing classes, causing the applications to run 20 times slower, and performing calculations on client machines instead of on the servers in distributed systems. Improper use of the technology can have a profound effect on its performance. When people learn to properly implement the technology, you will see much more of a movement towards object-orientation since the true benefits will be realized [35].

3.8.7 Problems and limitations

There are some problems with object-oriented technology, but they seem to be of a temporary nature. As people gain more experience and the technology becomes more widespread, these problems will no longer be an issue. However, these are problems that still need to overcome before the technology can advance.

Currently, the problem exists that there is a lack of a common infrastructure. Companies have kicked-off object technology initiatives and found that the effort was useless without a common infrastructure. Once it is put in place, companies will more readily deploy object-oriented systems [27]. Off-the-shelf components also figure into object-oriented solutions. They generally do not provide an exact match to system requirements, and therefore contain at least some unnecessary components that add to the system cost. The significance of those added costs depends on how well the available components match the application's requirements [29].

Many users have remained cautious, due to uncertainty of interoperability among different vendors products. This goes along with the fact that vendors have failed to provide clear goals and business justifications for using object-oriented products. They are not stating what the users can get out of the technology. The vendors must provide readily available reliable products that will interoperate with other vendor products [36]. When object-oriented technology is used in a distributed environment, there is much more complexity than within a single system. The data transmission must be minimized or more bandwidth provided, and servers must be able to get into and out of the transaction as fast as possible. The wide area links used to transport messages have a much lower bandwidth then the high speed bus within the system. There is almost an order of magnitude of difference between the two. This fact dictates that network traffic must be minimized to effectively reduce the traffic between nodes. This can be done by locating objects in the best locations. Distributed objects can work in one's favor in the sense that a small request can return the result of a substantial calculation at the remote server [34], [37]. Again, ATM technology will make available more bandwidth for the user, as discussed in the next chapter.

3.9 References

24   B.J. Cox, *Object-Oriented Programming, An Evolutionary Approach,* Reading, MA: Addison-Wesley, 1986.

25   D. Ingalls, "Object-Oriented Programming," *Distinguished Lecture Series, Volume II,* Cupertino, CA: Apple Computer Inc., 1989.

26   I. Graham, *Object-Oriented Methods,* 2nd Ed., Reading, MA: Addison-Wesley Publishing Company, 1994.

27   D. Taft, "Climbing Toward New Verticals," *Computer Reseller News*, January 30, 1995, page 39.

28   T. Budd, *An Introduction To Object-Oriented Programming,* Reading, MA: Addison-Wesley, 1991.

29   R. Lehrbaum, "Object Orientation Cuts Development Time," *Electronic Engineering Times*, April 25, 1994, page 50.

30   J. Lazar, "The Object is Productivity—Early Adopters of Modular Programming Report Encouraging Results," *Information Week*, January 3, 1994, page 36.

31   R. Peri, "Understanding Object-Oriented Programming," *Communications Week*, December 12, 1994, page 52.

32 P. Coad, and J. Nicola, *Object-Oriented Programming*, Englewood Cliffs, NJ: Yourdon Press, 1993.

33 C.A. Gunter, and J.C. Mitchell, eds., *Theoretical Aspects of Object-Oriented Programming*, Cambridge: The MIT Press, 1994.

34 R. Peri, "OOP… Revolution or Evolution?," *Communications Week*, December 12, 1994, page 49.

35 M. Marshall, "Developers Tackle Object Woes—Companies Scrutinize Basic Mistakes When Switching From Procedural Programming," *Communications Week*, June 19, 1995, page 4.

36 S. Girishankar, "Vendors Ready Object Software—Object-Oriented Software Standards Continue to Develop," *Communications Week*, May 9, 1994, page 13.

37 J. Rendleman, "Object-Oriented Projects by Local and Long Distance Carriers," *Communications Week*, November 20, 1995, page 76.

38 S. Gallagher "Seeing The Sexy Side of C++—The Object-Oriented Programming Language Displays Its Appeal to the Business World," *Information Week*, November 27, 1995, pages 60–63.

39 P. Lang, "Client/Server and Multi-distributed Databases," class project, Stevens Institute of Technology, Fall/Winter 1995–6.

40 D. Minoli, *Internet and Intranet Engineering*, New York, NY: McGraw-Hill, 1997.

41 P. Hennigan, "Object-Oriented Programming Principles," class project, Stevens Institute of Technology, Fall/Winter 1995.

42 D. J. Schmid, "Distributed Multi-Database Systems Including Client Server," class project, Stevens Institute of Technology, Fall/Winter 1995.

43 D. Minoli, *Analyzing Outsourcing*, New York, NY: McGraw-Hill, 1994.

44 D. Cook and D. Sellers, *Launching a Business on the Web*. Que Corporation, 1995.

45 S. Krantz, *Real World Client/Server*, Maximum Press, 1995.

46 J. Martin and J. Leben, *Client/Server Databases Enterprise Computing*, Englewood Cliffs, NJ: Prentice Hall, 1995.

47 W. Rosenberry, D. Kenney and G. Fisher, *Understanding DCE,* Sebastopol, CA: O'Reilly & Associates, Inc., 1992.

48 M. Betz, "Networking Objects with CORBA," *Dr. Dobb's Journal*, November 1995, pages 18 ff.

49 Smith and Guengerich, *Client Server Computing,* Second Edition, Carmel, IN: Sams Publishing 1994.

50 *Planning for Distributed Database.* First Edition, IBM Corp. 1992.

51 "Client/Server Data Base Design Review," *Data Management Review,* Vol. 4, August 1994.

52 "Optimizing Client/Server Performance," *Data Management Review,* Vol 5, January 1995.

53 "Middleware: Client/Server Bridge," *Data Management Review,* Vol 5, January 1995.

54 "The New Corporate IS Culture," *Data Management Review,* Vol 4, September 1994.

55 "System Manageability: A Client Server Issue," *Data Management Review,* Vol 4, September 1994.

56 "LAN of Opportunity," *INC. Technology,* Vol 17, September 1995.

57 "The Networked Corporation," *BusinessWeek,* June 26, 1995.

58 "Distributed Computing," *Relational Database Journal,* IBM, 1994.

59 "Enterprise C/S and C/S Developer," *DBMS,* Vol 8, November 1995.

60 "Client/Server Testing Tools," *Database Programming and Design,* Vol 8, November 1995.

PART II

ATM basics

chapter 4

An ATM primer

This chapter provides, for convenience, a short tutorial on ATM. It is assumed that the reader already has some working knowledge of the field, and so the description is limited in scope. The assumption is that the reader has investigated ATM and would be inclined to deploy the technology in his or her organization, but is not sure of the implications, as related to client/server support and the use of this technology for intranets. If more background on ATM is needed, the reader may refer to a number of texts, including [62]. More detailed background features are covered in the chapters that follow, as appropriate.

4.1 Background

ATM* is an evolutionary rather than a revolutionary technology, but it marks a major step beyond existing network architectures. At the wide area level, ATM technology takes full advantage of the large capacity potential of singlemode fiber optic media, while adjusting to the limitations of today's infrastructure—which will remain in place for a number of years. Specifically, interworking with legacy networks and protocols is a feature that has been built into ATM. At the local area level, ATM uses advanced encoding schemes to support 25, 100, and 155 Mbps on twisted-pair and multimode fiber media.

Private networks have evolved over the past quarter century. Successive architectures—all still in use—include X.25, Frame Relay, Ethernet, Token Ring, and FDDI. ATM technology is capable of overcoming its antecedent's shortcomings in bandwidth, scalability, traffic handling capabilities (this being called traffic management), and suitability for combined data, image, and voice traffic.

ATM standards were originally based on Broadband Integrated Services Digital Network (B-ISDN) standards, which in turn evolved from ISDN standards. For LAN and campus environments, a number of newly developed standards have also evolved in the recent past. ATM is an enabling technology for new networking applications; however, challenges, including efficient support of legacy networks, applications design, network management, and scalability, must be satisfactorily and fully addressed before ATM can be utilized comprehensively. This text also aims at describing ATM's ability to support client/server environments.

---

* This chapter is synthesized from a number of sources published by Mr. Minoli, including but not limited to [62], [63], and [65].

4.2 The emergence of ATM

Network hardware and computers rest on the same technological foundation: VLSI (very large scale integration). Just like computers, the crucial components in network hardware including adapter cards, switches, bridges and routers, are based on high density transistor chips and other electronic devices. Both technologies deploy this hardware in similar ways, obtaining comparable efficiency and performance.

Computing has, for the past dozen or more years, followed Moore's Law: the density (and, hence, the potential performance) of silicon-based microprocessors doubles every eighteen months. This observation, named after its originator, Intel cofounder Gordon Moore, is governed by technology. Another way of saying this is that power increases by an order of magnitude every four or so years. The price/performance of computers, reflecting competition as well as technology, improves at about the same rate as the Moore's Law cycle. This is especially true now that an increasingly wide range of computers is based on commodity microprocessors. Consequently, the obsolescence rate of computers, especially the desktop computers that respond most directly to Moore's Law, is very rapid. As every computer user is aware, however, the actual "mouse-end" utility of a computer is actually determined by software. Software, of both operating systems and applications programs, evolves much more slowly, ascending a much lumpier curve with numerous flat spots. Part of this problem is that software developers have focused on constantly adding new features to programs rather than keeping the feature level constant but improving speed. For example, increasingly more complex word processing packages are being developed to add many point-and-click capabilities, rather than keeping basic-but-nibble programs. In this example, such basic-but-nibble programs should not be to the exclusion of the more user-friendly version, but the option should exist for the advanced user to buy a (compatible) version of the software that focuses principally on speed. Many applications programs still in active use, often supporting billion-dollar industries, have remained fundamentally the same for ten or twenty years.

By contrast, networking technology has advanced more slowly than computer technology, as measured by, say, user-available bandwidth. It was shown in [61], in what might be called an equivalent "law," that bandwidth of a WAN has increased by an order of magnitude every 20 years (this "law" is based on an analysis covering 60 years). Raw bandwidth growth has been governed principally by technological factors. However, the traditional gap between computers and networks has also been influenced by the lack and ineffectiveness of a complete set of standards, their slow evolution, and their often-cautious adoption. As a result, ten-year-old networks are commonplace, and many are likely to remain in service for some time. Network software has, on the whole, advanced even slower than computer software.

Networking standards are needed to make it possible to connect systems of numerous manufacturers and facilitate interoperability of networks with different specifications. A network is also limited by the capacity of the transmission media through which data and other signals are transferred. These physical channels have evolved from twisted-pair wire, intended initially only for voice traffic, through more advanced uses of copper, to today's fiber optic facilities. Electronic switches have gradually displaced electromechanical equipment.

These diverse physical facilities of public networks, spread all over the world, represent a large investment. Telecommunications companies are accustomed to multidecade system lifetimes. Therefore, there is a tendency to retain embedded technology for a significant amount of time. However, in most relatively wealthy countries, national backbones and other WANs may be replaced or upgraded in the next few years. The capacity and overall cost-effectiveness of fiber are attractive, giving some impetus to the transition. Fiber is already predominant in major long-distance channels in the United States, and high-density countries like Hong Kong and Singapore that are anxious to gain a competitive advantage. The rest of the world may not catch up until well into the new century.

Many private networks are also moving to improve backbone as well as desktop capacity. Refinements in copper-wire technologies and the cost of replacing existing investments will, however, delay the introduction of fiber for private LANs, at the desktop level. Four recent developments are extending the practical lifetime of existing media in private networks:

- Improvements in carrying capacity and error reduction in copper-based LAN runs.

- Introduction of switching into the traditional shared media networks such as Ethernet Token-Ring and FDDI.

- Adoption and near-standardization of data compression techniques that now reduce the bandwidth demands of images and video as well as text, making 10Base-T and 100Base-T LANs at least marginally capable of supporting these media.

- At the backbone level, what has held back the introduction of dedicated fiber facilities is the availability of high-speed services from carriers, eliminating the need for companies to become their own carriers, outside of their core competencies. These days, given the international nature of the competitive horizon, companies have enough challenges in keeping up their own products and market postures, without having to be technologically advanced mini-telephone companies. Once upon a time, businesses produced their own (electric) power, say by using a river-based power plant, coal furnaces, etc. Now, nearly nobody does that; companies rely on the electric utility to supply power.

From the perspective of today's networks, the potential physical capacity of fiber media is very large, 10 Gbps now and 1 Tbps in a few years using technologies such as coherent modulation and wavelength division multiplexing. Distinctions between computing and networking will diminish. The challenges now facing network designers, operators, standards-makers, and hardware manufacturers are defined in large part by four contrasting, and to some degree contradictory requirements:

- Taking full advantage of the possibilities created by fiber
- Managing bandwidth efficiently via statistical multiplexing
- Adjusting to the capabilities of existing infrastructure
- Providing for optimal operation of networks that combine both older and newer physical foundations and systems technology

Physics and mathematics require that the Moore's Law cycle for microprocessor technology will at some not too distant point begin to stretch out and then reach a ceiling. Networking will be effected by its roots in the same basic microchip technology. It is also limited by the inescapable problem of transmission latency due to propagation delay imposed by distance.

Especially in WANs, the basic infrastructure is provided by telecommunications companies. Traditionally, data transmission has depended upon translation of the digital output of computers into the analog format of telecommunications facilities that were designed originally to support human voice. Now, there is a significant migration toward digital, at least for corporate (rather than consumer) networking. ATM is strictly a digital technology. The emergence of the Internet (and Internet's use of ATM) reinforces the trend toward high-speed digital comnmunications.

4.2.1 ATM's evolution

ATM has evolved from previous network architectures. Much has been done recently to upgrade LAN and WAN technologies. Both were originally based on copper wire, whether twisted-pair, shielded, or coaxial. The quality and carrying capacity of copper media have been improving steadily, and these solutions remain useful for smaller LANs and WANs (particularly the access portion to the WAN) that do not generate high volumes of traffic. In a longer perspective, however, both LANs and WANs are approaching their limits. Ethernet, Token Ring, and comparable networks are the foundation of today's routine network functions; sharing files, the client/server philosophy, and clustering workstations or other computers together to form a single distributed computational system.

FDDI, a technology based on fiber, went into use in the late 1980s. It is also based on a token ring philosophy. FDDI's nominal transmission limit, 100 Mbps, is ten times greater than the capacity ceiling of Ethernet. In the early 1990s it became clear that a faster LAN technology would be necessary to keep pace with in-building bandwidth demands. However, FDDI was deemed too costly and complex. Two "extender technologies" were proposed, each of which was based on the idea that the fundamental philosophy behind Ethernet could be extended to provide more bandwidth. These technologies were thus known as Fast Ethernet. As discussed in Chapter 2, one, called 100BaseT, was compatible with Ethernet (just at 100 Mbps). The other, called 100Base-VG, had additional functionality. These high speed LANs serve as an extension of legacy technologies. However, they do not have the capability to be an "enabling" technology because many of the intrinsic limitations of shared media remain.

ATM is an enabling technology, delivering a capacity level that could change the nature of networking. As it has been elaborated over a number of years, ATM is the next step in a progression. What makes the difference between ATM and the solutions from which it has evolved?

- ATM's architecture is different. It offers architected features such as quality of service (QoS), statistical multiplexing, and traffic loss prioritization.* ATM supports a connection-oriented service, rather than a connectionless service (these issues were first discussed in Chapter 2). With its "guaranteed" quality of service it is better suited to carry video and multimedia.

---

* ATM per se does not support per-cell cell-treatment priority from a performance point of view (there is a loss priority, but this is not directly related to expediting cells through the switch or rendering special treatment). To compensate for this, implementors have developed an "external" mechanism of providing per-session "traffic" priority discrimination. In a Permanent Virtual Circuit environment, the cells belonging to a session are implicitly assigned a priority at the switch by making a notation of the specific port on which the connection terminates; adding some supplementary cell-enveloping at the switch as the cell traverses the switch (this supplementary information is, however, removed as the cell exits the switch); and routing cells (based on the supplementary information) to different buffer pools. This implicit mechanism allows different traffic flows to receive different switching treatment (e.g., Constant Bit Rate, Variable Bit Rate, etc.). For Switched Permanent Connections, the treatment of the block of cells associated with a connection is based on the kind of service class called for in the setup message sent by the user for that connection, at the start of the session. Again, the switch will have to use extensions of ATM to service the different requirements; in addition, the priority is not on a per-cell basis. Hence, the issue of "priorities in ATM" has to be carefully worded: one can say that mechanisms exist to support a kind of connection-level grade of service which gives the appearance of supporting, from a performance point-of-view, a weak kind of traffic priority. It is important to also note that the QoS on one switch may not be the same as QoS on another switch (particularly for VBR, UBR, and ABR.)

- ATM's bandwidth scalability is capable of accommodating, with appropriate hardware upgrades, the expected growth in end-user bandwidth demand. This expected increase is driven by the rapid increases in performance and output of the computers served by the networks, and by the growth in numbers of users, as desktop systems are becoming almost universal.

- Desktop workstations based on the most powerful Reduced Instruction Set (RISC) microprocessors e.g., Digital Equipment's Alpha, can already swamp a FDDI connection when used for I/O-intensive functions. PCs will reach similar output in a generation or two. As desktop users have deployed applications like Microsoft Windows, IBM Lotus Notes, and even Netscape Navigator, with appended voice and video, demand for network capacity has accelerated. ATM will be able to better support these and similar applications than existing communication services.

- The demand curve will level off as Moore's law reaches its physical limits. Networks will bump up against similar ceilings as propagation delays over longer distances become a limiting factor. Nonetheless, ATM-based services are the best-suited, compared to all other currently available alternatives, to support high-performance applications.

- As bandwidth is increased, the laws of physics, as they relate to transmission, become an increased factor. Throughput does not increase in proportion with bandwidth at speeds in the hundreds of megabits/second. Because of this, it is imperative not to further add switching delays. Again, ATM technology is the best-suited, compared to all other currently available alternatives, to support high-performance services, by keeping the switching delay very small.

- It is essential that bandwidth be allocated to users and applications intelligently and efficiently. This feature cannot be added as an afterthought, but must be part of the original architecture—one of ATM's strongest features.

- ATM's basic philosophy is scalability, hence technological longevity. In addition to commoditizing the physical layers, the much simplified infrastructure made possible by ATM's basic philosophy permits a much longer productive life cycle for the cabling plant and networking hardware than for other (LAN) technologies. The cost and inconvenience of performance upgrades are reduced. For example, changing from ordinary Ethernet to Fast Ethernet requires a replacement of adapters and other hardware. In principle, ATM/SONET interface permits increases in speed with fewer, less costly adjustments. However, it must be understood that if the user purchased a 51.84-Mbps card, this card will most likely not support 155 Mbps or 622 Mbps; a new card would be required. The advantage of this approach is that the entry-level price is small, in that the user is not buying features which he or she does not immediately need. On the other hand, the user may choose to purchase a more powerful (but more expensive) card on day one which can, by design, support 51.84-, 155-, and 622-Mbps rates immediately. The user would initially only use this card at the lower rate. As needs increase, the user can then, without any hardware changes, upgrade the speed. It should be clear, though, that a tradeoff is required; nothing is ever free.

- ATM also strikes a balance between two related issues in network design: accommodation of traffic bursts and control of congestion caused by competition for resources among candidates for transmission, particularly in the presence of bursts.

Ethernet in the LAN and Frame Relay in the WAN cope with surges in network traffic, but can become congested if too many computers on the network wish to transmit at the same time. Token Ring has a monitor that controls access, but it can backlog computers, waiting until a token lets them on the network.* ATM, in contrast, supports a form of bandwidth on demand, up to the maximum speed of the access line or switch, and consequently can deal more easily with bursts.

Note: Some in the trade press seem to imply that ATM is "magical" in its support of bandwidth on demand. This could not be further from the truth. ATM, like anything else has a limited bandwidth equal (at the switch level) to the bus speed—say 2 Gbps; also there are a certain number of buffers—say 64,000 per line card or per fabric. As soon as the user puts in more than a certain well-calculable number of inputs and arrivals, he or she can become dead in the water, just like in Frame Relay and Ethernet. In addition, there are constraints based on both the access speed of the link (user/line side) and the speed of the trunk.

- Like any other technology operating at the Data Link Layer, ATM is independent of upper layer protocols (so in principle are Ethernet, Token Ring, etc.). This means that ATM will carry any Protocol Data Unit (PDU) that is handed down to it through the syntax of the ATM Service Access Point (SAP). From ATM's perspective, it is immaterial what is contained in the cell: IP, IPX, SNA, protocol control information, payload, etc. From the upper layer protocol's point of view, however, there has to be protocol compatibility matching; the protocol PDUs must conform to the ATM's SAP, hence, the upper layer protocol must know how to hand off its PDUs to ATM. Having noted this tautological observation, there is a desire to retain existing upper layer protocol (applications) unchanged. Hence, the developers have developed appropriate ATM Adaptation Layers to accommodate

---

* However, in Token Ring, the delay is deterministic and bounded, while in Ethernet it is stochastic and (theoretically) unbounded.

the interworking functions. AALs reside above the ATM layer and below the Network Layer. Note that ATM is a connection-oriented technology. This means that connections must be established (at the ATM layer) before information can be exchanged. There is also a desire to develop virtual LANs (VLANs), where the logical community definition is independent of the physical location of the user. A number of products already exist to support VLANs, but these are vendor-specific. Many hope that ATM (in particular LAN Emulation technology or MPOA) will become a vehicle to deliver vendor-independent VLANs.

- In ATM, the view of the network is "nearly" the same whether it is a LAN or WAN, public or private. Thus, although ATM is an evolutionary step forward from earlier networking technologies, it is a major step.

4.2.2 Packet transmission aspects

Private networking started with technologies like SNA (System Network Architecture, developed by IBM) and X.25-based packet services. SNA reflects its history and parentage. It was designed to provide communications within a corporation or other organizations, or between a limited number of large-scale hosts (usually a few dozen) and hundreds or thousands of users. Pathways are assigned to each data-transmission session. Routing is static, and the network must be reconfigured when a new host is added. This can be cumbersome, but it provides an efficient means to move large numbers of transactions to and from a mainframe computer in a stable environment.

X.25 refers to the packet-based protocol interface between devices called *Data Terminal Equipment* (DTE), which connects with the user's computer, and *Data Circuit-terminating Equipment* (DCE) which feeds data into the network. This 1970s technology supports transmission by segmenting data into variable length blocks called packets. After the packets navigate the network, they are reassembled at the other end. In a process similar to the operation of SNA, but more flexibly, X.25 establishes a pathway to the recipient and guarantees distribution. Typical implementations of X.25 are slow, generally around 64 kbps for user access. X.25 mechanisms can be used to send data over common-carrier circuits. It has, consequently, been popular in Europe and other countries in which telecommunications monopolies have been reluctant to lease dedicated lines and give up the substantial revenues collected by charging their regular tariffs. Processing and transmission overhead is high because X.25 was designed to deliver messages reliably in an era of low-quality connections with high error rates.

Being LAN technologies, Ethernet and Token Ring both transmit data in the form of possibly variable-length packets. Messages are encapsulated in packets, injected into the shared transmission stream and delivered to the recipient. This strategy makes it easy to add or delete nodes. On the other hand, congestion can occur if too many nodes are trying to heave packets onto the network at the same time. Token Ring is more structured; this makes for a more orderly flow of data but increases bandwidth overhead. Both Token Ring and Ethernet are multiaccess, connectionless technologies. Neither guarantees packet delivery. They are, however, based upon limited distance cabling with very low error rates. Furthermore, they are intended for data transmission; most protocols can recover from some data loss without serious impact to the application. It must be noted, however, that ATM also does not guarantee data delivery.

FDDI is a more recent token ring system for LANs based on fiber optic media, that has a nominal rating of 100 million bits per second. Like Ethernet and Token Ring, FDDI is limited to relatively short distances, from a single a building to a fairly compact campus, although extenders and other measures permit transmission over somewhat longer distances. Token Ring and FDDI both include a prioritization feature. Tokens can be utilized to accept packets with defined priorities in preference to other packets. Multiple packets with equal priority all obtain access. The prioritization feature has been used rarely on Token Ring because it was poorly documented, was given little emphasis by IBM, the sponsor of Token Ring, and did not seem to involve an important business requirement. On FDDI, the token algorithm is more complex as is its prioritization features, making it less cost-effective to implement. It must be noted, however, that ATM also does not explicitly support priority from a performance point of view as noted previously.

Other solutions, designed primarily to deliver improved bandwidth include Fast Ethernet, capable of a nominal capacity of 100 Mbps. Like Ethernet, Fast Ethernet lacks the technological scalability of ATM as bandwidth demands escalate out of the low hundreds of megabits per second toward gigabits per second. Direct scalability of Ethernet to "gigabit" rates is still unproven.

Shifting attention to WANs, Frame Relay is another technology intended to supplant legacy networks. It features lower overhead than X.25 and can support higher speeds—in the range from 64 kbps to 1.544 Mbps. It operates by transmitting frames (very much like packets) over virtual circuits. Frame Relay is viewed by some as a transitional technology. Some telecommunications companies and other vendors, in Japan for instance, where Frame Relay pricing is low, have embraced it because it can deliver increased bandwidth (compared to traditional packet switching) at relatively modest additional investment in infrastructure.

A high-speed technology called Fiber Channel has emerged in the past few years. Implementation remains limited at this time, but it has a potential role in LANs, primarily for functions like direct channels between large-scale computers and storage devices, or other peripherals. Fiber Channel could supplant High Performance Parallel Interface (HPPI), yet another technology developed to meet similar requirements. Both of these recent technologies, however, lack the versatility and flexibility needed for across-the-board competition with ATM.

So far we have discussed lower layer protocols (all, with the exception of X.25, residing at the Data Link layer). A brief discussion of upper layer protocols follows, since beyond the basic clocking rate/speed of the underlying media, the communication throughput is ultimately controlled by these protocols. TCP/IP (Transmission Control Protocol/Internet Protocol), designed in late 1970s, has been synonymous with the public Internet, but has also been extensively adopted by operators of private networks. It is a protocol intended to facilitate operation of transfer points (routers) between networks. TCP/IP was originally developed to meet Department of Defense requests for a network that could continue operation despite destruction of nodes on the battlefield. It thus tolerates low-quality, error-prone circuits. This also means, however, that overhead is relatively high.

TCP operates with packets up to 65,536 bytes (octets) in length. It includes an important provision that permits packets to be disassembled into smaller units without degrading the message, if a receiving or transit network cannot handle longer packets. IP by itself is a best-effort protocol; delivery of the data is not assured because it does not offer error detection and recovery features. (The responsibility for these functions rests upon TCP.)

In a parallel fashion, the OSI stack, first discussed in Chapter 3, is a set of protocols developed by the International Organization for Standardization (ISO) to serve objectives similar to those of TCP/IP. In the United States and on the global Internet (also for intranets) TCP/IP, not an international standard, has largely filled this niche, although OSI remains favored in Europe and some other areas. So, in the world of private corporate networks, many users are turning to TCP/IP, which is now supported by virtually all workstations and larger systems, including mainframes, to replace earlier, vendor-specific protocols.

For a while, at least, all the network architectures described above will continue to play roles in private networks. Increasingly, however, ATM will displace theses architectures or be utilized as an intermediate layer supporting other protocols such as TCP/IP and OSI. ATM offers the following features:

- Suitable for both long-distance and local networks
- Adapts to a wide range of physical media
- Accommodates voice, data, images, and video
- Supports QoS, congestion control, and other network management features

- Adjusts to bursty traffic and avoid congestion
- Scales to much higher bandwidths than Frame Relay or other competitive architectures

4.3 The standardization of ATM

Telecommunications could not take place without standards, but it is difficult to live with the current predicament of a large gamut of incompatible protocols. For data transmission, the ideal would be a universal or near-universal standard. *Note:* Although at face value it appears that the voice world has come up with a single standard, there are in fact many standards. However, there has been more emphasis to achieve interoperability so as to guarantee the ability to call anywhere in the world and be heard, than has been seen in the computer world.

Hundreds of official or de facto standards for data networks of various kinds are in wide use. This diversity may be tolerable within LANs, but local networks also provide the connections that lead to backbone circuits and thus to other computers all over the world. Negotiating internationally-accepted communications standards takes time. Procedures have been accelerated, but standard-setting is still much slower than the operation of Moore's Law. De facto standards have arisen, with TCP/IP the most conspicuous example. Although they may bypass the international consultative process, widely used de facto standards generally reflect a great deal of structured discussion by support groups, users, vendors, and others. Even if standards and other characteristics are different, bridges, routers, and associated software may provide interoperability and make it possible for networks to exchange data with other networks. These compromises may, however, slow everything down and cause complications.

4.3.1 The ATM standard

ATM took shape through the full international consultative procedure, although the standard specifications do not resolve every possible issue. This process took about 10 years (1985–95). It grew out of other well-established standards. Researchers in the 1980s were looking at the best method to achieve high-speed packetized data transmission.

It began with ISDN standards activities. ISDN is fully digital but is characteristic of its generation. Its Physical layer (level 1) is based on copper wire, and its bandwidth is limited to hundreds of thousands of bits per second. ISDN has been popular in Europe and Japan. The European Union has stimulated a program of universal or near-universal ISDN availability before the end of this decade. Adoption in the United States has been more spotty, although some regional telecommunications companies are turning to ISDN as a relatively low-cost means to increase bandwidth to subscribers.

ISDN allocates the available bandwidth into three channels using Time Division Multiplexing (also known as synchronous transfer mode) technology: two 64-kbps channels for data transport and one 16-kbps channel for signaling (housekeeping messages). The signaling channel is used to establish a connection; the data transport channels then supports transfer of the information. ISDN is strictly a circuit-switched service of defined bandwidth capabilities ($n \times 64$, $1 \le n \le 30$). ISDN was not designed to support broadband applications.

A decision was made in the mid 1980s to seek a new standard that could be based, to some extent, on ISDN principles and support optical fiber. Because of the media used, the supported speeds are much higher. The newcomer became known as B-ISDN (for Broadband ISDN). Although both are digital, ATM technology differs distinctively from ISDN in so far that ISDN is a "synchronous transfer mode technology" (namely, ISDN is a circuit-switched technology without any statistical multiplexing and statistical gains); ATM on the other hand is an "asynchronous transfer packet technology" with statistical multiplexing and gain. Because the user and the carrier "gamble" on statistical multiplexing, sophisticated traffic management capabilities are required by the carrier.

4.3.2 Background research

ATM concepts arose from research conducted in the mid 1980s. This work established that data units of fixed length were easier to switch at very high speeds than frames (like Ethernet, Token Ring, and FDDI) that could vary in length. This philosophy was influenced toward one direction by research done at IBM on a device called the PARIS (Packetized Automatic Routing Integrated System) switch, which serviced both variable and fixed-length packets. The PARIS project assumed, however, that all traffic would consist of data. It was a rationing-card system, in which senders could transmit only if they had received a token, awarded on the basis of an average data flow. (IBM later abandoned PARIS and embraced ATM.)

The B-ISDN debates were carried on between two factions. One faction, which could be identified as the X.25 faction, was concerned above all about more efficient, versatile, and less costly data transmission. The data faction was relatively unconcerned about time of arrival, and could tolerate some delay while packets are reassembled. They were very concerned with protecting the integrity of the information. The public telephone providers representing the other function emphasized time-sensitive information like voice, in which consistent sequence is crucial. Limited information loss was acceptable. There were, however, common grounds. For packetized video, packets must come through at a regular rate in order to avoid transmission "jitter." This is easier to accomplish with relatively short packets. The two factions solved this problem by deciding on a fixed-length packet, called a *cell*, that could be transmitted in an orderly, high speed fashion over a switched network. This solution would provide the cost advantages of data networks combined with the predictability of voice networks. But how long should those cells be? The data faction advocated a 64-byte specification, while the voice faction demanded 32 bytes. An agreement was finally reached where each cell would contain a 48-byte payload, accompanied by five additional bytes to identify the cell and carry other protocol control information.

For high-bandwidth networks based on fiber, ATM is frequently employed with a Layer 1 standard, called SONET. SONET defines a series of bandwidth levels for transmission over fiber networks. SONET rates consist of multiples of a base of 51.840 Mbps. Current ATM technology supports bandwidths at the OC-1 (Optical Carrier-1) level (51.840 Mbps), OC-3 level (155.520 Mbps), and at the OC-12 level (622.08 Mbps). SONET levels now targeted by systems developers would deliver 1244.160 Mbps (OC-24) and 2488.320 Mbps (OC-48). SONET standards are now nearly ready for OC-192 (about 10 Gbps) speeds.

Note: For user access, current ATM technology only supports the 155.520 Mbps; the 622.080-Mbps speed is only currently supported at the trunk level (although that should change in 1997).

Note: Outside the US, the SONET concept is described in the context of the Synchronous Digital Hierarchy (SDH). Effectively, this hierarchy uses building blocks of 155.520 Mbps rather than building blocks of 51.840. However, they are basically consistent for appropriate values of the aggregate bandwidth.

OC-24 and OC-48 would represent the gigabit network concept mentioned so often in public discussion. Applied with ATM technology, these bandwidth levels should be achievable later in this decade.

4.4 ATM as an enabling technology

ATM's architecture creates possibilities that have been beyond the reach of earlier technologies. As discussed, accredited standards bodies have developed the basic set of protocols. As is always the case, implementors workshops are then needed to complete the implementation details. In the case of ATM, the ATM Forum has focused on issues of interoperability. It appears that ATM will resolve these issues more quickly than was the case for predecessors. This is primarily due to two factors—focus and commitment. The ATM Forum consists of a plethora of vendor, user, government, and academic representatives whose commitment to the success of ATM is, in some people's view, unparalleled. FDDI, for example, has encountered some early difficulties in linking workstations from different manufacturers. Token Ring also had problems of this kind. (Ethernet, however, encountered fewer interoperability obstacles because of the inherent simplicity of its architecture.) This was due to the lack of an organization focusing efforts on implementation and deployment issues.

Because it can utilize fiber media to its full potential (at least in the long haul), ATM supports high speed. *Note:* In the campus environment, ATM uses multimode fiber to derive 100 Mbps (using FDDI-like encoding) or singlemode fiber to derive 155 Mbps (using FCS-like encoding), thereby not utilizing the fiber to its full potential. Also it uses UTP 5 twisted-pair to support speeds up to 155 Mbps; hence, ATM provides high speed when and only when it uses the underlying media to the full potential. These larger transmission capacities used in conjunction with appropriate switching technology make it easier to cope with bursty traffic. Ethernet, with its 10-Mbps ceiling, can also handle bursty traffic but is hindered by the contention issue and the easy-to-reach ceiling. As discussed, there are practical transmission (now 622 Mbps) and switching (now 2–20 Gbps) ceilings in ATM, but these are, at this time, more difficult to overwhelm. Token Ring and FDDI reduce contention compared to Ethernet but have much less capability to handle bursty transmissions. ATM's ability for *dynamic* allocation of bandwidth makes it easier to offer different classes of service to support different application classes. The transparency of the upper layers to ATM, when appropriate adaptation is provided (in pertinent equipment or software), makes it possible for ATM to be ubiquitous, employed in multiple types of LAN and WAN topologies and thus in every segment of the end-to-end connection.

ATM can be economically deployed in specific corporate environments, and its cost-effectiveness will increase over time. Error checking is performed only on the cell header, and not on the payload. This means that error-free reception of payload is not guaranteed at the ATM layer. It will be guaranteed at the TCP/IP layer. This is based on today's high-quality, low noise transmission media. Fiber media, used with the SONET Physical Layer protocol, makes available high capacity to the connected users. However, there is still a need to support statistical multiplexing and bandwidth overbooking, in order to obtain transmission efficiencies, particularly in the long haul. It follows that in ATM, sophisticated congestion control is needed to "guarantee" a very small probability of cell loss even under significant traffic levels. These characteristics add up to a technology that can permit users and applications developers to explore possibilities that have not been feasible until now.

4.5 Challenges facing ATM

ATM technology has not yet been developed to the point where *every* possible open issue has been resolved. Issues that require further work (as of press time) include:

- *Support of legacy networks*   In an interworking mechanism called LAN Emulation (LANE), Ethernet and Token Ring frames transit an ATM network (in a segmented fashion) and are delivered transparently to a similar legacy network on the receiving end. Furthermore, a user on an ATM device can send information to an Ethernet or Token Ring device. LAN emulation provides users with a migration path from existing architectures without passing through successive stages of large-scale reinvestment. To dispel some misconceptions, it must be noted, however, that the prospective user has to make immediate investment to acquire LANE technology in order to support some of the ATM functions at this time. The transition is then from Ethernet/Token Ring to LANE to ATM. Another approach would be for the user to save the funds invested in this partial migration to ATM, in order to be better equipped to then make the direct migration from Ethernet/Token Ring to ATM at a later date. The LANE solution requires investments just to support today's relative low bandwidth requirements; however, later it could be difficult to scale up to meeting the challenges of evolving network traffic patterns. Traffic concentration using ATM's higher capacity could overload tributary Token Ring and Ethernet networks by dumping bursts of information that choke the receiving network. Another approach is to use MPOA. The desire to protect investments must be traded off against the risks of poor overall performance. In addition, solutions must be found for problems of addressing brought about by connections with legacy networks. Even within the ATM domain, problems raised by address resolution and flow control have not been solved completely. It is also desirable to integrate

Frame Relay into ATM. Alternatively, ATM circuits might have to be utilized at lower speeds than SONET speeds in order to accommodate legacy traffic (LANE is treated in more detail later in the chapter and MPOA is covered in Chapter 6).

- *Applications design* Applications like traditional email may run well on ATM but do not take full advantage of its capabilities. Managers may choose to confine such traffic to alternative channels like the public Internet. This will be facilitated by the introduction of ATM APIs.

- *Security levels and quality of service* Considerations also need to be developed further for these in the context of ATM. Current capabilities are limited and some applications (e.g., transport of Motion Picture Expert Group 2 video) are utilizing their own security methods above the ATM layer. These considerations border on the classical polemic as to who should provide security; carriers argue that the applications should implement security measures; application developers argue that carriers should provide security.

- *Management and the network environment* Elementary management, when a port flashes red, etc., on ATM is not much different from earlier technology. In the past, however, crucial issues like traffic flows, quality of service monitoring and rendering, chargebacks, and other accounting procedures have not been addressed adequately. At this time there is little ATM work under way in these areas. Some users may be relatively tolerant of cell loss but require the fastest possible delivery. Others, pathologists who depend upon the resolution of medical images, for example, are sensitive to cell loss but may be willing to permit somewhat slower transmission or higher price. These issues can be addressed via the service classes supported by the carrier and/or switch (e.g., Available Bit Rate, Variable Bit Rate, Constant Bit Rate, Unspecified Bit Rate, etc.). However, equipment must be developed to support these services classes, in true accordance and in conformance with the standards. In particular, feedback mechanisms must be developed in both network and user equipment to support Available Bit Rate services. Traffic management issues related to the statistical management of the classes of traffic just enumerated are holding back the full implementation of ATM. In the opinion of many users, as well as service providers, the switch's ability of supporting class of service considerations with only minimal loss of cells is crucial.

- *Transparent Resilience* Problems that might occur during a transmission across multiple networks (e.g., a campus network and a WAN) are another issue. These relate to availability, quality of service and alternate routing in case of failure. ATM should provide resiliency from multiple failure situations within the network. If a problem occurs on the network, ATM hardware must be able to reroute virtual circuits which traverse the faulty path. This must be done transparently to the applications residing on the network. However, some problems remain. For example, is it best to remap a circuit to a different path, which might work but would not necessarily support the same grade of service? In the worst case, this could cause a loss of session. If that happens, what are the best recovery procedures? Some of these issues are being addressed by the Broadband Intercarrier Interface (B-ICI) work now nearly complete.

- *Scalability* It is not yet clear how far ATM performance will be able to scale upward with large increases in the number of devices and geographical size. Scalability in speed is not an issue, but at very high speeds switching and propagation delays could have limiting consequences. ATM's scalability can adapt to the distances characteristic of ordinary WANs, but will ATM scale to global dimensions? Another unresolved question is: do applications scale on virtual networks?

Questions like these are being addressed by the ATM Forum, by vendors, and by individual users. The search for solutions starts from the realization that ATM is a complex technology that can take many forms and be adapted to many uses. Until the implications of these complexities have been worked out fully, wide-spread adoption of ATM will take place gradually. As this process advances, however, ATM will increasingly become the solution of choice for a growing number of users.

4.6 Overview of key ATM features

This section outlines some of the principal features of ATM; later chapters will describe some of these features in greater detail. The features discussed here are:

- The structure of its 53-byte cells, or labeled information containers.
- The Physical Layer, ATM Layer, and ATM Adaptation Layer that organize appropriate Service Data Units (SDUs)/PDUs for transmission. Special attention is given to the Adaptation Layer, which governs the treatment of cells that require different quality of service to accommodate the special requirements of voice, video, and data traffic. The service layer sits on top of the AAL and uses specific AALs (e.g., AAL 1, AAL 5, etc.) to provide the appropriate services to the legacy protocols (e.g., IP) residing at the Network layer.
- LAN Emulation, in support of legacy LANs.

- Different technology solutions for ATM switches.

- The remaining agenda in the ATM arena: what needs to be done by the standards-making bodies to resolve issues like traffic management in a large network, additional LAN emulation features, support for twisted-pair media particularly at the higher ATM rates, interoperability, and congestion control.

ATM is a set of standards, defined originally by the International Telecommunication Union, Telecommunications (ITU-T). These standards establish basic specifications for ATM protocols and interfaces. The ITU-T standards for ATM specify the cell size and structure and the UNI. Note that there are two kinds of UNIs: one for access to public networks, and one, called Private UNI, for access to a customer-owned ATM network (specifically to a hub, router, or switch). For the public UNI the physical layer is defined for data rates of 1.544 Mbps, 45 Mbps, and 155 Mbps (SONET OC-3). For the Private UNI a number of physical layers for different media (UTP, STP, singlemode fiber, or multimode fiber) are defined.

ATM can be described as a packet transfer mode based on asynchronous time division multiplexing, and a protocol engine that uses small fixed-length data units known as cells. ATM provides a connection-oriented service (although it can also be used to support connectionless services such as IP). Note that LANs such as Ethernet, FDDI and Token Ring support a connectionless service. Each ATM connection is assigned its own set of transmission resources, however, these resources have to be taken out of a shared pool which is generally smaller than the maximum needed to support the entire population. This is the reason for the much-talked about traffic management problem in ATM. ATM nevertheless makes it possible to share bandwidth through multiplexing (multiple messages transmitted over the same physical circuit). Multiple virtual channels can be supported on the access link, and the aggregate bandwidth of these channels can be overbooked (ATM relies on statistical multiplexing to carry the load). Within the network, expensive resources are "rationed," and bandwidth must be allocated dynamically. ATM is thus able to maximize resource (bandwidth) utilization.

A virtual circuit can be either switched (temporary) or permanent. A connection is established through preprovisioning with the carrier or private devices (thereby establishing Permanent Virtual Circuits—PVCs), or through signaling mechanisms (thereby establishing Switched Virtual Circuits—SVCs). Connections supported by these channels (PVCs or SVCs) enable one computer or other system on the network to communicate with another computer or system.

Network resources such as inbound speed, outbound speed, quality of service, multipoint capabilities, etc. are requested as a connection is established. A connection is established if the network is able to meet the request; if not, the request is rejected. Once the virtual circuit is defined, the call connection control assigns an interface-specific

Virtual Channel Identifier (VCI) and Virtual Path Identifier (VPI) to identify the connection. These tables have only interface-specific meaning. Two different sets of VPIs/VCIs are assigned to the two end-point of the connection. Inside the network as many sets of VPIs/VCIs as needed (along the path) are used by the network, invisibly to the end users.

As long as the connection remains active, the assigned VCI and VPI represent valid pointers into routing tables in the network; the tables (accessed via the VPI/VCI) are used to accomplish cell routing through the network.

4.6.1 The ATM cell

ATM cell has a 48-byte payload, accompanied by a five-byte header that is divided into fields. Headers are of two types: the UNI and the Network-to-Network Interface (NNI). See Table 4.1.

Table 4.1 ATM cell structure

8	7	6	5	4	3	2	1
Generic Flow Control				Virtual Path Identifier			
Virtual Path Identifier (continued)				Virtual Channel Identifier			
Virtual Channel Identifier (continued)							
Virtual Channel Identifier (continued)				Payload Type Identifer			Cell-loss Priority
Header Error Control							
Payload							

Fields within the UNI cell are:

- The first field, of four bits, provides for generic flow control (GFC). It is not currently used and is intended to support a local bus ("extension") function to connect multiple Broadband Terminal Equipment to the same UNI as equal peers (note that multiple users can be connected to the UNI today by using a multiplexing, not peer, function). This is equivalent to the SAPI function in ISDN.

- A 24-bit routing pointing field is subdivided into an eight bit VPI subfields and a 16-bit subfield for VCI. It indirectly identifies the specific route laid out for traffic over a specific connection, by providing a pointing function into switch tables that contain further pointers related to the actual route.

- Three bits are allocated to the payload type identifier (PTI), which identifies whether each cell is a user cell or a control cell, used for network management.

- A single-bit cell loss priority (CLP) marker is used to distinguish two levels of cell loss priority. Zero identifies a higher priority cell that should receive preferred loss treatment if cells are discarded due to network congestion (ie., the cell should not be discarded). One indicates lower-priority cells whose loss is less critical (ie., the cell could be discarded).

- Header error control (HEC) is an eight-bit cyclic redundancy code (CRC) computed over the ATM cell header. The HEC is capable of detecting all single-bit errors and certain multiple bit errors. It can be used to correct all single-bit errors, but this is not mandatory. This mechanism is employed by a receiving device to infer that the cell is in error and should simply be discarded. It is also used for cell-boundary recovery at the Physical layer.

- The remaining 48 bytes are devoted to payload (in case of interworking some of the payload bytes have to be used for network-used AAL protocol control information).

- The NNI cell structure has one difference. The four-bit GFC field is dropped, and the VPI field is expanded from eight bits to 12.

4.6.2 Addressing

Addressing is a fundamental need in any network. The ITU-T ATM protocol calls for a hierarchical ISDN telephone numbering scheme, specified in ITU-T E.164, to be used in ATM. The standard permits the ATM address to be divided into an address and a subaddress. The ATM Forum recommends that the address describe the point of attachment to the public network (if connected to the public network) and that the subaddress identify a particular end station within a private network [64]. Note that the VPI/VCI

Table 4.2   The ATM Forum's addressing format for private ATM networks

1 octet	AFI	Authority and Format Indentifier
2 octets	DCC/IDC	Data Country Code/ Internation Code Designator
1 octet	DFI	Domain Specific part format identifier
3 octets	AA	Administration Authority
2 octets	Reserved	
4 octets	RD Area	Routing Domain
6 octets	ESI	End System Identifier
1 octet	SEL	(unused)

are just labels, not E.164 addresses; they are table pointers for the "relaying of cells" on to their destination, based on switch routing tables.

By contrast, the ATM Forum specification permits two address formats to be used as ATM address. One is the E.164 format, and the other is a 20-byte address modeled after the address format of an OSI Network Service Access Point (NSAP), as seen in Table 4.2.

Note: The end-system identifier contains a valid IEEE 802 MAC address. An alternative format allows the eight bytes after the AFI field to contain an E.164 address. This option permits both public and private subaddress to be combined into a single ATM address.

4.6.3 The physical and ATM layers

An extension of the conventional OSI seven-layer stack can be used to describe the structure of the ATM protocol: a reference model specific to ATM depicts its structure more clearly. This reference model distinguishes three basic layers. Beginning from the bottom, these are: the Physical Layer, the ATM Layer, and the ATM Adaptation Layer. Each is divided further into sublayers, as seen in Table 4.3.

Table 4.3   ATM reference model

Convergence	CS	AAL
Segmentation and reassembly	SAR	
Generic flow control (if/when imlemented) Cell VPI/VCI translation Cell multiplex and demultiplex		ATM
Cell rate decoupling HEC header sequence generation/verification Cell delineation Transmission frame adaptation Transmission frame generation recovery	TC	PHY
Bit timing Physical medium	PM	

The Physical Layer includes two sublayers:

- *Physical Medium sublayer*   Like any other Data Link Layer protocol, ATM is not defined in terms of a specific type of physical carrying medium, but it is necessary to define appropriate physical layer protocols for cell transmission. The Physical Medium (PM) sublayer interfaces with the physical medium and provides transmission and reception of bits over the physical facility. It also provides the physical medium with proper bit timing and line coding. There will be different manifestations of this layer based on the specifics of the underlying medium (e.g., DS1 link, DS3 link, SONET, UTP, etc.).

- *The Transmission Convergence (TC) sublayer* This layer receives a bit stream from the PM sublayer and passes it in cell form to the ATM layer. Its functions include cell rate decoupling, cell delineation, generation and verification of the HEC sequence, transmission frame adaptation, and the generation/recovery of transmission frames.

The ATM layer, in the middle of the ATM stack, is responsible for one of ATM's most "trivial" functions: to encapsulate downward-coming data into cells from a number of sources and multiplex the cell stream; conversely, it is responsible to deencapsulate upward-coming cells and demultiplex the resulting stream out to a number of sources.

The ATM layer controls multiplexing (the transmission of cells belonging to different connections over a single cell stream) and demultiplexing (distinguishing cells of various connections as they are pulled off the flow of cells.) ATM, as a Data Link Layer protocol, is medium-independent; it is capable of performing these functions on a variety of physical media. In addition, the ATM layer acts as an intermediary between the layer above it and the physical layer below. It generates cell headers, attaches them to the data delivered to it by the adaptation layer and then delivers the properly tagged cells to the physical layer. Conversely, it strips headers from cells containing data arriving on the physical layer before hoisting the data to the application layer.

ATM supports two kinds of channels: Virtual Channels and Virtual Paths. VCs are communication channels of specified service capabilities between two (intermediary) ATM peers. Virtual Channel Connections (VCCs) are concatenations of VCs to support end-system-to-end-system communication. VPs are groups (bundles) of VCs. Virtual Path Connections (VPCs) are concatenations of VPs to support end-system-to-end-system communication.

VCs and VPs are identified by their VCI/VPI tags.* The ATM layer assures that cells are arranged in the proper sequence, but it does not identify and retransmit

---

* Do not confuse VCs/VPs with connections. VC are channels; connections are instances of end-to-end communications. Connections are identified by Call Reference and Connection Identifiers included in the Setup message used in signaling. See [63] for a more extensive description.

damaged cells. If this is to be done, it must be accomplished by higher-level procedures. The ATM layer also translates VCI/VPI information.

Each ATM switch has its own routing table to identify each connection. In transit between switches, VPI/VCI identifiers (routing table pointers) will be different. Switches translate identifiers as they transfer cells onward to other switches.

Finally, the ATM layer performs management functions. If the PTI (Payload Type Identifier) identifies a cell as a control packet, the ATM layer responds by carrying out the appropriate functions.

4.6.4 Class of service: The Adaptation Layer

The ATM Adaptation Layer allows various network layer protocols to utilize the service of the ATM layer. As discussed earlier, the ATM layer supports only the lower portion of the Data Link Layer. Hence, in order for the Network Layer to use ATM, a filler sublayer is required. This is analogous to IP use over a LAN; the Medium Access Control (MAC) layer supports only the lower portion of the Data Link Layer, consequently, the Logical Link Control/SubNetwork Access Protocol layer is sandwiched in between.

Fundamentally, the AAL keeps the Network Layer happy by enabling it to use ATM transparently. The basic function of the AAL is to segment the downward-coming data (Network Layer PDU) into cells, and to reassemble upward-coming data into a PDU acceptable to the Network Layer.

It is critical to understand that AALs are end-to-end functions (end-system-to-end-system). A network providing pure ATM will not be aware of, cognizant of, or act upon, AAL information. (Only in case of service interworking in the network has there to be network interpretation of the AAL information.)

In one classical view of the ATM protocol model, a service layer resides above the AAL, in the end-systems. Hence, by further elaboration one can say that, in a coincidental manner, the AAL differentiates in the end-system the treatment of different categories of cells and permits responses to user-to-user quality of service issues. A number of AALs have been defined to meet different user-to-user quality of service requirements. Again, however, a network providing pure ATM will not be aware of, cognizant of, or act upon AAL information. (Only in case of service interworking in the network has there to be network interpretation of the AAL information.) Therefore, the AAL-supported service differentiation is among end-system peers, and is not the mechanism used by the ATM network to support network quality of service. We use the term *user-to-user quality of service* to describe the kind of end-system-to-end-system peer-to-peer connection service differentiation (this connection being viewed as "external" to the ATM network).

For example, an end-system TV monitor needs a continuous bit-stream from a remote codec to paint a picture; it may have been decided that an ATM network is to be used to transport the bits. Because of the codec/monitor requirements, the bits have to be enveloped in such a manner that clock information is carried end-to-end such that jitter is less than some specified value. To accomplish this, the bits are enveloped using AAL 1. From the ATM network's point of view, this is totally immaterial; the ATM network receives cells and carries them to the other end, the network delivers cells. The network does not render any different type of QoS to these cells based solely on the fact that the cells had AAL 1 information in them; the network was not even aware of the content. Naturally, it would be desirable if the network provided reasonable QoS to this stream, based on some kind of knowledge or arrangement. How is that accomplished?

The different QoS obtained via an ATM network are based on user-to-network negotiation, not by the content of the cell. In PVC this negotiation is via a service order. Here, the user would tell the network (with paper) that the user wanted to get reasonable service for a certain stream carrying codec video. The network provider would make arrangements to terminate this stream on a switch line card where, for example, its buffers are drained more regularly. The network provider then tells the user (with paper) to employ a certain VPI/VCI combination (say 22/33) for this specific stream. Here is what happens: The user sends cells over the physical interface terminated at the card's port. Certain cells arriving on the interface have VPI/VCI=44/66, these get some kind of QoS treatment. Then some cells arrive on the interface with VPI/VCI=22/33, these cells get the agreed-to QoS by receiving specific treatment by the switch. In SVC, a similar mechanism is in place, except that instead of communicating the information using paper, the call-setup message is used (with automatic call negotiation).

In any event, the QoS in the ATM network is not based on the fact that the cells carry a certain AAL. It is the other way around. The user needs a certain end-system-to-end-system QoS. The user then needs to do two things: select its (network-invisible) AAL, and separately inform the carrier of the type of QoS needed.

AALs utilize a small portion of the 48-byte payload field of the ATM cell by inserting additional control bits. In all AALs, the ATM header retains its usual configuration and functions. Notice that the data coming down the protocol stack is first treated by the AAL by adding its own header (protocol control information). This AAL PDU must naturally fit inside the ATM PDU. Hence, the AAL header must fit inside the payload of the lower layer, here ATM. To say that "Quality of service definitions are obtained at the cost of reductions in payload" is not exactly correct; AAL provides an appropriate segmentation and reassembly function. QoS is supported by the network switch, as discussed, and AAL classes support peer-to-peer connection differentiation.

In some instances, users determine that the ATM layer service is sufficient for their requirements, so the AAL protocol remains empty. This occurs, for example, if the Network Layer protocol can ride directly on ATM (this is unlikely for legacy protocols), or if the two end-systems do not need additional coordination. In the majority of cases, however, this AAL layer is crucial to the end-system protocol stack because it enables ATM to accommodate the requirements of voice, image/video, and data traffic while providing different classes of service to meet the distinctive requirements of each type of traffic.

Two sublayers make up the AAL: the Segmentation and Reassembly sublayer (SAR) and the Convergence sublayer (CS). The SAR sublayer segments higher-layer information into a size suitable for cell payloads through a virtual connection. It also reassembles the contents of cells in a virtual connection into data units that can be delivered to higher layers. Functions like message identification and time/clock recovery are performed by the CS sublayer. See Table 4.4.

Table 4.4   ATM Class of service

	Class A	Class B	Class C	Class D
Application	Voice Clear Channel	Packet Video	Data	
Timing (source-destination)	Needed		Not Needed	
Mode	Conneciton-oriented			Connectionless
Bit Rate	Constant	Variable		

The ITU-T specifications apply three broad criteria to distinguish four classes of ATM service, tagged as *A*, *B*, *C*, and *D*; these end-to-end (network-external) criteria are:

- Time relation between source and destination
- Bit rate
- Connection mode

In order to express these criteria in practical form, four AAL have been developed: AAL 1, AAL 2 (not yet defined fully), AAL 3/4, and AAL 5, focused upon data transmission. As covered preliminarily in Chapter 2, the four end-to-end (network-external) classes of service are:

- *Class A*   (For example, clear-channel voice and fixed bit-rate video, such as movies or high-resolution teleconferencing), a time relation exists between source and destination. The bit rate is constant, and the Network Layer-level service is connection-oriented.

- *Class B*   As in Class A, there is a time relation between source and destination, Network Layer-level service is connection-oriented, but the bit rate can be varied. Examples include audio and video with variable bit-rates (e.g., unbuffered video codecs with motion compensation).

- *Class C*   The Network Layer-level service is connection-oriented, but there is no time relation between source and destination, and the bit rate is variable. This can, for example, meet the requirements of connection-oriented data transfer and signaling.

- *Class D*   Intended for applications like connectionless data transport (at the Network Layer); none of the three parameters applies: service is connectionless, there is no time relation between source and destination, and the bit rate is variable.

These classes are general descriptions of types of user traffic. They do not set specific parameters or establish values. Equipment from multiple vendors based on different parameters may thus find it difficult to establish connections. AAL are end-to-end and generally external to the ATM network; considerations on AAL relate to consideration of end-user equipment. AAL are considered by the network only when there is service interworking. Examples include frame relay-to-ATM interworking in the network; legacy LAN-to-ATM interworking (specifically, LANE) in the network; private line-to-ATM interworking in the network. For example, in the first case, frames come in and cells go out. There is another case where AALs are used in the network, but this is totally transparent to the user. This situation (called by some network interworking) is when the network supports a "carriage function" over ATM. Examples include frame relay carriage over an ATM network; Ethernet carriage over ATM network (e.g., Ethernet bridging); private line carriage over an ATM network. For example, the frame relay user gives a frame relay frame to the (ATM-based) network; the network takes the frame and segments it into a stream of cells utilizing AAL 5 protocols; the stream is carried across the network and in proximity of the destination, the cells are reassembled into a frame relay frame using AAL 5; the destination is handed a frame. This type of service is called frame relay carriage over ATM or frame relay-to-ATM network interworking.

Three AAL protocols have been defined to support the three classes of service in the end-system: AAL1, AAL 3/4, and AAL 5. Routers and other devices must employ the same AAL in order to communicate with one another on an ATM network:

- AAL 1 meets the performance requirements of Service Class A. It is intended for voice, video and other constant bit-rate traffic, and its performance, to the upper layers of the end-system stack, is similar to today's digital private lines. Four bits in the payload are allocated to Sequence Number (SN) and Sequence Number Protection (SNP) functions.

- AAL 2 aims at Class B requirements; it has not yet been defined.
- AAL 3/4 is intended for connectionless data services. (e.g., for support of Switched Multimegabit Data Service). Four bytes are devoted to control functions, including a multiplexing identifier.
- AAL 5 is also intended for data communications, including services like Frame Relay and LANE. The ATM Forum and IETF recommend that AAL 5 also be used to encapsulate IP packets in the user's endsystem for Classical IP Over ATM (RFC 1577).

AAL 5 is specifically designed to offer a service for data communication with lower overhead and better error detection. It was developed because computer vendors realized that AAL 3/4 was not suited to their needs. In addition to the header, AAL 3/4 takes an additional four bytes for control information from the payload field, reducing its capacity by 8.4 percent. They also maintain that the error detection method of AAL 3/4 does not cope adequately with issues of lost or corrupted cells.

With AAL 5, the CS sublayer creates a CS Protocol Data Unit (CS-PDU) when it receives a packet from the higher application layer. The first field is the CS Information Payload field, containing user data. The PAD field assures that the CS-PDU is 48-bytes aligned. A one-byte control field remains undefined, reserved for further use. The two-byte Length field indicates the length of information payload, and the CRC field is used to detect errors. See Table 4.5.

When the CS sublayer passes the CS-PDU to the SAR sublayer, it is divided into many SAR Protocol Data Units (SAR-PDUs). The SAR sublayer then passes SAR-PDUs to the ATM layer, which carries out transmission of the cell.

When passing on the final SAR-PDU within the CS-PDU, SAR indicates the end of the CS-PDU transfer by setting to one the payload type identifier (PTI) in the header. By using the CS length field and the cyclic loss redundancy code (CRC) in the header's HEC (header error control), the AAL can detect the loss or corruption of cells.

Table 4.5   AAL Type 5 CS-PDU

Information Payload	PAD	Control	Length	CRC-32
0–64K	0–47	1 Byte	2 Bytes	4 Bytes

4.7 LAN Emulation

This section provides a basic introduction of key concepts. The chapters that follow provide a more extensive treatment of this topic.

4.7.1 Overview

Of the main specifications which The ATM Forum is developing, is LAN Emulation [66]. Traditional LANs provide a connectionless MAC service, supporting arbitration among end-stations for access to a shared physical transmission medium (e.g., the twisted-pair cable). ATM, on the other hand, offers a connection-orientated communication service based on switched point-to-point physical media. To achieve connectionless MAC service over an ATM link, a protocol layer emulating the connectionless service of a LAN must be placed on top of the AAL. This layer, depicted in Figure 4.1 is called the ATM MAC. This layer emulates the LAN service by creating the appearance of a virtual shared medium from an actual switched point-to-point network.

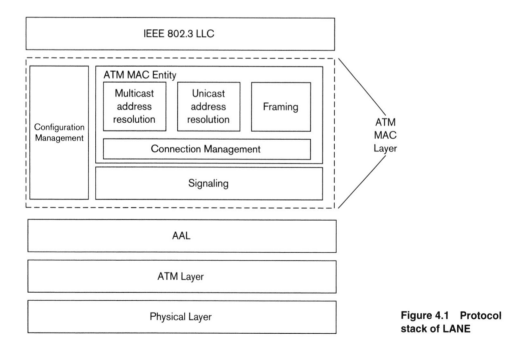

Figure 4.1 Protocol stack of LANE

Version 1.0 of LANE was adopted in 1995 and additional work is now under way on Version 2. The purpose of LANE is to provide users with a migration path to ATM without immediately incurring the high cost of implementing ATM to the desktop (however, LANE equipment must be deployed).

In legacy LANs, the membership of an individual station to a LAN segment is dictated by the physical connection of the station to the physical shared medium. Membership of a station to an ATM LAN segment is identified by logical connections to the multicast ATM virtual connection. Hence, membership of an ATM LAN segment is defined logically rather than physically; the membership information is stored in some management database. This capability of ATM LANs offers terminal portability and mobility. LANE does provide transparent support for LAN-based applications since it functions at layer 2, like a bridge. Effectively it is a converting-bridge technology between the connectionless Ethernet/Token Ring environment and the connection-oriented ATM environment. It also supports ATM-enabled devices to communicate with LAN Emulated devices. LAN Emulation allows for logically separate emulated LANs to coexist on the same physical ATM network.

LAN Emulation does not allow users to leverage the end-to-end class of service functionality which ATM provides in end-systems, however, it will provide for a higher bandwidth and a more stable network infrastructure for large building and campus backbones. It also requires that Ethernet, Token-Ring, and FDDI be connected by traditional routers, since it does not provide transparent bridge functions between these technologies.

4.7.2 Components of LAN Emulation

Traditional LANs use the 48-bit MAC address. The MAC address is globally unique. This nonhierarchical LAN address assigned by the manufacturer, identifies a network interface in the endstation. The use of a MAC address is practical in a single LAN segment or in a small internet. However, large bridged networks become difficult to manage and experience large amounts of broadcast traffic for the purpose of attempting to locate endstations. The address space of a large network is preferably hierarchical. This makes it easier to locate a particular point on the network, however, it restricts the mobility of the network users. The E.164 address used in public ATM is hierarchical.

To emulate a LAN, the ATM network must support addressing using MAC address scheme; each ATM MAC entity must be assigned a 48-bit MAC address, from the same address space, to facilitate its identification. As noted, an ATM network, whether public or private, uses a hierarchical address. The address resolution operation in LANE binds the endstation MAC address to the physical address of the ATM port to which the endstation is currently connected. When an endstation is attached to an ATM switch port, a registration protocol exchanges the MAC address between the ATM network and the end station.

The LAN Emulation service consists of several pieces of software and hardware operating on one or more platforms. Prior to explaining the operation, some definitions are necessary:

- *LAN Emulation Client (LEC)*   The LEC is software that resides at the edge device. The edge device is where the emulated service is rendered in terms of the conversion between protocols.

- *LAN Emulation Server (LES)*   The LES provides address registration and address resolution functions. Since ATM and legacy LANs use very different addressing schemes, a way to map the two is important, particularly with a view to *subnetworks*, where the addressing capabilities of ATM, may be lacking.

- *LAN Emulation Configuration Server (LECS)*   The LECS provides initialization and configuration functions.

- *Broadcast and Unknown Server (BUS)*   The BUS provides the mechanism to send broadcasts and multicasts to all devices within the Emulated LAN.

- *LANE User-Network Interface (LUNI)*   The protocol used by the LEC to communicate over the ATM network.

In a traditional LAN, all frames (unicast, multicast, and broadcast) are broadcast to all stations on the shared physical medium; each station selects the frames it wants to receive. A LAN segment can be emulated by connecting a set of stations on the ATM network via an ATM multicast virtual connection. The multicast virtual connection emulates the broadcast physical medium of the LAN. This connection becomes the broadcast channel of the ATM LAN segment. With this capability, any station may broadcast to all others on the ATM LAN segment by transmitting on the shared ATM multicast virtual connection.

4.7.3 LAN Emulation operation

Background considerations   Address resolution in LANE can be implemented in principle by either a broadcast mechanism similar to IP Address Resolution Protocol (ARP) or a distributed database mechanism. In both mechanisms, the source sends an address resolution request containing the destination MAC address and its own MAC and ATM addresses [64].

For unicast address resolution, a broadcast mechanism requires that the source broadcasts the requests to all stations on the local ATM LAN segment and to all ATM LAN segments connected via bridges. After self-checks, the station that owns the requested MAC address replies with its current ATM address. The reply may be sent on the broadcast channel for the ATM LAN segment, or the destination may set up an ATM connection to the source. For multicast ARP, an algorithm may be specified to convert from a group MAC address to a group ATM address; alternatively, a simple server mechanism may be implemented for multicast addresses.

In database address resolution, the method actually recommended by The ATM Forum, requests are received by an address server in the network. The server keeps a table containing MAC-to-ATM address mappings. The table is updated as part of the registration protocol whenever a station joins or leaves the network. The server may support both unicast and multicast address resolution. The address server must be implemented as a distributed database to protect against failure. In turn, this requires a more complex implementation than a broadcast implementation.

The situation where the destination is not directly attached to the ATM network but is attached to a LAN connected to the ATM network via bridge is more complex. When using a broadcast ARP implementation, the bridge can reply to the address request with its own ATM address, as a proxy for the destination, on the assumption that the bridge contained the destination MAC address in its forwarding table. In the database ARP approach, the address server on the ATM network must contain entries not only for the directly attached devices but also for all stations attached on internets. To sustain this, each internet device must continually update the address server with the contents of its forwarding table; this could be demanding in large bridged networks.

The two approaches to ARP can be transparently combined. Here endstations can assume that a broadcast mechanism is in use. The multicast server can also act as an address server. The multicast server can intercept ARP requests submitted for broadcast to an ATM LAN segment and respond with the required address from its database. The address resolution database can be built from the exchange of addresses in the registration protocol, and also by learning processes used by transparent bridges. If no entry is found in the database, then the server can use the broadcast address resolution mechanism.

LUNI operation   The LUNI* operates in five stages:

1 *Initialization*   Prior to information transfer, the LEC must perform some housekeeping operations. This begins the initialization stage. The LEC must find the

---

* This is the UNI that is employed by a LEC.

LECS. It first uses the Interim Local Management Interface (ILMI) to attempt to obtain the address from the switch. If that fails, it will attempt to use what's known as the *well-known ATM address*. This is a predetermined address which is used on all ATM networks. If that fails, it attempts to use the PVC with VPI/VCI=0/17. This is a well-known PVC. Finally, if that fails, it will try the LES.

2 *Configuration*   Upon initialization, the LEC must determine the type of emulated LAN and maximum frame size. It must also send its ATM address, MAC address and LAN types and requested frame sizes. It can also optionally request to join a particular emulated LAN.

3 *Joining*   Once the LEC has passed through the initialization and configuration stages, it can then "join" the emulated LAN. The LEC sends a join-request to the LES. This request contains its ATM address, LAN information, MAC address and proxy information (if appropriate). Proxy information is appropriate if the LEC is acting on behalf of additional end stations. The LES responds with a join response containing the results.

4 *Registration and BUS Initialization*   Upon successful join, the LEC must register all MAC addresses with the BUS. The MAC address 0xffffffffffff (broadcast address) will then be mapped to the BUS ATM address. The LEC establishes a point-to-point connection with the BUS. The BUS then adds the LEC onto its point-to-multipoint circuit for the specific emulated LAN.

5 *Information Transfer*   After the housekeeping functions are complete, the LEC can transfer data. Data can be transferred either to a specific address, or broadcast to all devices of the emulated LAN. In a unicast, the LEC determines the destination ATM address either by checking its ARP cache, or through a LAN Emulation Address Resolution Packet (LE-ARP). It then establishes a SVC (if not established) to the destination and begins transferring information. To send a broadcast, the LEC will forward the information to the BUS to be sent out on the point-to-multi-point circuit.

A LAN segment could be emulated by directing all of the traffic for the segment on the broadcast channel. However, most LAN traffic is unicast; therefore it is more efficient to support unicast communications. Not only does this reduce traffic, but greater security is achieved because the unicast traffic appears only at the two pertinent stations. An ATM LAN segment can then support higher aggregate bandwidth than would be the case if all traffic were transmitted on the same broadcast channel. Furthermore, the use of individual virtual connections for unicast traffic allows greater control of the quality of service. To establish a point-to-point ATM virtual connection for each instance of unicast communication, the current location of the destination end station must be discovered and expressed as a destination address that the ATM signaling service can understand; this operation is called address resolution [64]. The ATM signaling service must then be initiated to establish a point-to-point ATM virtual connection, with the appropriate quality of service, to the destination. Within the end station, this operation must be implemented in the software of the ATM MAC layer, in order to offer a transparent service to the LLC sublayer.

4.8 Narrowband ATM access

The ATM protocol is most efficient when operating at high speeds. As stated before, these cells are 53 bytes long, with 48 bytes of payload and five bytes of header information. This is almost a 10% overhead for the header information, just at the ATM layer (there are other inefficiencies at the AAL and Physical layer). The ATM-level inefficiency is not considered excessive when operating at high speeds given the ability to mix voice, video, and data.

Currently, low speed access links are the norm for most WAN environments. ATM's overhead becomes burdensome at these speeds, typically 56 Kbps to T1 (1.544 Mbps). The ATM Forum addressed this requirement by developing a new UNI aimed at increasing the efficiency for low speeds links. This new UNI is called the Frame UNI (F-UNI), and operates on frames which can have payloads of up to 4,096 bytes. Frame Relay, Data Exchange Interface (DXI) and FUNI are all frame-based standards:

- Frame Relay defines HDLC as part of its specification and adds a header to support DLCI (Data Link Control Identifier) addressing.

- DXI/UNI is an evolution of the ATM DXI (e.g., see [62]) which defines router interfacing to an ATM CSU (through HSSI), though the DXI/UNI also defines V.35 and $n \times 64,000$ (via a regular CSU). For $n \times 64,000$, frames are carried all the way to the switch at the Central Office. AAL 5 Convergence Sublayer and VPI/VCI addressing scheme is used. The ATM DXI/UNI allows a customer to access a network supporting ATM technology based on HDLC frames. The purpose of this interface is to provide HDLC access to ATM at low speeds.

- FUNI is separate from DXI/UNI. It can be thought of as a superset to DXI/UNI. The difference between the two is that FUNI also extends Q.2931 signaling for SVCs. It also carries AAL 5 Convergence Sublayer PDUs. Hence, FUNI defines an alternate HDLC-based protocol for access to ATM.

Using ATM DXI one can support legacy DCEs by encapsulating frames and giving them to a Central Office-interworking unit which then prepares them for ATM transport. This approach is good for PVCs, but not for SVCs. For SVCs one should use FUNI; here the same encapsulation is used for the User Plane and for the Control Plane, it entails a dual-stack interworking unit at the switch/Central Office.

Figure 4.2 depicts the protocol stacks involved in DXI/UNI and FUNI. The FUNI supports full ATM signaling, enabling frame-oriented devices such as bridges and routers to set up switched circuits, and negotiate class of service within the network. The FUNI header contains flags to indicate standard ATM features such as cell-loss priority, congestion notification, and the presence of operations and maintenance traffic. The FUNI specification details the appropriate mapping function to go between frame headers and cell headers. It also supports adaptation layers 3, 4 and 5. For management, FUNI supports the Interim Local Management Interface (ILMI).

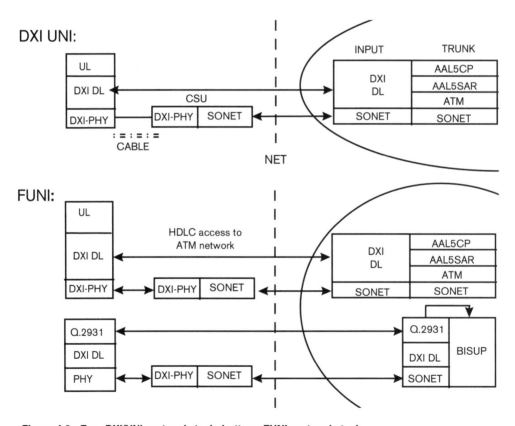

Figure 4.2   Top: DXI/UNI protocol stack; bottom: FUNI protocol stack

CHAPTER 4   AN ATM PRIMER

4.9 ATM switches

End-users requiring ATM service can either secure the service from a carrier, or build their own network. In campus situations it may be reasonable for an organization to develop its own network. This would entail the acquisition of a number of ATM switches and ancillary support equipment (e.g., NICs for routers, PCs, servers, etc.). For WAN applications, carriers tend to be the best option. In any event, ATM switches must be deployed. To support ATM, a switching architecture must meet the following requirements:

- The switch must be able to support high aggregate throughput with a small switching delay. In addition to supporting the multiple Gbps internal speeds (0.5–80 Gbps) required for multiple ports, the processing time to switch a single cell from one port to another must be less than three microseconds. Processing time must be less than 1.5 microseconds if the cell is to be switched between two switches.

- Support of broadcast and multicast is also necessary. Only point-to-point connections are allowed in classical switches. ATM systems, however, are required to broadcast or multicast information to many destinations. Applications that require this capability include distribution of rates on financial markets to branches and individual traders, as well as email.

- Non-blocking operation is another important consideration for ATM switches. In some cases, switching fabrics are unable to establish a connection even though two ports are available. This may be caused by a lack of resources within the switch, leading to inefficiency. In ATM the concept of non-blocking is slightly different than in a traditional circuit switch, however, there is still a need to support a connection with a specified grade of service, if pertinent resources are available.

- Resource contention. Many cells may be destined for a single output port within the ATM switch at the same time. The ATM architecture assumes a low cell-loss rate, so it is important to provide a queuing mechanism that stores the cells competing for the same out-port. Another way of saying this is that the switch must guarantee the stipulated grade of service. All this arises from the fact that statistical multiplexing with a medium-to-high level of overbooking needs to be supported.

There are two forms of ATM switch—backplane-based systems and matrix switches. In backplane-based systems, ATM cells are transported across a high speed bus linking ATM modules. Each ATM module receives cells according to VPI/ VCI values that identify connections and their paths. Backplane-based ATM systems are relatively simple and inexpensive to develop, but this architecture does not scale well. For example, in order to support 16 ports operating at OC-3 (155 Mbps), the backplane speed must be 2.480 Gbps. The same number of ports at OC-12 (622 Mbps) would require a backplane speed of 9.952 Gbps. These speeds are now out of reach for backplanes, so it would be a bottleneck, preventing ATM's ability to operate at high bandwidths.

Matrix switching is the preferred method for meeting this high-speed capability. The switching architectures for traditional PBX systems using STM (synchronous transfer mode) are well understood, but these architectures may not be suitable for ATM switching. First, an ATM switch must accommodate much higher speeds than a PBX. Moreover, the statistical behavior of the ATM streams passing through an ATM switching system differs from traffic through a PBX. Consequently, researchers are now proposing a number of ATM switching architectures.

Buffering can be done at the input or output or in a central portion of the switching element. Each philosophy involves a different degree of complexity and probability of cell loss. Balancing all these considerations, output queuing is gaining support as the preferred method. The end-user has little control on these factors, beyond the initial selection of the switch; the architecture is a design factor which is controlled by the switch manufacturer or by the carrier (this one having selected a specific switch). The user may not even be technically equipped to undertake the detailed research needed to determine what the switch vendor is doing and if this is a good architecture. It should be noted that while there is basically one switching architecture for voice switches (namely, Time-Space-Time, i.e., all voice switches are the same), there is no consensus as to the ATM switching architecture and every vendor uses a different approach or twist.

4.10 Tasks receiving continuing attention

As noted earlier, the ITU-T definition of standards for ATM left a number of gaps and ambiguities that await final resolution. For example, LAN traffic that passes over an ATM backbone or other intermediary network now depends upon proprietary implementations by various vendors; there is no interoperability between equipment made by different vendors. (LANE technology will address that problem.) There also is interest in supporting Virtual LANs (VLANs) in a standardized fashion; this will also be possible using LANE principles. Also one wants to transport IP and other Network Layer protocols over ATM.

The ATM Forum was established as a vendor group, focusing primarily on the development of ATM implementor's agreements. These agreements extend and implement ITU-T specifications. For example, The ATM Forum has published two extensions to the UNI standard. Current ATM Forum projects include traffic management in a large network, LAN Emulation Version 2, and more extensive UTP (unshielded twisted-pair copper wire) support.

A large scale network, including private internets, requires a comprehensive method for end-to-end traffic management if overbooking is utilized. It must be able to resolve congestion in two segments—between the user workstation and the switch, and between multiple switches. This requires flow control throughout a network, including all end devices and intermediate devices.

LANE, also on the active agenda of the ATM Forum, would permit LAN traffic (typically generated by legacy technology like Ethernet or Token Ring) to be switched transparently over an ATM network as if it were passing through a bridge. This would replace current vendor-specific proprietary solutions that obstruct interoperability. The ATM Forum seeks to provide a clean migration path from existing LAN architectures to ATM without the high cost of fiber cabling and/or ATM implementation all the way to the desktop. This approach will provide higher bandwidth and a more stable network infrastructure for large backbones on the building or campus scales. The first version has been completed and work was under way at press time for version 2. LANE does not, however, make it possible for users to leverage ATM's end to end class of service functionality. Classical IP Over ATM and MPOA make better use of ATM features.

In any discussion of ATM a clear distinction must be made between WAN ATM and LAN ATM. WAN ATM technology has been available since the late 1980s, and the service has already undergone price deductions. ATM LAN technology, including LANE and ATM to the desktop are relatively newer; their price performance points still need to improve. By 1997 this technology should reach commodity status.

ATM is not the most economical or practical solution in the near term for relatively low-speed (and, preferably low-cost) access, directly to the desktop. Niche users with special requirements including multimedia or high traffic volumes will need to adopt hybrid solutions—ATM for their special purpose applications and legacy LANs for connections to the backbone. Products that support convergence between ATM and non-ATM hosts are not yet stable enough for large scale production network usage.

ATM's original objectives, reflected in current products, focus on high speed fiber connections. Prices for ATM adapters are declining rapidly, but running fiber to the desktop and supporting it with ATM hardware would nevertheless be costly. In the near term, moreover, much of the bandwidth made available would be unused surplus. Most of today's workstations and servers are not likely to fill the bandwidth that ATM makes possible. The ATM Forum and vendors are addressing solutions that would bring ATM functionality to the desktop at moderate speeds over less expensive media. The ATM Forum is devising a physical basis for ATM traffic over various categories of unshielded twisted-pair cabling (UTP). This contrasts, for example, with the more expensive shielded or coaxial cables which were traditionally used by early deployment of LAN technologies like Ethernet.

Several alternative were explored for the support of 51-Mbps (OC-1) traffic over Category 3 UTP. Support of 155-Mbps (OC-3) traffic will require Category 5 UTP. In an effort originally separate from The ATM Forum, IBM has pursued a standard for 25 Mbps over Category 3 UTP. Now The ATM Forum has also standardized a 25 Mbps Physical Layer. The IBM proposal departs from the SONET-type signaling advocated by the AT&T-Hewlett-Packard project for 51 Mbps. IBM remains loyal to the Manchester coding associated with Token Ring for its 25 Mbps ATM standard.

UTP error-rates and carrying capacity have been increased substantially in recent years, but UTP is nevertheless limited. None of the low-speed/UTP proposals is scalable to higher bandwidths beyond 155 Mbps. However, 155 Mbps to the desktop should be adequate for a number of years. For example one can support good-quality video at 1.544 Mbps (with MPEG-1), and can support HDTV at 21.5 Mbps.

The ATM Forum is also discussing other issues. These include:

- It has developed a schedule for interoperability that allows vendors to ensure that, over time and in a series of steps, customers can count on multivendor interoperability.

- At the logical level, the ATM Forum has developed specifications for:

  - Intercarrier interchange of information,

  - A private UNI that defines the originating system to a private switch interface,

  - A private NNI (Network to Network Interface) that defines the interface and protocols between private switches.

  - Congestion control, which ensures reduction in data loss to levels from minimal to zero, even in heavily loaded networks.

  Other standards are also under development:

- Network management to support networks using ATM.

- An Application Programming Interface, defining an interface to upper (application) layer processes to send and receive information over ATM.

- Multiprotocol Over ATM, to support IP and other protocols more effectively over an ATM network, and make use of one-hop routing.

4.11 Carrier-provided ATM services

Utilizing ATM one can support a family of switched broadband data services. The services supported at this time by many carriers include:

- Ethernet interconnection (bridging) at specified throughput rates
- FDDI interconnection (bridging) at specified throughput rates
- FDDI to Ethernet interconnection (bridging) at specified throughput rates
- LAN Emulation
- MPOA, for IP and other protocols
- Frame Relay transport and grooming
- Native ATM (DS3 and OC-3) UNI

These switched data services are provided over an ATM/SONET backbone for wide area applications. Typically, a carrier's ATM infrastructure consists of three modules:

- Customer-location concentrators
- Multiservice edge ATM switches
- Core ATM switches

These devices segment and adapt all supported user streams into ATM cells. At the destination, the cells are reassembled into the original frame (type). In effect they support appropriate AALs. The tiered architecture consists of ATM-LAN concentrators deployed at the customer sites, which collect or deliver the user traffic, and of Central Office Switches that aggregate and switch customer traffic between sites. The ATM-LAN concentrators at the customer sites are connected by a trunking system utilizing ATM NNI at speeds from 45 Mbps through 155 Mbps. Bandwidth capacity is scalable at the concentrator level, both *Constant Bit Rate* and *Variable Bit Rate* services are supported by many carriers. Advanced methods of congestion avoidance, flow control, and traffic shaping enable carriers to support the service contracts established with the customer.

Native ATM services are supported by connecting the user over transmission links that terminate on the ATM switch. Legacy services (e.g., LAN interconnection) are supported by installing the remote concentrators on customer premises (either at a specific location or in common space).

4.12 Relation to SONET rings and other transport technologies

Public ATM-based services can be offered over a variety of transport media. On the access side, DS3 and OC-3 links can be employed. Typically OC-3 is provided over an access SONET ring; however, it is also possible for the access to be provided on a simple span (at least for a portion of the access facility). The DS3 can also be derived from a SONET-based access infrastructure. The interoffice (inter-ATM switch) transmission system is over a SONET-ring apparatus.

The ATM switch supports a SONET protocol peer. Hence, an arrangement where two ATM switches are connected at the ends of a fiber span, affords most if not all of the SONET management capabilities. Although this direct connection of switches is doable (and may make good sense in a strict campus-environment), in general, the switches will be connected in conjunction with a pair of SONET add/drop multiplexers. This affords the ability to get better utilization of the access/backbone fiber (e.g., getting an OC-12 or better, rather than just an OC-3), and allows the insertion of other services at the add/drop multiplexer location. Figure 4.3 depicts the two scenarios.

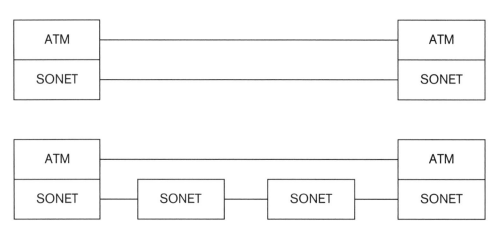

Figure 4.3   SONET used in conjunction with ATM. Top: Switch without ancillary SONET equipment. Bottom: Switch with ancillary SONET equipment

4.13 Commonly asked ATM service questions

This section summarizes the preceding material in the form of a Q&A discussion.

What is ATM? In the narrow sense, ATM is a cell-based Data Link Layer (DLL) protocol. A Data Link Layer protocol has the job of moving information across a single link (in a reliable manner), using well-defined frames (here, cells). In this view, ATM fulfills only the lower portion of the Data Link Layer. The Data Link Layer protocol relies on a Physical Layer (PHY) protocol, which can operate on any number of media, including DS3, OC-3, TAXI/FCS multimode fiber, and UTP (CAT5). Protocol-wise, ATM and the PHY taken together, correspond to a MAC layer of a LAN (except that the former is connection-oriented at the DDL, while the latter is connectionless at the DLL). In general, there is a need to fill out the DDL, before a network layer protocol (e.g., IP, IPX) can be carried. This is done using an AAL set of protocols. It should be further noted that the protocol model has three stacks: the User Plane, the Control Plane, and the Management Plane. ATM can be used in all these planes as the common link protocol, although the upper layers would be different.

In a more colloquial sense, ATM is the entire technology that supports fast packet broadband communications. It is a statistical multiplexing technology, where the industry has agreed on how to support open multiplexing. With this technology, providers can overbook user bandwidth, thereby reducing network facilities; this in turn reduces provider costs, which in the final analysis, can reduce the cost to the user.

What are the benefits of ATM to end-users? ATM technology affords the following benefits, among others: it supports high speed communications (DS3, OC-3, and higher in the future); it is a scalable technology, so that higher speeds can be supported without having to obsolete the underlying technology infrastructure; it supports both WAN and LAN systems, enabling the user to deploy a single technology for all the enterprise-wise needs; it supports multimedia communications; it supports multipoint communications; it supports quality of service contracts; and it can be used as a multi-service platform to support a variety of legacy services such as LAN bridging, LAN Emulation, frame relay, and circuit emulation.

Additionally, the technology is cost-effective (because of the overbooking described in the previous question), reliable, and well-supported by the industry.

How does an ATM platform support other services? An ATM platform can be used to support a variety of legacy services, such as LAN bridging, LAN Emulation, MPOA, frame relay, circuit emulation, etc. The switch or CPE (Customer Premises Equipment) concentrator provide interworking (protocol conversion) functions which enable the legacy frames (and/or bit streams) to be mapped into ATM cells. This is done by using appropriate AAL protocols.

Is ATM new? Use of ATM technology officially started in January 1985, although trial work started a few years earlier. By 1989 many of the standards required to support WAN data communications, were available and equipment started to appear. Additional standards and equipment have appeared ever since. For WAN data applications, ATM technology is well into the second generation of equipment, with a third generation expected by the second half of 1996.

What standards are important in ATM service? Several entities have published relevant standards, specifications, and requirements including ITU-T and ANSI (ATIS). The ATM Forum (ATMF), The Frame Relay Forum, and Bellcore have published relevant documentation.

Carriers require support of the ATMF User-to-Network Interface Specification Version 3.1 (with Version 4.0 to follow in 1996), Broadband Intercarrier Interface (B-ICI) Version 2, and (for internal connectivity only) Private Network Node Interface (P-NNI) Version 1.0 or higher. UNI 3.1 supports the ITU-T Q.2931, which is important. LAN Emulation Version 1.0 or 2.0 is also generally required.

What is the distinction between PVCs and SVCs? Communication in ATM occurs over a concatenation of virtual data links called Virtual Channels; this concatenation is called a Virtual Channel Connection. VCCs can be permanently established by an external provisioning process, entailing a service order (with desired traffic contract information) and manual switch configuration. Such a VCC is called a Permanent Virtual Circuit. When the Control Plane mechanisms are implemented in both the user equipment and in the switch (specifically ITU-T Q.2931 and/or ATMF 3.1), the user will be able to establish connections automatically on an as-needed basis. This type of connection is called a Switched Virtual Circuit (SVC).

What is the difference between VC and VP switching? In VC switching, each VC is switched and routed independently and separately. VP switching allows a group of VCs to be switched and routed as a single entity. This switching concept applies only to ATM and not to the other services available over the ATM platform.

When is a remote concentrator used?   LAN bridging, LAN emulation, MPOA and FDDI bridging requires a remote concentrator that supports the AAL functions. Frame relay can be done over an access line (but currently a nonchannelized-only service is supported). Native ATM UNI service does not generally require a remote concentrator, unless there are enough customers at one location that it is more effective to use a concentrator/multiplexer in common space than to use a multitude of transmission facilities.

How is bandwidth allocated in an ATM network?   For ATM services, the customer can specify the equivalent of the Sustainable Cell Rate (SCR), the Peak Cell Rate (PCR), and the Maximum Burst Size (MBS). The switch allocates various resources (e.g., trunk capacity, buffers) on a statistical basis. This involves the use of traffic shapers, traffic policers, and tagging for discard. The carrier has the obligation to deploy enough resources in the network to guarantee the type of quality of service and the kind of service required (e.g., Constant Bit Rate, Variable Bit Rate, Available Bit Rate, Unspecified Bit Rate, etc.). Non-ATM services are allocated in a similar manner, but the user has no direct control on the ATM traffic parameters.

How does a carrier provision an ATM service?   ATM (and ATM-based) services entail five levels of provisioning. First, appropriate physical lines must be deployed to the sites in question (this can entail more than two user locations and the physical bandwidth to each location can be different). Second, the Central Office switch must be configured (port, slot, switch capacity, trunk capacity, etc.). Third, the concentrator must be configured (port, slot, switch capacity, trunk capacity, etc.). Fourth, the QoS parameters (SCR, PCR, MBS, service type, etc.) must be configured into the network Management station. Fifth, the virtual connectivity must be specified (the PVC/SVCs, workgroups, etc.).

What is meant by ABR, VBR, UBR, and CBR?   For native ATM, a number of services are available, in support of different use requirements. CBR provides constant bit rate in support of a service that provides the equivalent of a private line at T1 or T3 rates. VBR is a variable bit rate service in support of data applications such as frame relay and LAN interconnection. ABR provides available bit rate service at a discount basis; here the amount of bandwidth in the network is not guaranteed, and is managed via a feedback mechanism. UBR is unspecified bit rate with only "best-effort" characteristics.

Physically, how are different services supported?   ATM services are supported over a fiber DS3/OC-3 link; the user adds equipment supporting the ATM peer. Frame relay services are supported over a T1 line; the user adds equipment supporting the frame relay peer. LAN-based services are supported by installing the concentrator at customer sites. The concentrator is connected with the network over an appropriate ATM trunk; the user connects to the concentrator over an RJ-45 and/or SAS/DAS FDDI connection.

What user equipment is needed to access a carrier's cell relay service? LAN bridging service? For ATM cell relay, the user can use an ATM-ready hub, ATM-ready router, or workgroup switch. For a legacy service, the user delivers an Ethernet or FDDI connection to carrier's site-located concentrator.

What is the relevance of P-NNI? Does it matter that our switch does not communicate over the P-NNI to another switch? Carriers have not, hereto, supported access by the user to the trunk side of their switches (e.g., voice switches, packet switches, frame relay switches, SMDS switches). They will not likely allow access to the trunk-side of an ATM switch. Carriers may only offer a UNI service, not a P-NNI service. Hence, it does not matter that a switch may not interwork with another switch over the NNI; this in not relevant to the service a carrier provides. The only relevance of P-NNI is in the event the carrier decides to use P-NNI as an NNI to connect equipment *within* the carrier's network (but not outside of it).

What is LAN Emulation? LANE is an interworking capability that allows Ethernet/Token Ring stations to communicate directly with ATM stations (and vice versa) as if they were using the same protocol. The interworking switch supports the conversion between the two protocols.

Does ATM support multimedia, and if so, how? Video and multimedia information can be carried either over an ATM UNI, an FDDI interface, or an Ethernet interface. The ATM switch supports a high grade of service which makes it a good platform for these media.

Does ATM support multipoint services and how? ATM supports multipoint connections. The ATFM UNI 3.1 specifies the use of signaling messages to establish such connections. Many ATM switches do not currently support ATM UNI multiconnections (it does support a kind of internal multipoint service for LAN support).

4.14 References

61   D. Minoli, *Telecommunications Technologies Handbook,* Norwood, MA: Artech House, 1991.

62   D. Minoli, M. Vitella, *Cell Relay Service and ATM for Corporate Environments,* New York, NY: McGraw-Hill, 1994.

63   D. Minoli, G. Dobrowski, *Principles of Signaling For Cell Relay and Frame Relay*, Norwood, MA: Artech House, 1995.

64   Peter Newman, "ATM Local Area Network," *IEEE Communications Magazine*, March 1994, pages 86 ff.

65   D. Minoli, T. Golway, *Planning and Managing ATM Networks*, Manning/Prentice Hall, 1997.

66   D. Minoli, A. Alles, *LAN, LAN Emulation and ATM Technologies*, Norwood, MA: Artech House, 1997.

PART III

ATM-based approach to client/server

chapter 5

LAN Emulation and Classical IP over ATM

This chapter discusses methods that can immediately be used to run existing client/server applications over an ATM network. If a network designer plans to deploy ATM in the near future, a major technical issue that must be addressed is how hosts locate each other. Standards bodies quickly realized a need for finding simple techniques for dealing with a relatively complex technology. The ATM Forum and the IETF have devised two approaches that can be used today for rapid deployment of ATM networks. The work of these two bodies is the major focus of this chapter. The topics covered include:

- LAN Emulation developed by the ATM Forum
- Classical IP Over ATM developed by the Internet Engineering Task Force

Both approaches have strengths and weaknesses that should be considered by network managers when selecting a migration path from existing LAN infrastructures to ATM based LAN internetworks. The chapter is divided into three sections. The first two cover the details of how LAN Emulation and Classical IP would be used in a Client/Server environment. The concluding section addresses techniques and issues to consider when migrating to an ATM framework.

5.1 LAN Emulation motivation

In an effort to speed the deployment of ATM technology, the ATM Forum had to face the problem of providing a means to connect the installed base of LANs to newly acquired ATM attached hosts and routers. The connection had to be done so that the LAN attached hosts had no idea that they were communicating with ATM attached hosts. In addition, applications running on ATM hosts were also unaware that they were using ATM as a network media. This problem was solved when the ATM Forum developed a technique for emulating the behavior of legacy LAN protocols, and carrying the data over an ATM network. The result of this work is the LAN Emulation (LANE) specification.

LAN Emulation's goal is to help ATM adopters who are faced with the problem of interconnecting their installed base of LAN protocols over a new ATM media while minimizing the impact to existing systems. In a client/server environment, LAN Emulation can be summarized as follows:

- LAN Emulation provides a mechanism for existing LAN based Client/Server applications to run over ATM networks without modification.

- LAN Emulation uses ATM as a backbone to interconnect existing legacy LANs together to achieve higher bandwidth.

- LAN Emulation permits several emulated LANs or Virtual LANs (VLANs) to concurrently share the same ATM network. This allows one physical network to appear as several logical networks.

- LAN Emulation must be deployable in ATM networks immediately.

LANE is very successful in meeting these goals. It is expected to be widely deployed since it provides network designers with proven techniques for building multiprotocol ATM network.

5.1.1 LAN Emulation problem space

Initially, early implementors encountered significant difficulty using ATM prior to LANE due to the connection oriented nature of ATM. Most network protocols such as Ethernet or Token Ring, are designed to operate on connectionless networks. On connectionless networks, any host can communicate with any other host simply by placing a packet onto the network. The packet is transmitted to all hosts attached to the network by virtue of the fact that they all share a common virtual "wire." Transmitting data to all hosts simultaneously is called broadcasting. Being able to transmit a message to all hosts on the network via broadcasts is not possible with ATM because it is connection oriented. With a connection-oriented network, a path between hosts must be established by some means before they can communicate. In addition, because virtual circuits provide for one-to-one communication, a host that is broadcasting to a set of other hosts must be aware of any additions or deletion to the set. Lack of a broadcast capability is what prevented network managers from running existing applications over ATM easily.

One can consider today's telephone network as an example of a connection-oriented network. Users of the telephone network must manually place a call before they are able to communicate. In an ATM network, the connections, or virtual circuits, are either established by operators in advance or they are dynamically established by hosts. Operator controlled virtual circuits typically remain in place for long periods of time and are referred to as Permanent Virtual Circuits (PVCs). PVCs are usually created by a management interface to the ATM switch and exist until deleted by the network administrator. Virtual circuits that are dynamically created and deleted, are called Switched Virtual Circuits (SVCs). SVCs make an ATM network function like a telephony network and greatly increase the flexibility of inter-host communication. However, with the addition of SVCs comes the cost of increased complexity. SVCs introduce problems such as call routing, call control, and billing, to hosts so that they can correctly format call setup messages. If a network designer intends to use ATM, then these extra complexities should be anticipated.

The constraints imposed by ATM's connection-oriented methodology, coupled with a lack of SVC software support, dictated that the first prototype networks built use only PVCs. Higher layer protocols, like Telnet, were intentionally kept ignorant of the fact that they were using ATM as transport. In some first generation ATM networks, routers were attached to the network by HDLC to ATM converters. These frame-to-ATM conversions effectively hid ATM from the router. However, as the ATM networks grew, establishing more and more PVCs became cumbersome. For each pair of hosts wanting to exchange data, a new bidirectional virtual circuit needed to be created. While this could be tolerated for networks with dozens of computers, it quickly became difficult to manage in a network of hundreds of hosts in which any host can communicate with any other host. Lack of SVCs and static configuration proved effective for prototype systems but it was far from easy to use and was not scalable.

To improve the ability to "plug and play" and increase scalability, the ATM Forum formed a working group called the Local Area Network Emulation Over ATM. It was chartered with developing protocols that allowed quick and easy use of ATM. The requirements set forth by the ATM Forum LANE group were that the solution be:

- Based on the UNI 3.0 specification
- High performance, highly scalable facility backbone
- Capable of protocol independent switching across logical LANs
- Capable of seamless interworking with legacy LANs via bridges
- Capable of supporting PVCs, SVCs or combinations

LANE* version 1.0 is the first specification from this group and is now a protocol that is available in products from dozens of ATM vendors. The goal of LANE version 1.0 is to simplify attaching legacy devices to the ATM network in a manner that would be no more difficult than making attachments to an Ethernet or Token Ring network. Specifically, LANE allows the addition of end stations or bridges to the ATM network as shown in Figure 5.1.

The LANE protocols can also be extended to run over wide area connections. By extending LANE over the WAN, users have the capability of transparently attaching

---

* LAN Emulation is work in progress. While the ATM Forum has produced a workable specification, still more work needs to be done. Additional specifications will be produced and modifications may be made to existing documents.

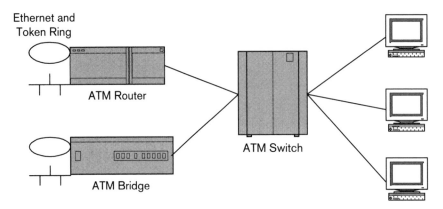

Figure 5.1 LAN Emulation network of hosts and bridges

remote hosts to the various campus ATM LANE networks. Hosts that are part of an emulated LAN over a wide area connection are not treated any differently than hosts directly connected to the campus network.

All devices attached to a LAN Emulation network can function in a plug and play fashion with minimal configuration. Because client/server application programs using the network services will interface with MAC device drivers, the LAN Emulation service does offer the same MAC driver service interface to upper protocol layers. To do this, LAN Emulation client software must intend on using its services and be loaded onto hosts that are attached to an ATM. The LAN Emulation protocol stack (Figure 5.2) provides all of the functions of commonly used device driver APIs, NDIS, and ODI [NDIS]. In essence, the problem of hiding ATM from applications is solved by replacing the NDIS device driver with LAN Emulation. The new device driver hides ATM by recreating the traditional API that is used between applications and Ethernet or Token Ring device drivers.

5.1.2 Issues with LAN Emulation

Emulation of Ethernet and Token Ring is very attractive if users are interested in migrating their production network to ATM. However, it is important to realize the implications, both good and bad, of hiding the ATM network from clients and servers with LAN Emulation. By hiding ATM, hosts are not required to understand all of the potential complexities of operating on a connection oriented network that supports multiple qualities of service. On the other hand, hiding ATM may be problematic since

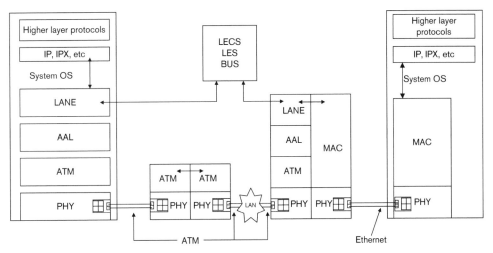

Figure 5.2　LAN Emulation protocol stack

there is no way for a host to make use of quality of service. There are no provisions made in LAN Emulation for communicating quality of service requests, which is, ironically, one of the fundamental strengths of ATM. The question of direct interaction between client/server applications with the ATM network's quality of service features has been deferred to LAN Emulation version 2.*

A video server using TCP/IP over ATM is an example of the potential problems encountered due to the lack of quality of service. This configuration is illustrated in Figure 5.3. The video server has no way of assigning a higher priority to the video packets as they cross the ATM network.† The video could easily be interrupted by electronic mail or a large file transfer. If, on the other hand, the video server application was developed as a native ATM application, then the server would have the ability to communicate with the ATM network. When the native application communicates with the network and dynamically creates its connection, it can then specify that it is a video server and designate the data stream as a high priority that should be transmitted with consistently low latency. Of course, an obvious short term advantage is that LAN Emulation devices make use of ATM's superior bandwidth and scalability while not incurring additional cost for modifications.

While the technique of hiding ATM is useful for quick migration to an ATM network, LAN Emulation is a protocol that may have a limited lifetime. LAN Emulation,

---

* LAN Emulation version 2 was later aligned with the Multiprotocol over ATM group in the ATM Forum and now they are colaborating on the specification development.

† Excluding the use of RSVP as described in Chapter 7.

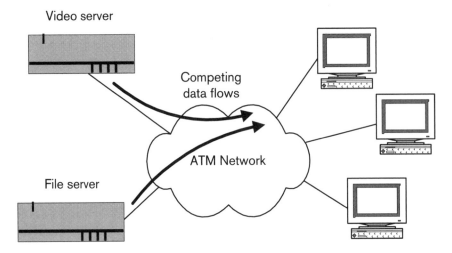

Figure 5.3   Multimedia Over ATM

in its most basic form, is just a high speed replacement for Ethernet. One could argue that 100BaseT, or some other technology, would be just as effective for high speed communication. Therefore, it is key that protocols that provide access and control of quality of service, like MPOA, be developed and quickly deployed.

LANE also suffers from the drawback that it behaves like protocol independent bridging.* Years of network design have shown that bridging, while effective for interconnecting small workgroups, does not scale on large internets. As bridged networks grow, they are prone to experiencing a large load of broadcasts as hosts try to resolve MAC addresses into layer 3 address mappings. It should also be noted that LANE only supports emulation of one type of network at a time. If a host on an emulated Ethernet wants to communicate with a host on an emulated Token Ring, the packets must pass through a router that is a member of both emulated LANs.

The positive side to bridging is that LAN Emulation will support any layer 3 protocol that is designed to operate on a connectionless network (e.g., APPN, IPX, IP, AppleTalk, etc.) without modification. An additional strength to LAN Emulation is its support for multicast. Because it is emulating connectionless behavior, applications that make use of broadcast or multicast can still function in a LAN Emulation network. Also, LANE does not support the concept of a collision or transmission of tokens and beacon frames. Collisions occur on Ethernet networks when two hosts try to transmit at

---

* LAN Emulations supported bridging methods include both Transparent Bridging and Source Routing Bridging [61].

the same time. On the Ethernet, the problem is handled with CSMA/CD [68]. In an ATM network the collision is dealt with by buffering the data inside the network.

Because LAN Emulation is recreating the behavior of legacy networks, it is also very good at recreating the problems of the legacy network. However, the LAN Emulation version 1.0 specification expressly avoids solving the networking problems that existed long before its conception (e.g., conversion from Token Ring to Ethernet). LAN Emulation is limited to the degree it emulates the legacy network and it will not support all functions of the layer 2 protocol being emulated. The limited support is often due to the paradigm shift from a connectionless network to a connection oriented one.

Examples of what LANE will not support:

- Solve existing Ethernet/Token Ring/FDDI bridging problems
- Allow a station to receive all frames on a logical LAN
- Support exiting MAC layer protocols such as SMT/Token Management

5.2 Address resolution basics

Before discussing the details of the LAN Emulation protocol, a brief review of address resolution is outlined. The ability to resolve the location of hosts and addresses is a fundamental accomplishment of the LAN Emulation specification.

The current LAN Emulation specification is capable of emulating Ethernet (802.3) or Token Ring (802.5) networks. With an Ethernet or Token Ring LAN, membership to the network is determined by physical points of attachment. Hosts are added or removed from the subnetwork by physically adding or removing them from a hub or cable segment. Once a host is attached to a LAN, it identifies itself via its Medium Access Control (MAC) [67] address. When communicating with other hosts the most basic address used is the MAC address.

MAC addresses are globally unique numbers. Blocks are assigned to vendors to be hard coded into computers and routers at the time of manufacturing. MAC addresses are considered flat addresses because they can be found in a network in a more or less random fashion. For example, two physically adjacent hosts can have MAC addresses that are numerically very different. Flat addresses have very little significance for large scale routing because they have no hierarchy.

In order for hosts to communicate on a connectionless network they must locate remote MAC addresses. The process of resolving addresses usually follows these steps:

- Determine host name of destination computer
- Translate the text host name into a network layer address

- Translate the network layer address into a MAC address
- Establish communication to remote host using the acquired MAC address

The Address Resolution Protocol (ARP) [68] is a technique for transmitting a request onto the network to ascertain if any host is willing to accept packets containing the destination layer 3 address. Network layer addresses, or layer 3 addresses such as IP, are typically used to identify hosts on a network in a somewhat human readable format. Layer 3 addresses are also used to build a hierarchical view of the network. The hierarchical view facilitates routing and locating hosts.

As an example, consider a legacy LAN in which clients wish to access a database on a remote server. The user of the client specifies a host name in a human readable format, for example, `www.uiuc.edu`. The client next determines the network layer address of the server. It does so via its domain name server [68]. The name server is given the text host name and replies with a layer 3 address. When a network layer address has been determined, the originating client will utilize ARP in an attempt to locate where to send the database query. If the address returned from the name server is believed* to be local, then the originating client will use ARP to find the MAC address. If the originating host believes that the destination server is on a remote network, it will transmit the database query to its gateway† which will forward the request to the server.

ARP packets are specialized requests that are transmitted to the "broadcast" addresses on the network. The broadcast address allows the ARP request to be forwarded to all hosts on the subnetwork. On an Ethernet, the broadcast address is all ones. Any packet containing all ones as a destination address will be accepted by all hosts on the subnetwork and the contents examined. ARP packets contain the source MAC address of the client attempting to locate the server and they also contain the requested destination address. ARP broadcast packets are forwarded through bridges and hubs, but typically will not pass through routers.

When a host receives an ARP packet, it examines the contents to determine if the source of the ARP is attempting to locate itself or if it is some other host. If the destination layer 3 address matches the host (i.e., the self check is true), it responds to the ARP, then notifies the ARP originator that it has successfully located the destination. If the requested address does not match the host's layer 3 address, then the ARP requests are ignored.

When a client has received a successful reply to an ARP message it can update its internal ARP table with a layer 3 to MAC address mapping. The ARP table is referenced

---

* Determination of local versus remote is done by comparing the source and destination layer 3 addresses taking into consideration the sub network mask.

† The MAC address of the subnets' router is found with ARP as well.

when the client has additional packets to transmit. If an entry for the server exists in the clients local ARP cache, then the packet is immediately transmitted. If no ARP entry exists, the address resolution process will be repeated. ARP table entries have a limited lifetime and, if not used, are periodically deleted to allow for changing layer 3 addresses.

The preceding description of ARP illustrates how it was designed for connectionless networks and how it works in that environment. When hosts are moved to a connection oriented ATM fabric, they lose the ability to transparently broadcast to all hosts. Special techniques need to be used to mimic connectionless behavior. In an ATM network LAN Emulation is one of those techniques.

5.3 LAN Emulation components

To overcome the lack of broadcast capability LANE provides the ARP function via three servers. As shown in Figure 5.4, the servers that perform the functions of LAN Emulation and addresses resolution are:

- A single LAN Emulation Configuration Server (LECS) provides configuration information.
- LAN Emulation Server (LES) implements Address Registration/Resolution.
- Broadcast/Unknown Server (BUS) performs all broadcasting and multicasting functions.

These three servers are independent applications running on one or more hosts attached to the ATM network. Typically, all three servers are located on one device, however, they can be separated to improve reliability. Currently, the servers are run as additional processes on an ATM attached router. However, in some cases, to reduce the load on the router, the servers are run on ATM attached workstations.

5.3.1 LAN Emulation configuration server

The LAN Emulation Configuration Server acts as a central point for maintaining configuration information in the ATM network. The LECS is the first point of contact when new clients boot and need to register on their ATM network. The LECS is responsible for keeping a database of all clients and knows which emulated LAN the host is a member of. The LECS can connect clients to different virtual LANs because its

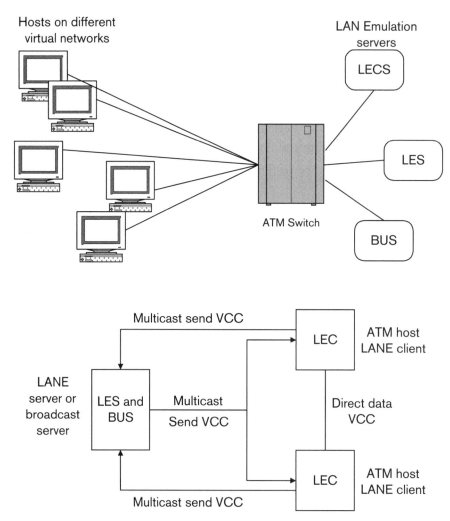

Figure 5.4   LAN Emulation servers

response to a client wishing to be configured, is the ATM address of an individual LAN Emulation Server. By maintaining a database that contains mappings of clients to LAN Emulation servers, the LEC is capable of subdividing the ATM network into several virtual LANs. This allows the ATM network administrator to break the network into administrative groups such as accounting, engineering, marketing, etc.

Knowing which emulated LAN to assign hosts to is done by the LEC's own policies, configuration database, and information provided by clients. The mapping of host identifiers to virtual LANs is typically done once by the LECS administrator. The LECS will also notify the LEC what type of LAN, Ethernet or Token Ring, it has been assigned. The emulated LAN type information is then used by the clients to correctly generate packets that are similar to the native emulated LAN technology.

5.3.2 LAN Emulation Server

The LES is the focal point of the address resolution process and acts as the central repository of address mappings from an ATM identifier to a MAC identifier. Once a client has been assigned to a LES, it registers its address with that server. The client may also register other LAN destinations that it represents, if it is acting as a legacy bridge. Clients then use the LES to mimic the behavior of ARP by querying the LES when it has an address to resolve and/or a route descriptor to an ATM address. If the LEC knows the mapping, it will respond to the client. If not, it will forward the request to other LECs on the Emulated LAN in an attempt to locate the address mapping information.

5.3.3 LAN Emulation Broadcast and Unknown Server

The BUS is the final component used to make a connection-oriented network appear connectionless. It is used to reproduce the mass distribution behavior of multicast, broadcast, and initial unicast frames. To accomplish this, each host on the Emulated LAN establishes a virtual circuit to the BUS serving its Emulated LAN at registration time, and joins the BUS's broadcast group. Frames that are to be broadcast are sent to the BUS; then the BUS has the responsibility of forwarding them to all hosts in the group. The BUS can also be used to begin immediate communication with a remote server on the emulated LAN. For example, a client is permitted to begin sending traffic to a server via the BUS while that same client is concurrently attempting to locate the server via the LES. Once the LES responds, it is recommended that the client allow the traffic sent to the BUS to get passed to the server, cease using the BUS, then establish direct communication with the server.

Frames that are forwarded by the BUS must be serialized and redistributed one at a time in the same order they were received. The reason for forwarding the frames this way is that LECs receive them from the BUS over only one AAL 5 virtual circuit. By serializing the traffic, the semantics of Ethernet and Token Ring are better preserved and packets from different hosts are not intermixed when converted into cells. It is also recommended that the BUS's multicast function be tightly coupled with the ATM network's intrinsic multicast capabilities. This allows the ATM switches to reproduce ATM cells rather that having the BUS reproduce each frame internally for each destination.

5.3.4 LAN Emulation Clients

The LANE servers described above interoperate with LANE's fourth component, the actual devices attempting to communicate on the ATM network. These are called the LAN Emulation Clients (LEC). The LAN Emulation client is software that resides on host computers or bridges. It performs data forwarding, address resolution, and other control functions to emulate Ethernet or Token Ring. On a bridge, it represents, or proxies for, all of the legacy attached devices and acts as their agent to the LECS, LES, and BUS. The LEC software buffers the network layer from the layer 2 protocols as shown in Figure 5.2.

5.4 LAN Emulation User Network Interface operation

A host or bridge connected to an ATM network that supports LAN Emulation services is said to be connected to a LAN Emulation UNI (LUNI) (Figure 5.5). For this interface to provide ARP-like functions, a set of requirements and procedures have been defined that each LEC must execute sequentially.

In a LAN Emulation network, the operation of the LUNI allows all member components to correctly interoperate.

The processes of LANE can be subdivided into four areas.

- Initialization on the ATM network

- Registration with the LANE server

- Address resolution via the LANE server

- Data Transfer with other LANE clients

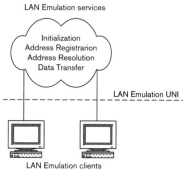

Figure 5.5   LAN Emulation UNI

5.4.1 LAN Emulation procedures

The operation of a LANE network can be broken down into the four processes listed above. Each of these processes can be further subdivided into a virtual circuit establishment phase and an information exchange phase.

The first step to using the LANE service is the establishment of a Configuration Direct VCC to the LECS. The VCC is called direct because it refers to a point-to-point circuit between two hosts. In this phase the LEC establishes the VCC to the LECS, passes its MAC address to the LECS, then is assigned to a LES by the LECS. It should be noted that this phase may be omitted if the LEC is staticly configured with the ATM address of the LES.

There are several techniques used by a LEC to find its LECS. The host wishing to initialize itself on the network first uses the ILMI [70] protocol to find the address of the LEC. Via ILMI messages, the ATM switch can provide the LEC with an ATM address that is used to establish a SVC to the LECS. If ILMI fails, the next step is to establish a virtual circuit using a well-known address. This address can be configured into the ATM network to point to the LECS. If the call setup to the LECS using the well-known address fails then the client can default to communicating to the LECS by using a PVC with the VCI equal to 17. Once a connection is established to the LECS, the LECS can exchange messages with the LEC to obtain the LEC's MAC address. The LECS then checks its database to determine which virtual LAN the client belongs to and returns to the client the ATM address of its LAN Emulation server along with what type of emulated LAN the LEC is joining.

In the next phase, the LEC establishes a VCC to the LES and enters the join state. In the join state, the LEC is assigned a unique LEC identifier (LECID), it is told the type of Emulated LAN to which it has connected, and the maximum frame size for intra LAN communication. Once joined, the LEC must register* at least one MAC address with the server. The LEC can optionally register additional MAC address for devices it is bridging to the Emulated LAN. The addresses registered by the member LECs will be referenced by the LECS when it receives ARP requests.

Initialization is completed when the LEC performs its first ARP to locate and connect to the BUS. The LEC issues a LAN Emulation ARP message (LE-ARP) to the LES to request resolution of the BUS's address. The LES replies to the LEC with an LE-ARP message which contains the desired ATM address of the BUS. Then the LEC establishes a VCC to the BUS and registers itself with the BUS. At this point, the BUS establishes what is called a uni-directional multicast forwarding VCC to the LEC. The multicast forwarding VCC is used to forward all broadcast traffic received by the BUS on to clients of the Emulated LAN. Once the multicast forwarding VCC establishment is complete, the initialization process is finished, and the LEC can begin to communicate with other hosts on the ATM network.

---

* The LEC may also unregister addresses as the state of the network changes.

5.4.2 Address resolution

When a client is a member of an emulated LAN, it can then begin the process of address resolution and inter host communication. The outcome of address resolution will be a mapping of a MAC address to an ATM address that the client can use to establish a direct VCC to carry data. When a client has data to transmit to another client who has an unknown ATM address, the originating host first transmits a LE-ARP request to the LES containing the unknown destination address. The LES then returns to the LEC the desired ATM address.

The LES has two possible ways to deal with this request. First, if the destination host has registered with the server, then the server can respond to the originating client directly. The response is called an LE-ARP reply and contains the destination ATM address. The second possibility is that the server does not contain the translation. In this case, it should then forward the LE-ARP request to clients in the group it believes contain the MAC address. When a client receives a LE-ARP from a server and it possess the destination address it must respond to the query. The response is sent to the originating client and the LES so that both can update their local ARP caches.

5.4.3 Multicast and unicast address forwarding

After the process of address resolution is complete, the originating client can establish direct VCCs to destinations and use the new VCCs to exchange data with the destinations. Alternatively, if the originating host does not yet have a VCC established to the destination, it can begin communicating by transmitting data to the BUS. The BUS then forwards the data to the correct destination, if the location is known, or the BUS forwards the data to all clients in hope that the destination will be found by the LES.

Forwarding frames to all registered clients is acceptable and desirable behavior in an emulated LAN due to the connectionless nature of the bridged networks being emulated. When the destination is unknown in an 802.1D [67] transparent bridge, the frame reaches its destination by forwarding it in every possible direction. The flooding process is critical to the correct operation of bridged networks, but it is also one of their major weaknesses.

If a client elects to use the BUS to flood data throughout the emulated network, it must stop the mass forwarding once it receives an LE-ARP response to its original query. When the LE-ARP reply is received, the originator should establish a direct VCC to the destination. If the client wishes to send multicast frames, then it must use the BUS's forward capability. This is the logical approach because, the BUS establishes a uni-directional VCC to all host on the emulated LAN. The LEC should exercise this option in favor of establishing a unique VCC to all possible destinations for multicast flooding. In the case of unicast frame being transmitted between two hosts, the originating host must stop using the BUS as soon as it has established a direct VCC to the destination.

The final process in data forwarding involves a protocol for clearing out data that may be buffered in the BUS. The originating host can issue a request to the BUS to expedite the transmission of all frames it has received from the originator. This process is called flushing and is designed to prevent data from being delivered out of order. Without flushing, the originator may receive a response to the LE-ARP, establish a direct VCC and begin transmitting additional frames while data is pending transmission in the BUS. With flushing, the originator can establish a direct VCC, issue a flush, momentarily pause, then begin communicating with the destination.

5.5 Scalability and reliability

A key issue to developing a network based on LANE will be its performance capabilities related to scalability and reliability. In terms of scale, LANE by design is intended to emulate the operation of a legacy LAN segment. As bridged LANs grow, the number of broadcasts generated by ARP can become overwhelming. An additional problem is posed when the network is used to carry multicast traffic. For example, if a LAN network was used for video distribution, it is conceivable that the BUS could quickly become overloaded. Both of these conditions have the potential to overload LAN Emulation servers.

To date, very little practical experience has been gained with large scale production LANE networks. Most of the work has been focused in test beds and making single points of attachment to legacy LANs. For example, using a LAN Emulation edge device to connect the ATM backbone to a campus Ethernet or Token, as shown in Figure 5.6.

LANE does provide the benefits of far superior line speeds coupled with a switched environment. Hosts connected to an ATM LANE network can support interface speeds of 155 Mbps. Because LAN Emulation is not associated with a physical media's speed, it is potentially scalable from 64 Kbps to 622 Mbps. And when properly implemented, the network is used in a statistical mixing fashion thus providing for very high speed inter-host communication channels with little congestion. ATM LANE also holds the promise of allowing servers to attach to the network via 622-Mbps connections which will

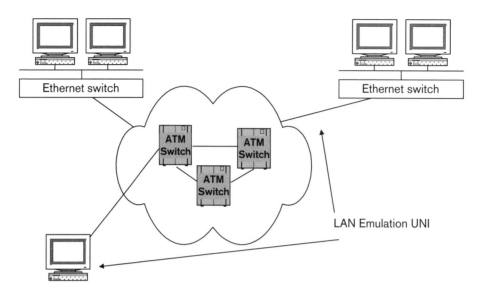

Figure 5.6   Small scale LANE network

further reduce congestion and improve performance. These high speeds may facilitate a migration back to centralized servers capable of providing information to thousands of clients.

5.6 Classical IP over ATM

5.6.1 Overview

In the previous section the problem of APR over ATM was addressed with the LANE suite of protocols. In this section an alternate technique, Classical IP Over ATM, is discussed. Classical IP and ARP over ATM [72] predates LANE and has been developed by the Internet Engineering Task Force (IETF). The IETF specification is defined to provide native IP support over ATM and is documented in RFC 1577 and RFC 1483, Multiprotocol Encapsulation over ATM Adaptation Layer 5. These protocols are designed to treat ATM as wire with the special property of being connection oriented and therefore require unique means for address resolution.

In the Classical IP Over ATM model, the ATM fabric interconnecting a group of hosts is considered to be one Logical IP Subnetwork (LIS). The idea behind Classical IP Over ATM is that network administrators will build networks with the same mind set they use today, dividing hosts into groups called subnets according to administrative and workgroup domains and then interconnecting subnets via routers. A LIS in Classical IP Over ATM is made up of a collection of ATM-attached hosts and ATM-attached IP routers which are part of a common IP subnet. Policy administration such as security, access controls, routing, and filtering will still remain a function of routers.

Much like the LANE protocol, each LIS has an ARP server that maintains IP address to ATM address mappings. All members of the LIS register with the ARP server, and subsequently all ARP requests from members of the LIS are handled by the ARP server. This mechanism allows direct IP to ATM address mappings; see Figure 5.7.

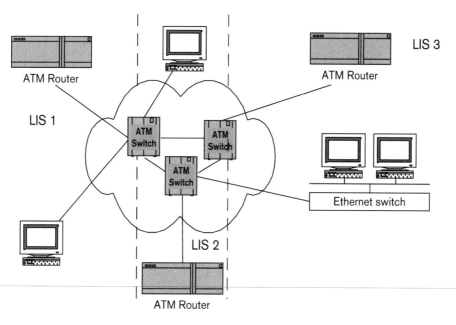

Figure 5.7   Classical IP over ATM LIS

In the Classical IP Over ATM model, IP ARP requests are forwarded from hosts directly to the LIS ARP server. The ARP server, which can simply be a process running on a ATM attached router, replies with an ATM address. When the ARP request originator receives the ATM address, it can issue a call setup directly to the destination host. As opposed to LANE, the Classical IP Over ATM model's simplicity reduces the amount of broadcast traffic and interactions with various servers. By reducing communication with the LECS, LES, and BUS, the time required for address resolution and subsequent data transfer can be greatly reduced. However, the reduction in complexity does come with a reduction in functionality.

Classical IP Over ATM has the drawback that it can only support the IP protocol because the ARP server is only knowledgeable about IP. Communication between LISs must be made with ATM attached routers that are members of more that one LIS. One physical ATM network can logically be considered several LISs but the interconnections, from the host's perspective, are via another router. Using an ATM attached router as the path between subnets prevents ATM attached end stations in different subnets from creating direct virtual circuits between one another. This restriction has the potential to degrade throughput and increase latency.

The creation of direct virtual circuits is a key design goal of ATM and techniques for addressing this problem are discussed in Chapter 6. Classical IP Over ATM also suffers from the lacks of support for multicast traffic. This shortcoming is being addressed in the IETF's IP over ATM working group [73]. More information on Multicast Address Resolution is given in Chapter 6.

There are also questions about the reliability of the IP ARP server in that the specification has no provisions for redundancy. If the ARP server were to suffer a catastrophic failure, all hosts on the LIS would be unable to ARP. Finally, Classical IP Over ATM suffers from the drawback that each host must be manually configured with the ATM address of the ARP server as opposed to the dynamic discovery allowed in LANE.

5.6.2 Operation

In the Classical IP Over ATM model, data transfer is done by creating a VCC between hosts, then using LLC/SNAP [71] encapsulation and AAL 5 segmentation, and reassemble. Mapping of IP packets to ATM cells is specified in RFC1483, Multiprotocol Encapsulation Over ATM. The advantage to RFC1483 is that ATM is treated as a data link layer that supports a large Maximum Transfer Unit (MTU). Because the network is not emulating an Ethernet or Token Ring, like LANE, the MTU has been specified to be as large as 9180 bytes. The large MTU can improve performance of hosts attached directly to the ATM network.

RFC 1577 specifies two major modifications to the traditional connectionless ARP. The first is the creation of the ATMARP message used to request addresses. The second is the InATMARP message used for inverse address registration.

When a client wishes to initialize itself on a LIS, it establishes a virtual circuit to the server. Once the circuit has been established, the server contains the ATM address of the client and then transmits a InATMARP request in an attempt to determine the IP address of the client that has just created the virtual circuit. The client responds to the InATMARP request with its IP address and the server uses this information to build its

ATMARP table cache. The ATMARP cache is used to answer subsequent ATMARP requests for the clients IP address. Clients wishing to resolve addresses generate ATMARP messages which are sent to their server, and locally cache the reply. Client cache table entries expire and must be renewed every fifteen minutes. Server entries for attached hosts time-out after twenty minutes.

5.7 Migrating towards ATM LANs

The discussion above on LAN Emulation and Classical IP Over ATM illustrates techniques that can be used to make existing client/server applications work on ATM networks. Analysis of ATM network architectures and protocols is important. However, more importantly, network managers are faced with plotting a migration strategy from existing LAN infrastructures to ATM-based LAN internetworks.

In migrating to ATM LANs, users will typically start with a pilot network based on ATM, and then expand as this network proves to be stable. When the demand for bandwidth and enhanced management capabilities grows, the pilot network will need to be expanded into a production system. In pursuing such a plan, one has to undertake the following:

1 Plan for interconnecting Legacy network to the net ATM fabric

2 Select a model for Address Resolution (LANE or RFC 1577)

3 Plan for upgrading the pilot ATM network

First, one needs to understand the various models outlined above, and decide which is appropriate for one's environment. Performance, features, and product availability have to be considered. For IP only networks that are looking for good performance, the Classical IP Over ATM is a strong candidate. For companies that have a campus network supporting multiple internetworking protocols, like IPX or AppleTalk, and where performance is not as critical, the ATM Forum's LAN Emulation model is a good starting point. Finally, companies which have multiple protocols and need to consider performance and scalability, should target the multiprotocol over the ATM model. However, implementations of standards-based MPOA products on a corporate network will, in all likelihood, be delayed until mid 1997. The reason for this delay is the expected completion of the final specification in early 1997, followed by a short lag time until standards based products are available.

It is important to note that Classical IP Over ATM and LAN Emulation are not mutually exclusive. For example, network planners may choose to have ATM-attached hosts run Classical IP and LAN Emulation simultaneously. However, the different models will not directly interoperate without the intervention of a gateway device. An ATM host that speaks "Classical IP over ATM" will not be able to communicate to a host that speaks "ATM Forum LAN Emulation" without going through an IP router that understands both these models. A host in a LAN Emulation network communicating with a host in the Classical IP Over ATM network will have to go through an edge device or router that uses both these protocols. But when all the devices using the same protocol are using the same model, this interoperability issue is not as critical. In fact, most environments will continue to need bridging and routing, and it is likely that the ATM Forum LAN Emulation model and the new multiprotocol model will continue to coexist in many environments.

Key components to assist the migration from today's LAN internetworks to these newer models are edge devices with legacy LAN and ATM interfaces, and routers with native ATM support. Both of these devices allow existing LAN internetworks to interconnect with the new ATM based LAN internetworking solutions. With the LAN Emulation model, one can link to legacy LANs through a LAN-to-ATM bridge or through a router with an ATM interface that understands LAN Emulation. With the Classical IP over ATM model, one must use an IP router to link legacy LAN internetworks to the Classical IP hosts. In the multiprotocol model, one can link to legacy LANs through a LAN-to-ATM network-layer intelligent switch or through a traditional router with an ATM interface that understands the multiprotocol over ATM protocol.

Finally, network managers must have guarantees from vendors that the products they are buying will be upgradeable to support the functionality planned for the long term. For example, a user may start by implementing MAC-layer LAN Emulation today, but have plans to deploy Multiprotocol over ATM as the standard becomes finalized. If the products he buys today are not designed to accommodate network layer intelligence, a significant upgrade may be needed some time in the future. While initial networks are likely to be fairly simple, customers need to understand their vendor's rollout plans for new features, as well as their own long-term architecture before making significant investments.

5.8 References

67 ISO/IEC 10038: ANSI/IEEE Std. 802.1D Information processing systems-Local Area Networks-MAC Sublayer Interconnection (MAC Bridges).

68 W. Richard Stevens, *TCP/IP Illustrated,* Reading, MA: Addison-Wesley, 1994.

69 D. L. Spohn, *Data Network Design,* New York, NY: McGraw-Hill, 1993.

70 The ATM Forum, "ATM User-Network Interface Specification," Englewood Cliffs, NJ: Prentice Hall, 1993.

71 J. Heinanen, Request for Comments: 1483, "Multiprotocol Encapsulation over ATM Adaptation Layer 5*,"* July 1993, `http://www.ietf.org`

72 M. Laubach, Request for Comments: 1577, "Classical IP and ARP over ATM," January 1994, `http://www.ietf.org`

73 G. Armitage, Request for comments 2022, "Support for Multicast over UNI 3.0/3.1 based ATM Networks," November, 1996, `http://www.ietf.org`

chapter 6

Virtual LANs and Multiprotocol Over ATM

As described in Chapter 5, running Client/Server applications over ATM networks is possible today; however, the techniques of LAN Emulation and Classical IP Over ATM are only starting points. To take advantage of ATM's tremendous potential, new paradigms in network design and in new product development must be undertaken.

Multiprotocol Over ATM (MPOA) is a product of this paradigm shift and will revolutionize the way client/server networks are built. MPOA can be viewed as solving the problems of establishing connections between pairs of hosts that cross administrative domains, and enabling applications to make use of a network's ability to provide guaranteed quality of service. In the ATM Forum the work on these next generation protocols has been assigned to the MPOA working group.

These changes in paradigms are already beginning to be felt, as manufacturers release products that separate switching from routing, and allow applications to designate their required quality of service.

This chapter will present new ideas that are being applied to network design and routing problems. It will also discuss one of the more interesting developments in ATM, the Multiprotocol specification, and how network managers can apply the concepts in this specification to build next generation networks and applications. Before describing the details of MPOA, the goals from the perspective of virtual LANs are reviewed.

6.1 Virtual LANs

The concept of virtual LANs is a generic idea referring to the ability to partition one physical network into several logical networks. While many vendors claim to have unique virtual LAN models, in most cases, the models reduce to the logical addresses of clients and servers being separated from their physical location.

There are at least two ways to view virtual LAN models:

- Port-centric, referring to a collection of distributed network ports that are administratively configured to appear to all come from one common hub.

- Device-centric, in which the virtual LAN is associated with the computers network address and is not associated with the network point of attachment.

The port-centric model defines a virtual LAN as a collection of physical ports either associated with LAN or ATM switch interfaces. Clients are manually assigned to a virtual LAN, and the ports that make up the virtual LAN are kept in a database. This model operates as a MAC layer bridge transporting messages between members of the virtual LAN. In the port model, a client's address is static. It is the network's responsibility to correctly partition clients and forward ARP messages. Moving a client from one port to another removes it from its virtual LAN, requiring managed virtual LAN database to be manually updated to reflect the change.

In the device-centric model, hosts are identified by their either their MAC (e.g., IEEE 802.3) address or their Network Layer address [74] (e.g., IP address). In the device-centric model network, the administrator assigns clients to a virtual LAN group using their address as an identifier. Both the location of clients and the transport of data between clients are managed by the network and are based on the client's address. Clients are automatically grouped into their proper virtual network when they are moved because the network recognizes the address disappearing from one location and later reappearing in a different location. Because it is network controlled, the device-centric model requires no configuration by the network manager to deal with moves.

In either the port or device virtual LAN model, the network is not just a transparent pipe but is knowledgeable about the connected devices. For this reason, the network is capable of detecting duplication of addresses or the addition of unauthorized addresses. This can be a very useful feature to help network administrators cope with the problem of incorrectly addressed hosts which can disrupt correctly addressed hosts. More importantly, the network can detect when a malicious user has attached a device to the network in an attempt to eavesdrop. By creating virtual LANs, the ability to eavesdrop is reduced, and security can be much higher than for conventional shared media.

An additional use for virtual LANs is in the area of policy administration and security. Virtual LANs can be used to divide the network into a group of hosts, and to restrict the servers that these groups can access. In this way, the virtual LAN acts like a firewall to provide additional security. Without virtual LANs the network administrator needs to establish filters and access lists in routers or on servers. Device-centric or port-centric virtual LANs allow the network administrator to support filtering functions at the granularity of IP addresses, TCP port numbers, or MAC addresses. Virtual LANs are limited only by the security of the database and the facilities in the network layer protocol (e.g., TCP port numbers) for their support. The major drawback of the techniques described above is that they are nonstandards-based and potentially limited in how large the total system can grow. Whereas, MPOA provides the same function with standards based technology and is not limited with regards to scalability.

6.1.1 Virtual LANs with ATM

While virtual LAN capability is possible over almost any network media, it is especially suited to the connection-oriented nature of ATM. ATM is well suited because administratively controlled virtual circuit connection setup is required before two hosts can communicate. Additional administrative control can be maintained on an ATM network because addresses are dynamically assigned via the Interim Local Management Interface (ILMI) [75] protocol and ARP/Broadcast servers are used to segregate and locate other hosts.

Applying ATM to virtual LANs is attractive from both a manufacturer's and network designer's perspective. Manufacturers view virtual LANs as an opportunity to focus their skills on building a specialized device that is less complex than a conventional multiprotocol router, as shown in Figure 6.1. For example, a LAN Emulation bridge is a product that only understands how to register itself on the ATM LAN and communicate with the ATM servers. With only these capabilities, and no knowledge of routing protocols, it can participate in a complicated campus network. To a network designer, virtual LANs are attractive because they provide the ability to invest in one common fabric for the enterprise network. For example, several ATM switches may be interconnected on a campus network. The attached devices may be a set of routers and a set of high performance workstations. The network administration, through virtual LAN technology, can use one network to interconnect all of these devices, however, the workstations can be isolated from the routers. The network is centrally managed but is logically firewalled into many administratively separate sections.

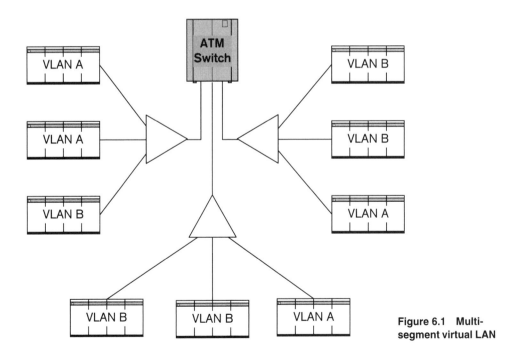

Figure 6.1 Multi-segment virtual LAN

Virtual LANs empower the ATM network designer with several new capabilities for:

- Dividing the processes of routing from switching as data passes through the network

- Subdividing working groups by administrative boundaries with one common network infrastructure

- Providing the potential to aggregate large amounts of traffic, on very high-speed connections, towards servers which are members of many virtual LANs

- Providing the capability to act as a filtering or firewall device

- Providing centralized maintenance of work group membership, making moves, adds, and changes easier

- Being virtual LANs standards based

At a minimum, segmenting the enterprise ATM network into multiple virtual LANs is desirable to improve scaling. Dividing the network is useful so that broadcast/multicast domains are limited to a reasonable size, hence, the total network load from this traffic is localized. Limiting the distribution of broadcast traffic may be especially important in the LAN Emulation model, where broadcasts may be more frequent. Stopping multicast traffic will play an increasingly important role as bandwidth hungry multimedia client/server applications become more prevalent. Lastly, virtual LANs provide new capabilities that simplify configuration and management of LAN internetworks.

The two techniques for building ATM networks discussed in chapter 5, LAN Emulation and Classical IP Over ATM can be used to build basic virtual LANs. In the ATM Forum's LAN Emulation model, a virtual LAN is equivalent to an emulated LAN. Inter-emulated LAN communication requires a router that is a member of two or more emulated LANs.

In the Classical IP Over ATM model, the philosophy is very similar. In this model, a virtual LAN is a group of hosts aggregated into a Logical IP Subnetwork or LIS. Membership in the virtual LAN is controlled by the ARP server. Like LAN Emulation, intervirtual LAN communication is made by routers which are members of multiple Classical IP Over ATM networks. When dealing with routeable protocols, each of these virtual LAN models is applied to networks on subnet boundaries or domains.

6.1.2 Virtual LAN with Multiprotocol Over ATM

In the Multiprotocol Over ATM model, a virtual LAN is similar to a virtual subnet or virtual network. However, intervirtual LAN connections are not necessarily mediated by routers. With MPOA, hosts are capable of directly communicating with each other, even in the case where the path is between different LISs. In the MPOA model, hosts on different LISs are empowered with the ability to communicate without passing data through routers.

By decoupling the tight association between logical and physical address mappings of subnets, a single subnet can span multiple physical ports. This allows virtual LANs to cleanly support virtual offices that can be secure and mobile. With MPOA, any layer 3 protocol will be able to communicate across the ATM network without using routers, and make quality of service requests.

The MPOA model operates by relying on route servers to maintain knowledge of the location of devices. When the location is found, the ATM network can be used to place a call directly between hosts. This model is very similar to using directory assistance on a voice network. The directory assistance agent is asked for the phone number of a destination and returns the value. With the phone number, a call can be place to the desired destination. However, with MPOA there will be no restriction on local versus long-distance directory assistance.

The work on MPOA is still proceeding within the ATM Forum. However, the Forum has specified the protocol model and decided on the interaction between the various components. The Forum has also decided that the LAN Emulation specification will form the foundation of MPOA. The protocol specification is being released in two versions. The first addresses inter-LIS communcation. The second concerns quality of service.

6.2 Comparing Multiprotocol Over ATM with LAN Emulation

When comparing the MPOA model to LAN Emulation, it is important to consider the following points:

- MPOA is an evolution of the LAN Emulation model. MPOA will make use of LAN Emulation services.
- LAN Emulation operates at OSI layer 2 [76], hence, it is bridging.
- MPOA operates at both OSI layer 2 and layer 3, hence, it is both bridging and routing.
- LAN Emulation hides ATM/QoS, MPOA exposes both.

Clearly, virtual LANs, using LAN Emulation or MPOA, are extremely useful tools for building multiprotocol corporate networks. The challenge now is to devise methods to successfully develop and deploy technology to meet the requirements. MPOA is a first step in meeting that challenge.

6.3 Introduction to Multiprotocol Over ATM

The choice of LAN Emulation versus Classical IP Over ATM is primarily based on the type of traffic carried on the network. If performance is important, then Classical IP Over ATM should be used. However, if more that one network layer protocol is being used, then LANE is the only viable solution. LANE emulation enables the network designer to treat ATM as a bridged legacy LAN. Classical IP Over ATM treats ATM as a point to point link between hosts.

Because LANE provides an emulated layer 2 bridge, it is clearly the technique for running client/server applications over ATM in a multiprotocol environment. LAN Emulation is also the only one that is currently capable of supporting multicast traffic. If IP is the only internetworking protocol, then the simplicity and lower latency of Classical IP Over ATM is very desirable. However, both approaches are limited in deployment because both methods utilize increasingly antiquated models of network design.

The advantages of MPOA are as follows:

- Clients can establish direct connections to remote servers without using routers
- Lower latency in establishing connections between devices
- Reduced amount of broadcast traffic
- Flexibility in selection of Maximum Transfer Unit size to optimize performance

LAN Emulation and Classical IP Over ATM still suffer from the traditional mind set of segregating networks into subnetworks, interconnected by routers. While this paradigm was the logical transition from bridged interworking, and has worked well for over a decade, it may soon be replaced by techniques that allow clients to communicate directly across administrative domains without using routers. Direct communication means clients and servers will reduce both processing delays and bottlenecks introduced by interconnected routers. Also, and potentially even more powerfully, clients and servers interconnected by ATM switches can utilize ATM's quality of service.

The benefits of the MPOA solution are:

- It provides the connectivity of a fully routed environment
- It takes advantage of ATM, direct interdomain connection, and QoS
- It separates switching from routing
- It provides a unified approach to layer 3 protocols over ATM

The standardization of this new paradigm has been ongoing for several years in multiple standards bodies. Only recently have these forces come together to develop a common set of interfaces and protocols. The ATM Forum is a major focal point for this effort and their work on new protocols has been allocated to the Multiprotocol Over ATM working group. This group is influenced by, and works closely with, the IETF's Routing Over Large Clouds (ROLC) [78] group and the Internet Services group [77]. The two groups have been working on solutions to address the shortcomings of LAN Emulation and IPv4. The cooperative effort has yielded the Next Hop Resolution Protocol (NHRP) [78] and the MPOA protocols that will form the basis of the next generation of networks.

6.3.1 Cut-through routing

Consider the scenario where every time two people wanted to talk, they had to use an interpreter as a middleman. In this situation, delays in getting messages passed and increased complexity would be the norm. Ironically, this mediated conversation example is very similar to running client/server applications over existing IP router networks. As discussed in Chapter 5, both Classical IP Over ATM and LAN Emulation suffer from the limitation that hosts in different logical subnets, but attached to the same ATM network, must communicate through routers. The traditional model of routing is shown in Figure 6.2.

Directly establishing communication between a client and a server in different subnets without using a router is very desirable because of the potential improvements in performance and scalability. This technique is referred to as *cut-through* routing because it bypasses routers and cuts a path through the ATM network. This is illustrated in Figure 6.3. Cut-through allows hosts to find the address of the destination, even if it is in a different administrative domain, and establishes direct communication with that destination. Cut-through uses route servers to acquire information about the host on the network, but then relies on layer 2 technology to communicate with the remote host.

Establishing a direct virtual circuit that crosses multiple administrative domains is a very complex problem which is referred to as the *large cloud problem*. One can appreciate this problem by considering conventional routing protocols. Typically, routing

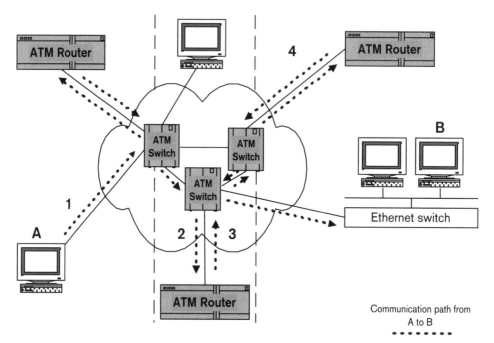

Figure 6.2   Large clouds

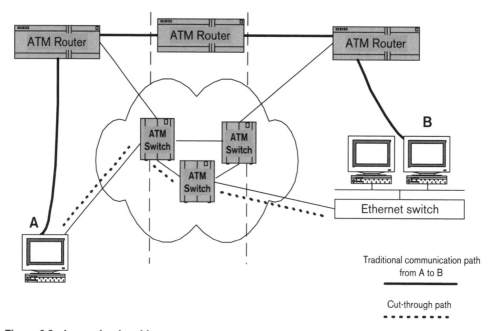

Figure 6.3   Large cloud problem

protocols operate by summarizing or aggregating information to build their routing tables. When information is summarized, details about the layer 2 technology are either lost or hidden by the routing protocol. For applications to establish direct communication across an ATM network they need the details of exact locations of destination, not summarizations.

MPOA, in performing cut-through, also needs these details (e.g., ATM addresses) to set up virtual circuit between hosts. To cope with this problem, MPOA has an associated query protocol. The query protocol is used as a probe to follow the routed path to the destination. When the query protocol reaches the final route server, it asks that server for the layer 2 address of the destination computer. When the ATM address is returned, the source can establish a virtual circuit that can cut through the ATM cloud.

The NHRP is a protocol designed to deal with networks like Frame Relay, X.25, and ATM, since it supports direct virtual circuits between attached hosts. In a network supporting virtual circuits, devices attached to the same network must establish paths or calls in order to exchange data but, unlike LANs, the network lacks the ability to easily broadcast a message to all hosts. In the NHRP model, these networks are called *non-broadcast, multiaccess* (NBMA) [78].

The NBMA NHRP allows a host or router to determine the internetworking layer addresses and NBMA addresses of suitable "NBMA next hops" toward a destination station. A subnetwork can be nonbroadcast either because it technically doesn't support the function, as is the case with Frame Relay and ATM, or because broadcasting would not be feasible, as is the case with large SMDS networks [81]. If the destination is connected to the NBMA subnetwork, then the NBMA next hop is the destination station itself. Otherwise, the NBMA next hop is the egress router from the NBMA subnetwork that is "nearest" to the destination station.

NHRP describes a next hop resolution method that relaxes the forwarding restrictions of the LIS model. For example, when the internetwork layer address is IP, once the NBMA next hop has been resolved, the source may either immediately start sending IP packets to the destination on a connectionless network, or may first establish a connection to the destination with the desired bandwidth and QoS characteristics, if the hosts are connected to a connection-oriented network.

The last topic that needs some explanation before examining the MPOA protocol in detail is the concept of a "Distributed Router." Distributed routing is the realization of breaking apart the higher level functions for route determination from the lower level functions of switching data as, or before, it passes through a network. A distributed router consists of a central route server that controls multiple edge devices, as shown in Figure 6.4. In a distributed router, the edge devices do most of the switching. Routing servers run routing protocols and supply routes to the edge devices. Together, the route server and edge devices can be used to build layer 3 protocol independent distributed

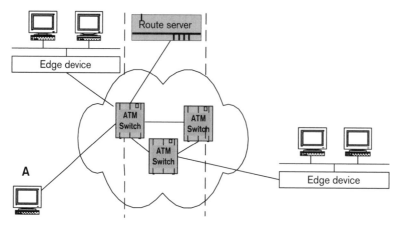

Figure 6.4 Distributed router

architectures. As will be shown, this distributed router is an excellent way of conceptualizing MPOA. In MPOA, functions are defined and the actual implementation of these functions is distributed throughout the cloud.

6.4 Multiprotocol Over ATM requirements

The goals and model framework of MPOA were established in late 1995 by the ATM Forum. Two of the principal goals of MPOA are allowing different administrative domains to concurrently exist on one physical ATM network, and supporting communication between any two devices running layer 3 protocols. An additional goal is the ability for hosts to make use of ATM ability to support different qualities of service. MPOA plans to leverage much of the knowledge gained by the ROLC work and to extend its model to allow multiple protocols and distributed routing architectures. This will all be accomplished in the realm of lower-cost edge devices that are network layer intelligent. The remainder of this chapter focuses on the MPOA model. Details of using quality of service and additional information on applications driving quality of service are deferred to Chapter 7.

MPOA's key requirements are:

- Allowing MPOA devices to establish direct ATM connections
- Integration with LAN Emulation

- Support for firewalling and protocol filtering
- Support for multicast and broadcast traffic
- Support for automatic configuration of ATM hosts
- Separation of switching and routing concerns

As can be expected, the product of the joint work between the ATM Forum and the IETF has generated substantial interest within the industry. The completed specification will reduce limitations found in previous models. In addition, it will provide a higher performance, scaleable solution for LAN internetworking over ATM that will enable next-generation applications.

6.5 Multiprotocol Over ATM overview

In the MPOA model, the ATM fabric is considered one physical network capable of supporting many virtual LANs. In a sense, the ATM network can be visualized as an emulated multiprotocol bridge/router with the addition of quality of service and very high bandwidth capabilities. An MPOA network (Figure 6.5) consists of several network layer aware components. These can be subdivided into router servers, edge connection devices, broadcast servers, and LIS coordinators.

Edge devices and ATM attached hosts, communicate with the MPOA servers to perform address resolution analogous to LAN Emulation. However, MPOA adds two

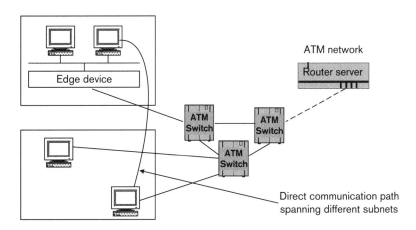

Figure 6.5   MPOA network

major capabilities. First, the MPOA system actively helps find destinations that are not a member of the LIS. Second, MPOA supports direct mapping of network layer addresses to ATM addresses. This allows for the construction of virtual LANs based on layer 3 parameters, and does away with the need to map layer 2 virtual LAN and layer 3 subnets as in LAN Emulation. Because layer 3 addresses are mapped to ATM addresses, boundaries on layer 3 subnets are also eliminated.

The result is the ability to support global virtual LANs that operate independent of and beyond traditional router boundaries. Hosts that are members of different subnets can communicate directly across the ATM network without passing through an intermediate packet-based bridge/router. The MPOA model also provides for the support of legacy physical layers and legacy routing protocols which ensures interoperability with pre-existing networks.

The MPOA model is similar to RFC 1577 because it supports direct association of IP addresses with ATM addresses. However, the MPOA model goes beyond the Classical IP specification because MPOA clients are empowered with the knowledge of the ATM addresses belonging to devices outside of their subnet. MPOA also provides mechanisms for Broadcast/Multicast support that are lacking in Classical IP Over ATM. The MPOA client protocol stack is shown in Figure 6.6.

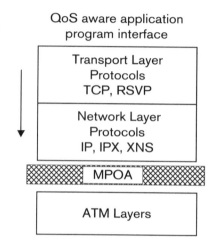

Figure 6.6   MPOA client protocol stack

6.6 Components and architecture

MPOA is work in progress and this description should be considered as a statement of direction of the protocol as it existed at the time of writing. The first version of MPOA will be limited in functionality and only include LANE with the addition of cut-through routing. Subsequent versions will address the problems of layer 3 protocol to ATM mappings for quality of service and multicast.

MPOA is built from special purpose servers, new software on ATM attached devices, and the information flows between these components. The implementation and separation of actual processes running on devices is left to the implementor. The MPOA model only defines logical components, not products. To subdivide the set of processes that makes up the MPOA system, the term *functional group* is used. A functional group is just a collection of closely interrelated tasks. The key architectural components are:

- Edge connection devices that are used to physically connect legacy networks to an MPOA system. These are similar to LANE bridges.

- Route servers which contain topological information gained by running routing protocols and distributing state.

- Internet Address Summarization Groups (IASG) which are logical subnets administered similarly to LANE's server.

- IASG coordination functions which are the logical information flows between all of the devices in the MPOA system.

From a high level of granularity, MPOA's logical components can be broken into clients and servers such that:

- An MPOA server maintains global knowledge of the layer 2 and layer 3 protocols and topologies for the areas they serve.

- An MPOA client is only responsible for maintaining a listing of layer 2 addresses to layer 3 for the hosts with which it is communicating.

6.6.1 Multiprotocol Over ATM functional groups

In the MPOA protocol suite, the concept of functional groups is used to coordinate which aspects of the protocol should be performed by which devices. Components of a functional group are closely related so that they are provided by a single logical component of the MPOA system. A functional group is only conceptual and the actual implementation of the group's duties may be allocated to one or many devices. It is left to manufacturers to decide where in the MPOA systems applications will run. The defined functional groups are shown in Figure 6.7.

The defined groups are:

- *Edge Device Functional Group (EDFG)*   A device that is used to connect a legacy LAN to an MPOA network. This device understands how to operate in an MPOA network and buffers the legacy LAN devices from MPOA specifics.

- *ATM attached Host Functional Group (AHFG)*   This functional group is concerned with the set of properties understood by hosts directly connected to the ATM MPOA network.

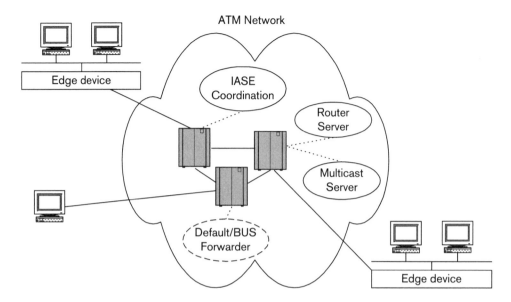

Figure 6.7 MPOA functional groups

- *Internetwork Address Subgroup Coordination Functional Group (ICFG)* This is the group of functions that is required to support the distribution of a single "subnet" across multiple legacy LANs and ATM ports. This functional group is similar to a LANE Server.

- *Default Forwarder Function Group (DFFG)* This functional group is very similar to LAN Emulation's Broadcast and Unknown Server (BUS). It is responsible for the operation of forwarding data in the absence of direct client-to-client connectivity.

- *Router Server Functional Group (RSFG)* This group of procedures is at the heart of MPOA/NHRP and is responsible for distribution of layer 3 (e.g., IP, IPX) information in the system. This group will participate with legacy peering sessions using legacy routing protocols, and communicate the results among the MPOA route servers. It will also answer queries to locate hosts. It can be considered the glue that connects two LANE servers.

- *Remote Forwarder Functional Group (RFFG)* This group is tightly coupled with the RSFG and is responsible for forwarding traffic from an originating client, then across the MPOA system, and finally to the destination client in the absence of a direct virtual circuit. This functional group can be considered as a global DFFG.

6.6.2 Multiprotocol Over ATM
information flows

An MPOA system utilizes several information flows between the various functional groups listed above. The information flows describe how the functional groups exchange MPOA state information. The information flows can be categorized as:

- *Configuration Flows*   All functional groups use these flows to retrieve configuration information and register themselves in the network.
- *Data Transfer Flows*   The actual transmission of information between hosts using an MPOA system.
- *Client Control Flows*   These flows are used after configuration to query the MPOA servers and inform servers of state change.
- *Server Control Flows*   Informational flows between MPOA servers which contain routing information and assist in client-to-client connection establishment.

The above information flows can be further subdivided into "sub-flows" that perform detailed operations.

Clients that are members of an MPOA system will need to pass information to:

- Their route servers to obtain address resolution information
- Their ICFGs for destination resolution of intra-IASG traffic
- A default forwarding device, which like a LANE BUS, will forward data in the absence of a direct point to point VCC

MPOA servers pass information used to:

- Establish peering conversation with other RSFGs
- Communicate with ICFGs to communicate topology information to ICFGs that serve a given subnet

6.7 Multiprotocol Over
ATM operation

As previously discussed, the MPOA system works by allocating tasks to functional groups and then defining the protocol's operation by specifying information flows between the functional groups.

In defining the information flows between functional groups, the ATM Forum has broken the problem into specific cases that correspond to different states of the protocol:

- Startup and configuration
- Registration and discovery
- Host to host data exchange
- Routing protocol support

6.7.1 Startup and configuration

Like LAN Emulation, devices in an MPOA network must contact a configuration server at boot time. The configuration server knows which clients are associated with which virtual networks and notifies the client of its server's ATM address. When route servers and subnet coordination servers (ICFGs) are initialized, they will need to be given the identity of the subnets they control along with the layer 3 protocol types used. In addition, the route server is a member of the subnets so it also acquires a layer 3 address.

When legacy bridges and ATM attached hosts are initialized on an MPOA network, they will need to be given information about which protocol they should be using (e.g., IP or IPX), and what host is providing the function of intra-subnet coordination. In addition, the ATM address of the Route server and Default Forwarder will be required.

6.7.2 Registration, discovery, and routing

The registration and discovery state occurs just after initialization and concerns the set of exchanges that is used by functional groups to inform each other of their existence, capabilities, and domains. The term discovery, when related to edge devices, describes reporting their legacy attached devices to the subnetwork coordination function. As ATM attached hosts join the network, they register themselves with the subnetwork coordination function servers that they learned about during startup. When an ATM attached host registers, it is providing layer 3 protocol addresses that it supports and placing these address into the ICFG database. At this point, the clients have acquired address/group information and are registered with their servers. They can now begin to communicate among themselves.

6.7.3 Data exchange

Data flow through an MPOA system can be either one of two types: uni-cast or multi-cast. In the MPOA system, uni-cast, or point-to-point communication, can further be subdivided into two categories: default flows or short cut flows. The default flow mechanism is similar to a LAN BUS and is used whenever short cut flows are not possible. Default host-to-host data communication is done using one of the default forwarding servers, either the RFFG or the DFFG. The use of the RFFG is intended for remote hosts, otherwise the data is sent to the DFFG.

All EDFGs are to use the LANE BUS default forwarder. When a packet arrives at a DFFG it checks to see if the destination ATM host is one that is registered to that DFFG. If it is registered, then the data is forwarded to the ATM host. If the address has not been registered, the packet is forwarded using the routing system (e.g., the RFFG). If data arrives at a DFFG and destination is registered as an EDFG, the data is forwarded to the destination using LANE.

The MPOA Route Server is responsible for executing traditional routing protocols with hosts on the legacy media reachable through EDFGs or with directly connected ATM hosts. The route server determines which subnets it is responsible for, via information flow between itself and the ICFGs. In order for short cut data transfer to work, the ICFG and RSFG must interoperate very closely.

Short cut data transfer is accomplished by establishing a virtual circuit across the ATM network and communicating directly with the ATM destination. After the ARP process is completed, short cut completely does away with intermediate default forwarding systems and should therefore provide lower latency and higher quality of service.

When a source attempts to locate another computer in the MPOA system it asks its local ICFG. The ICFG then forwards the request, on behalf of the source, to the Route Server (RFFG). If the destination is in another IASG handled by the RSFG it will generate a response to the ICFG. The ICFG in turn forwards the response to the source which can then establish a VCC. If the RSFG believes that the destination is reachable via another RSFG, it forwards the query to the other RSFG. This pattern is followed until a RSFG is reached which contains the sources IASG. When the RSFG responds to the query, it saves the ATM address of the requester so that if there are any changes in routing or reachability, the source can be notified. When changes occur, the source will be forced to disconnect the VCC between itself and the destination and reestablish a new VCC after repeating the address resolution process.

6.7.4 Multicast support

Multicast data transfer can be accomplished by either:

- Having the source create a multicast tree with itself as the root
- Using a multicast server

The technique used to create a multicast session is governed by the complexity of managing multiple VCCs versus load placed on the network and the availability of the multicast server.

In the case of source created multicast trees, the originator can establish several point-to-point connections to all of the multicast destinations. The source in this case either creates several point-to-point connections that originate from itself, or optionally, it may use the capabilities of the ATM network in creating the multicast tree. Utilizing the network to create the multicast tree is done either by issuing UNI 3.1 add party messages [79], or a UNI 4.0 [80] third party call setup message.

There are several potential problems with this approach. The first is that a mechanism is needed for sources to determine which clients want to be members of the multicast tree. This facility can be provided by a multicast server that maintains group information. The server would operate by gathering ATM addresses from hosts periodically. If a client wanted to create a multicast session, it would ask the multicast server for the members of the group. The servers response would need to be a reliable transmission of a data structure containing all of the group members. Implementing this scheme on a large network has yet to be accomplished so no one can be sure of the exact performance. However, if the multicast group contains thousand of destinations, a great deal of time may be spent in just transmitting and processing group membership messages.

The second major problem with source created multicast trees is their ability to effectively utilize network bandwidth. When trees are created by clients using point-to-point virtual circuits, the network may not be utilized efficiently. For example, if several hosts wanted to participate in a video conferencing session, they would need to be able to exchange data among themselves. Over an ATM network this would require that a virtual circuit be established between each host on the conference. Without a full mesh of circuits, some participants would be cut off from the conference. This again raises serious concerns about the network's ability to scale, both from the standpoint of bandwidth capacity and complexity.

One potential technique to improve the ability to multicast in an ATM network would be to use a multicast server. A multicast server would be similar to the address maintenance servers described above, however, it would be the focal point of the multicast session. When hosts wanted to create a multicast session, they would contact the server with the list of clients that are to participate. The multicast server would then create virtual circuits from itself to all of the destinations. By using the multicast server as the focal point, the total number of virtual circuits needed is reduced, and additional members can transparently be added without informing all participants. However, a multicast server will be limited by the bandwidth of its link to the ATM network, and its internal processing ability. If a multicast server was the focal point for several concurrent video conferences, it is not unrealistic to think that with today's technology it will only be able to handle 5–10 concurrent sessions.

6.8 Summary

The goals of MPOA are to bring together several different interworking technologies to achieve a level of functionality that to date is unparalleled. To recap, MPOA provides network designers with the capability of building systems that will:

- Allow for the creation of virtual LANs on one physical network.
- Empower applications with the ability to use quality of server parameters and standardize quality of server requests between the clients and ATM networks.
- Allow clients to directly communicate with servers in different domains, without passing all data through routers.

As described in Chapter 5, LANE and Classical IP Over ATM specifications are effective in allowing users to quickly deploy ATM. However, the speed in deployment is a compromise and the user must be willing to give up ATM's rich quality of service capabilities. Exposing the ATM layer and allowing applications to make use of quality of service parameters, while supporting virtual LANs, is a major benefit of MPOA.

Corporate implementation of MPOA should be viewed from two perspectives. First, the network administrator will need to understand the various servers and work with their vendors to build the system infrastructure. The basic components of the MPOA solution will be ATM switches and ATM hosts. These can be the same devices that are currently connected to a LANE or Classical IP Over ATM network. The migration to MPOA will involve adding the MPOA servers to the network, which, may be as simple as upgrading the ATM switch control software. The third hardware component will be the addition of MPOA bridges. In all likelihood, basic MPOA bridging will be achievable via software upgrades to LANE bridges.

Initially, MPOA and LANE networks are very similar and actually start to differ only when their size grows, or users execute applications that use quality of service. Because MPOA and LANE are so tightly coupled, it seems reasonable for corporate planners to deploy LANE today, with the intent on migrating to MPOA. As the network grows, administrators will be able to create additional virtual workgroups that can all share one ATM switch fabric.

The ATM Forum has take a very aggressive role in developing implementation agreements and the MPOA specification is expected to be completed in the first quarter of 1997. Compliant products will most likely follow shortly thereafter. However, because the fundamentals of the protocol, and the interaction between components has been specified, products may be available at the same time as a completed specification.

The second area where MPOA planners will play a key role is the deployment of applications that utilize quality of service. In order for applications to fully exploit quality of service on an MPOA system, they must be able to communicate their traffic characteristics to the network. This requires that a new application program interface (API) be developed along with new applications designed to use the quality of service API.

Currently, the work of defining a common API used to support real time traffic and resource reservations is *primarily* being done in the IETF.* The ATM Forum plans to use the IETF's API, and associated networking mechanisms, as a basis for application developers to write programs that use quality of service. The resulting solution from these groups will be a multiprotocol LAN internetwork scheme that scales in size, and better leverages the capabilities of the ATM fabric. Applications that make use of the new API, coupled with a network that can support quality of service, will have successfully migrated away from the traditional shared media paradigm.

6.9 References

74 W. R. Stevens, *TCP/IP Illustrated,* Reading, MA: Addison-Wesley, 1994.

75 The ATM Forum, "ATM User-Network Interface Specification," Englewood Cliffs, NJ: Prentice Hall, 1993.

76 M. Rose, *The Open Book,* Englewood Cliffs, NJ: Prentice Hall, 1992.

77 R. Braden, L. Zhang, S. Berson, "Resource ReSerVation Protocol (RSVP)-Version 1 Functional Specification," http://www.isi.edu/rsvp

78 D. Katz, D. Piscitello, and B. Cole, "NBMA Next Hop Resolution Protocol (NHRP)," ftp://ietf.cnri.reston.va.us/internet-drafts/

79 The ATM Forum, "ATM User-Network Interface Specification," Englewood Cliffs NJ: Prentice Hall, v3.1, 1995.

80 The ATM Forum, "ATM User-Network Interface Specification," v4.0, http://www.atmforum.com

81 D.L. Spohn, *Data Network Design*, New York, NY: McGraw-Hill, 1993.

---

*   Resource reservation is covered in more detail in Chapter 7.

chapter 7

Client/server technology over ATM, the Internet models

Currently, there is an explosion of growth in distributed client/server applications. The Internet and World Wide Web have accelerated this growth with easy-to-use Web browsers, distributed computing environments, and widespread availability of network service providers.

This chapter discusses client/server applications over IP, and integrated IP/ATM networks. The first section reviews multimedia programs, standards, and network requirements. The second section places IP and ATM integration into common infrastructure to support multimedia applications.

The data communications industry is moving towards interconnecting audio, video, and existing techniques to produce more powerfully integrated environments. These uses are much more demanding of network resources, like bandwidth, than their predecessors. To meet the demands of future applications, the underlying networks and protocols must provide facilities for deterministic delivery of data.

Existing Internet software is based on the TCP/IP protocol suite with little focus on the underlying network technologies. While TCP/IP does not provide the necessary real time data delivery features to enable these technologies, it is clearly the most successful standard protocol suite for Internet applications. In contrast, ATM was designed with features that support real time data delivery but does not have a widely installed base. Despite ATM not being fully integrated with TCP/IP at the software or network levels, this integration is in progress.

7.1 The client/server model

The client/server model of interest is the application level client/server model, shown in Figure 7.1. In this model, clients and servers are programs running on different computers in a mixed ATM-IP network. Users interact directly with client software, which in-turn interacts with server programs over the network to retrieve data for presentation. In fact, a single client may interact with many servers in different locations in the network, and may, in turn, be a server to other clients. This model should not be confused with the system level client/server model, where network server computers provide services (such as Networked File Systems) to client computers. There are four key applications that can be associated with this model:

- Video/audio teleconferencing
- Resource discovery or World Wide Web searching
- Information distribution (ie. those found in stock/commodities trade distribution)
- Electronic gaming

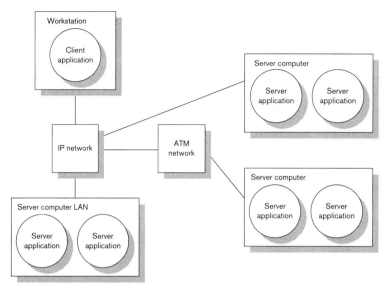

Figure 7.1   The client/server application, model

Each of the above applications requires different characteristics of the underlying network technology. Both one-to-many and many-to-many semantics are utilized with the additional complexity of dynamic joining and leaving of a communication group.

7.2 Real time communication: Standards and applications

Applications, such as real time video delivery, virtual reality, and real time simulations are increasingly becoming commonplace on the Internet. These programs involve real time constraints on the delivery of data that were unheard of only a few years ago. Though, IP does not directly support the features to provide real time constraints, these facilities are being developed so that the Internet can continue to expand the types of services it provides. ATM presently supplies the necessary support for real time applications, but since Internet applications are programmed for IP, they may require modifications to utilize ATM's QoS features.

In order to support multimedia, subtle features of both IP and ATM need to be understood at the application level. This chapter will discuss the issues and models for the integration of IP, ATM, and real time services. Before beginning a detailed analysis of protocols, a review of applications and standards that are driving this IP/ATM interconnection will be discussed.

7.2.1 Browser applications

Advances in multimedia application technology have taken place since the introduction of easy to use Internet Web browsers, such as NCSA Mosaic [92] and Netscape Navigator[93]. These programs integrate multimedia document access, file transfer, network news services, email, and other protocols into single hyper-text software with an easy to use point and click interface.

These software programs have been based on a download-and-view model, where the data is transferred from servers on the network to the local client which displays the data on the users computer. TCP/IP has supported them well because it has no timing or real time constraints on data delivery. However, the perceived acceptable performance may be short lived because browser technologies are now beginning to provide support for "live" interactive transmission, in which data and applications are delivered in real time over the network. Real time delivery is necessary for continuously changing data, or data that is too large to store on a local machine.

The next section covers common standards for these types of applications, then discusses the issues relating to ATM.

7.2.2 Browser protocols

HTML   HyperText Mark-up Language (HTML)[91] is a document composition language used to compose portable multi-media documents for the World Wide Web. HTML allows composition of multimedia documents consisting of text, images, graphics, special characters, and hyperlinks to other HTML documents on the network. HTML documents can bind data from multiple sites into a single document. In a client/server system, the document can be thought of as the client, with the ability to access multiple servers in multiple locations. The attractive features of HTML programming include:

- Combining text, graphics, images, and sounds
- Binding data from multiple servers into a single document
- Formatting language in text-based documents, making documents portable
- Providing built-in extensions for special purpose programming

An HTML document consists of text interspersed with HTML mark-up tags that define the presentation of the document and the location of data, and links within the document. Figure 7.2 shows a minimal HTML document with a link to the "HTML Beginners page." Figure 7.3 illustrates the result of viewing this document in the Netscape Navigator.

```
<TITLE>A simple HTML example</TITLE>
<H1>This is a level-one heading</H1>
Welcome to the world of HTML
This is one paragraph.<P>
This is a second paragraph.<P>
<h3>
<a href="http://www.ncsa.uiuc.edu/General/Internet/WWW/
HTMLPrimer.html">
This is a link to beginners information on HTML. </a>
</h3>
```

Figure 7.2 A simple HTML Document

HTML includes tags for the presentation of many data types, including:

- Titles and headings
- Paragraphs
- Links to other documents
- Numbered and unnumbered lists
- Preformatted text
- Extended quotes
- Email addresses
- Inline images and sounds
- Forms for communication to the server

Programming large HTML documents with text, graphics, images, and sound can become complicated due to cryptic HTML commands. Fortunately, there are a number of HTML editors that provide graphical *what you see is what you get* interfaces for creating HTML documents. To facilitate creating HTML documents, many editors supply template documents and forms that can be customized to suit the individual application. In addition, there are numerous tools for converting common document formats (i.e., Microsoft Word) into HTML.

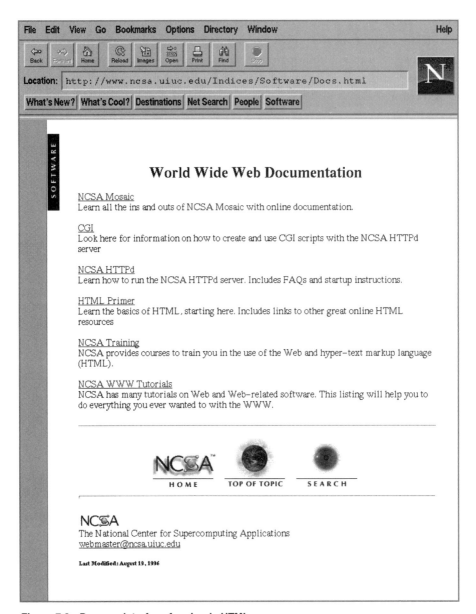

Figure 7.3   Browser interface for simple HTML

HTML, being a text description language, does not provide direct support for ATM networks. Information on ATM servers is supplied by IP over ATM solutions like those in RFC 1577. It is unlikely that the World Wide Web will adopt an end-to-end native ATM support in the near future. However, as more real time applications are introduced into the Web, there will be a demand for real time data delivery using IP/ATM networks. The demand will come from a need to have the World Wide Web (i.e., the Internet in general) provide different degrees of service depending on the application or the cost of the service. Applications will likely be adapted to real time services that are being developed for the integrated services model using IP and ATM. This is discussed in greater detail in Section 7.3.

It is only possible to speculate on the future of the World Wide Web's support of QoS, however, two possible paths are clear. The first direction includes integrating QoS parameters in the HTML language which can be communicated to the network, depending upon the type of application executed. In this case, HTML would have the ability, for example, to signal the network the special parameters to replay a video clip. The second possible path involves the tight coupling between underlying transport protocol, and HyperText Transfer Protocol (HTTP). In this case, it is the applications that are responsible for signaling QoS parameters to the network.

VRML　Virtual Reality Modeling Language (VRML)[95] is a language for interactive virtual reality applications that adds 3D capabilities to the World Wide Web. It provides the ability to program multi-user, interactive, virtual worlds hyper-linked with the World Wide Web. Virtual worlds can have hyper-links to other virtual worlds and HTML documents, and can contain text, images, sound, and animation. Currently, VRML 1.0 is available, along with a number of VRML browsers and plug-ins (Section 7.3). VRML 2.0 is still undergoing development, and numerous browser manufacturers have committed to supporting VRML 2.0 in their browsers or as add-ons.

It is likely that VRML applications will benefit from real time data delivery and multicast services. As with HTML/HTTP, it is unlikely that there will be native ATM support for VRML in the near future. However, as an integrated IP/ATM network with real time services is being developed, VRML and other real time applications might benefit from adaptive protocols (Section 7.3) for real time delivery of data over IP.

Java　The has been a great deal of activity centered around Java language [94], developed by Sun Microsystems. Java was developed to solve common problems in object-oriented languages such as C++. It is very similar to C++, with additional features that overcome common programming problems, such as memory management and multi-threading, and features that are attractive to distributed programming, such as built in security and network awareness.

Java is an object-oriented language, based on C++ with extensions from Objective C. It is both a compiled and an interpreted language. The Java compiler produces an architecture-independent byte code program that can be run on any platform to which the Java interpreter has been ported. The byte code contains type information and other compile time information from the program, allowing the interpreter to perform type checking and other security checks when running the program. For performance sensitive programs, the byte code can be translated into native machine code by the interpreter, which yields performance equivalent to that of the native C++ code. Java also includes built-in support for multi-threaded applications, synchronization, dynamic loading, and network protocols, such as HTTP and FTP.

Java Features   Java includes security features that are useful for distributed and Web programming. When a program, or applet, comes in to the interpreter, it undergoes a series of security checks. First, byte code verification is completed on the incoming byte code to ensure it is a safe Java file. Java checks that the file does not violate type or memory safety, that its language interfaces are properly utilized, and all the parameters are correctly used within the code. The Java loader inserts each new class into a separate name-space, and enforces a name resolution scheme that forbids the incoming code from replacing a built-in class. Finally, its networking package can be set up to allow or disallow all network access, permit access only to the host where the incoming code originates from, or admit access externally if the code arrives externally.

Java and the Network   Java is a network-aware language, allowing its programs to be transmitted over the network and run on any computer. This enables more complex, dynamic applications that take advantage of resources on both clients and servers. An applet can dynamically modify its behavior on the fly, responding to events at the client or server. For example, a Java applet can perform animation in the client, or can be used to dynamically assemble HTML documents.

A subset of the Java language, called JavaScript, is endorsed by leading companies as an open object programming language for the World Wide Web. Java has gained its wide popularity as an Internet programming language and this trend is expected to continue. The attractive features of Java, including the simplified programming model, portable applications, fast execution, network security, and threaded application support are already bringing a flood of new real time interactive applications. As these applications become available, there will be a push for real time data delivery services over an integrated IP/ATM Internet.

The main strengths of Java include portability, industrywide support, and the ability to make mini applications, or applets, available to download and run over the Internet. Although Java does not support real time applications directly, it is expected that these facilities will be integrated into the language as they become available at the application level in IP.

Plug-Ins Although browsers can integrate many protocols and data formats, they are limited to supporting common formats and protocols because of program size and complexity. To accommodate additional applications, most browsers provide support for external "helper applications." The browser handles data transfer, and starts the appropriate application to view the data. Since these applications are not part of the browser, they are not controlled through its interface or integrated with the supported data types. To support additional media types, algorithms, and browser extensions in an integrated environment, developers have moved toward a more modular and open approach that permits support modules to be plugged into the browser dynamically.

Plug-in technology provides software interfaces and hooks into the browser for programming new media types and applications. New data types and algorithms can be supported without requiring them to be compiled into the browser application. The plug-in interface allows third party developers to create new media types and algorithms while leveraging the browsers' facilities for handling the user interface, HTML, etc. The result is a seamless application interface that supports new data types and programs. There are numerous plug-ins available, ranging from MPEG players and speech synthesis to virtual reality systems based on VRML. Some of the plug-ins available for the Netscape Navigator include:

- *Adobe Acrobat Reader*   Supports access to PDO documents
- *Lightning Strike*   Wavelet image encoding and decoding
- *Live3D*   VRML interaction within the browser
- *OLE Controls*   Support for embedded OLE languages
- *Vosaic*   Support for real time audio
- *QuickTime*   Video support

What are the differences between Java and plug-ins? Both are browser extension technologies, but they are used in different ways. Plug-ins are binary program plug-ins that take advantage of the browser for HTML and interactive display. They provide more implementation freedom at the expense of portability. On the other hand, Java provides an environment within the browser for program execution. Its programs provide portability, but are limited to facilities in the Java environment within the browser. The differences are shown in Table 7.1.

Table 7.1 Differences between Java and plug-ins

	Java	Plug-ins
Portability	High	Low
Performance	Good	Better

Table 7.1 Differences between Java and plug-ins (continued)

	Java	Plug-ins
Security	Java security	Programmer implemented
Customization	Within environment	Fully customizable

7.2.3 Audio/video applications

Audio and video are being integrated into many new applications, including:

- *Telecommunications*   Audio/video conferencing
- *Distance learning*   Remote educational applications
- *Distance medicine*   Remote imaging and diagnosis
- *Remote security*   Remote observation
- *Remote control*   Industrial and robotics control
- *Entertainment*   Video/audio on demand

These programs utilize computers and networks to capture, manipulate, store, then transmit pictures, videos, and sound in a digital form. The issues to be considered for the integration of digital audio and video include data format, and transmission of the data over the network for real time display.

7.2.4 Audio/video standards

There are many standards [83] for digital audio/video capture, storage, and transmission, each targeted for specific applications. This section will discuss the following common formats: JPEG, MPEG, and H.261.

JPEG   JPEG [87] (from Joint Photographic Experts Groups) is a standard for compressing still, real-life color, gray-scale, and black and white images. JPEG is a lossy compression algorithm, meaning that the reproduced image is not exact. Instead, it is a close approximation of the original. A lossless variation of JPEG also exists, but is less widely used. It is possible to vary the degree of loss in a compressed JPEG image by varying the *quality* parameter, which in turn affects the compression ratio.

Higher quality results in less compression and an increased size of the resulting compressed image data. JPEG can achieve 20:1 image compression without visible loss of quality, thus making it suitable for compression of transmitted images.

Motion JPEG   Video can be compressed using motion JPEG, which applies the JPEG compression to each frame of the video, independently. In the past, real time compression or decompression of motion JPEG at full rate (30 frames or 60 fields per second) was beyond the capabilities of most computers, and required additional hardware support. This is no longer the case with fast processors and those processors with built-in multimedia instructions [88], [89].

For ATM applications there are a number of standalone motion JPEG encoder/decoder devices available that sit directly on the network, reducing the need for computer processing. These devices have inputs for audio and video, as well as an ATM interface. Some examples of these devices and their features include:

- *EMMI (Lucent)*   OC-3C ATM interface operating with AAL 5. The EMMI has a SCSI interface used for data transfer to a computer and to control the device.

- *MMX (STS)*   OC-3C ATM interface operating on a null AAL. The MMX is controlled through a serial port on the box; SNMP control is in development.

- *AVA/AVD (Fore)*   The AVA is an encoder device with a 155-Mbps interface operating on AAL 5. The AVA includes software to present audio/video on many computer platforms. The AVD is a stand-alone decoder companion device. The AVA and AVD devices are controlled over the ATM network by GUI applications.

MPEG   MPEG [85] is a bit-stream representation for synchronized digital video and audio. MPEG is designed to compress audio and video into a bitstream with a bandwidth of 1.5 Mbps, corresponding to CD ROM or DAT performance. MPEG is one of the standards on the Internet for video clip exchange, and produces picture quality similar to VHS video recording. A critical point to consider with MPEG is that it is currently the only video compression technology that the ATM Forum has developed a standard around.

The MPEG standard consists of three parts: video, audio and synchronization protocols. Video encoding compresses the video stream to about 1.15 Mbps. Audio encoding and synchronization data make use of the remaining bandwidth.

MPEG video encoding in the US uses a 352- by 240- pixel resolution at 30 frames per second. In Europe the resolution is 352- by 288- pixels at 25 frames per second. The MPEG algorithm does both inter- and intra- frame compression, and the resulting data format is bidirectional, allowing for rewind, fast forward, etc. The MPEG video stream results in three types of frames. *I* (intra) frames consist of compressed still images similar to motion JPEG frames; *P* (predicted) frames consist of compressed changes from the most recent *I* or *P* frame; and *B* (bidirectional) frames consist of interpolations between *I* and *P* frames, allowing for bidirectional playback. The amount of compression is adjustable by controlling the frequency at which *I* frames are encoded in the stream, because *P* and *B* frames are smaller than *I* frames. When the data generated by an MPEG encoder are transmitted across an ATM network, it resembles the graph shown in Figure 7.4.

The MPEG encoding algorithm is computationally intensive, so it is difficult to encode MPEG in real time without MPEG hardware encoder support. Decoding is less demanding, but still intensive enough to require high performance machines to view MPEG at the full rate of 30 frames per second. This will be less of a problem as CPU performance continues to increase and the CPU manufacturers integrate multi-media instructions into their hardware.

The MPEG-2 standard is similar to MPEG-1, with extensions to support broadcast quality video, HDTV, and interlaced video. MPEG-2 compressed video delivers 720- by 480- pixels at 30 frames per second and requires bandwidth between 4 and 9 Mbps. MPEG-2 algorithms provide better coding efficiency, and permit video to be compressed into multiple bit streams encoded at different resolutions, picture quality, and frame rates.

H.261   The H.261 standard[84] is developed for video encoding over low bandwidth communication lines like ISDN. Its main purpose is video phone and video conferencing applications where image quality is not the primary concern.

H.261 defines encoding and decoding methods for bandwidths that are multiples of 64 kbps, $p \times 64$ kbps, where p varies from 1 to 30. Video phone applications can be achieved using $p = 1$ or $p = 2$. For video conferencing applications, higher picture quality requires p values above 5.

There are two picture formats defined in H.261-CIF (Common Intermediate Format) encodes 288- by 360- pixels and QCIF (Quarter Common Intermediate Format) encodes 144- by 180- pixels.

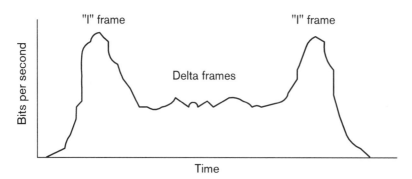

Figure 7.4   MPEG data stream

The H.261 encoding algorithm is similar to the JPEG and MPEG encoding algorithms, although none of these encoding schemes are compatible. The H.261 algorithms were designed to require substantially less CPU power than motion JPEG or MPEG algorithms. The algorithm includes a mechanism to provide a constant bit rate encoding which trades picture quality for picture motion while keeping the data rate constant.

7.2.5 Application issues related to QoS

While real time audio and video communications are a subset of continuous media applications, they are excellent candidates for ATM's ability to simultaneously provide QoS and high bandwidth connectivity. Continuous media applications are demanding of computational and network resources due to data volume, format and compression schemes, and the timing constraints necessary to present, or process, the data. For example, a real time broadcast quality running at 30 frames per second requires frames to be transmitted, decompressed, and displayed approximately 33 ms apart. The timing of audio data is even more critical since it is continuous, and jitter or delay in the audio presentation is more noticeable to the user than delay, or jitter, in video.

For applications involving multiple sites, such as video conferencing, multicast communications are required. Multicast can drastically reduce the network resources necessary for an application with many sites, such as a global video broadcast where it would be impossible to establish a connection between the broadcast point and each recipient. IP has multicast capabilities based on the Mbone [90] multicast facilities. Native ATM has point-to-multipoint capabilities, in which there is a single sender and multiple recipients, but does not support multicast with multiple senders.

To achieve the goal of supporting real time data delivery for multimedia applications, the IP application layer and ATM real time delivery layer must both be supported in the context of existing applications.

7.3 Integration of IP, ATM, and Quality of Service

Next generation applications running over IP, ATM, and mixed networks will require facilities available to applications, that do not currently exist across both IP and ATM. Routing, multicast, and Quality of Service facilities need to be accessible at the application level regardless of the underlying network technology. In addition, these facilities will need to be interoperable across mixed networks. Native ATM networks provide Quality of Service mechanisms, but do not supply IP routing or multicast. IP protocols provide routing and multicast, but lack support for Quality of Service. In this section the focus will be on integrating IP and ATM networks into a seamless environment for applications, including support for Quality of Service and traditional IP services.

7.3.1 The integrated IP/ATM model

As described, there is currently a need for integrated real time service support that includes IP routing, ATM style Quality of Service, and multicast features. These services should be available to applications running on ATM networks, IP networks, IP over ATM networks, and mixed networks. The integrated IP-ATM network model is shown in Figure 7.5. In this model, there are the following possible communication paths between hosts:

- ATM host to ATM host
- IP host to IP host
- ATM host to ATM host over a non-ATM IP network
- IP host to IP host over an ATM network
- ATM host to IP host

To enable an integrated IP/ATM network, the features of the ATM model, the IP model, and QoS must be interconnected within the network and available at the

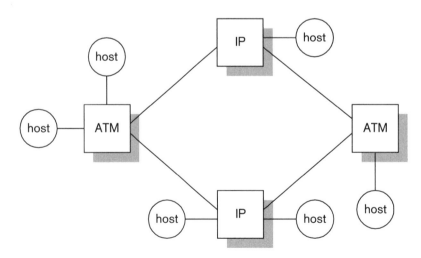

Figure 7.5   The integrated IP-ATM model

application level. The goal of the integrated services model is to mask the underlying technology from the application while still providing the following features:

- Internetwork routing, which allows applications to achieve their desired performance from the network via optimal path section

- Multicast capability, which allows one-to-many, or many-to-many communication flows

- QoS facility, which are parameters that describe the desired characteristics that applications can expect from the network

Routing   Internetwork routing is a critical consideration because QoS constraints are specified by applications, communicated to the network, and guaranteed chiefly through route selection, and then through resource reservation. The best path must be chosen by a routing algorithm that is QoS aware, that is, it will understand that different paths leading to the same destination may provide very different QoS characteristics. Internetwork routing between ATM and IP has been solved, in part, by providing IP best-effort services over ATM networks using Classical IP (RFC 1577), and LAN emulation. Although IP routing is supported, as pointed out in Chapter 5, both of these solutions fail to make the ATM real time service facilities available to IP applications.

An integrated model that utilizes an ATM network will, in all likelihood, be implemented by combining one of the QoS negotiation protocols covered in this chapter with the ATM Forum's Private Network Network Interface (PNNI) protocol. PNNI is a ATM routing protocol designed to support QoS on a global ATM Internet. The protocol is divided into two sections:

- PNNI routing that supports hierarchical, link state, source based decisions with QoS support

- PNNI signaling which uses Q.2931 as a foundation, allowing ATM switches to exchange reachability information

The key to the operation of the protocol and its ability to support QoS is centered on hierarchical views. At a high level of abstraction, the protocol operates by subdividing the total set of interconnected ATM switches into subgroups.* Within each group, the members are referred to as peers and a leader is selected to act as the spokesman for QoS negotiation on behalf of the peer group. Each peer group can then exchange state information among themselves to establish knowledge of network load and reaffirm the consequences of establishing new connections with strict QoS requirements.

---

* The subdivision is usually done on administrative boundaries (i.e., engineering, marketing…)

The concept of *hierarchical views* is used by the peer group leader when it examines the state of its members, then passes that information on to its adjoining peer group leaders. The outcome of this aggregation and dissemination of information is that individual ATM switches can establish connections across the ATM network with a high degree of certainty that desired QoS requirements will be met.

When connections are established in a PNNI environment, a computer or router attached to an ATM switch will issue a call setup message. This message, with its associated QoS values, will be examined by the switch using the global knowledge gained by being a member of the PNNI network. Then, the switch will determine which path has the highest probability of meeting or exceeding the desired QoS, based on its understanding of the current state of the network. Afterwards, the switch forms the path through the network as it passes the call setup message to the next switch. Because the first switch the host encounters attempts to calculate the entire path for the connection, the PNNI protocol is said to be source based routing (see Figure 7.6). As the call setup message traverses the network, it is passed to peer group leaders that check their current state, and then forwarded to the appropriate next hop. In the case in which a change in the state of the network makes the switch along the path unable to meet the QoS requirements, the call is *cranked bank* one hop and the path calculation is repeated.

Multicast   Multicast capabilities are supported in both IP and ATM, although in fundamentally different ways. IP was developed on broadcast network media, and since it provides connectionless facilities, its multicast implementation is more mature than ATM. IP supports multicast groups with multiple receivers and any-cast that permits sending to all hosts. ATM provides point-to-multipoint services, with a single sender and multiple receivers. However, ATM does not supply native multicast with multiple senders, and has no support for any–cast without employing multicast servers. LAN Emulation gives multicast capabilities on ATM networks, but it is a link layer technology, thus may potentially suffer scalability problems.

It is likely that the multicast facilities in integrated networks will be based on the IP multicast model.

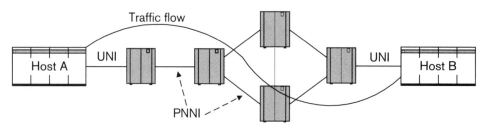

Figure 7.6   PNNI

Quality of Service   Quality of Service provisions allow an application to specify resource requirements, and to reserve resources to ensure correct operation. Quality of Service mechanisms are useful for applications that operate on real time data, such as audio and video transmission. There are three classes of Quality of Service.

Guaranteed services provide quality guarantees and can be explicitly stated in a deterministic or statistical representation. Deterministic bounds are specified by a single value, such as average bandwidth. Statistical bounds are determined by a statistical measure, such as the probability of errors. Predictable services are based on past network behavior. QoS parameters for reliable services are estimates of the consistent behavior based on measurements of past behavior.

Best effort services have partial or no guarantees. Most traditional network protocols, such as TCP/IP, supply best effort services.

ATM defines five quality of service classes:

- *Constant Bit Rate (CBR)*   Emulates leased lines, where data flows at a constant rate
- *Variable Bit Rate (VBR)*   Where data flows continuously but at a varying bandwidth with tight delay constraints
- *Variable Bit Rate/Non Real Time (VBR non-real time)*   For applications with variable bit rate without delay constraints
- *Unspecified Bit Rate (UBR)*   For best effort as in traditional IP
- Available Bit Rate (ABR)   For using available bandwidth on the network while minimizing loss and utilizing the ATM Forum's Traffic Management 4.0 mechanisms. Details on ABR are covered in Chapter 8.

The Q.2931 ATM signaling specification offers the following QoS parameters:

- Maximum end-to-end delay
- Cumulative end-to-end delay
- Peak cell rate, forward direction
- Peak cell rate, reverse direction
- Max. PDU size, forward direction
- Max. PDU size, reverse direction

Conversely, IP version 4 (IPv4), the protocol used on the Internet today, does not support Quality of Service provisions. The newest TCP/IP standard, IP version 6 or IPng (next generation), lends support for QoS specification within the protocol, but the particular QoS model and implementation are not yet standardized. In all likelihood, the ATM model will be the basis for Quality of Service in an integrated network environment. The ultimate solution must be able to communicate with any network capable of QoS support, regardless if the application is running on an ATM attached host or not.

The Integrated Services (int-serv) group of the IETF and the MPOA group of the ATM Forum are developing protocols for QoS support. In addition, these bodies are deciding how to integrate IP and ATM networks. To effect this end, they can either require changes in IP to support Quality of Service, in ATM to support IP services, or in the application interfaces to supply an integrated interface. As this issue evolves, it is likely that all of the above approaches will be necessary. For an IP solution, the IETF is working on integrated support for real time services on the Internet via protocols that are independent of ATM. For ATM, the MPOA group is working on integrated real time services via the UNI interface and Q.2931, but this approach does not address how higher layer protocols such as TCP/IP should make use of signaling desired QoS. The solution creates an environment where software developers can begin to implement new applications that are QoS aware.

The IETF work is focused on enhancements to the IP networking model which allows support of real time and delay sensitive traffic flows. Their motivation is driven by the problem that best effort coupled with over engineering networks is no longer viable. Their intent is to move towards a new paradigm where network resources are optimized by empowering applications with QoS knowledge.

The next section will concentrate on two models that the IETF is reviewing, *integrating IP/ATM Internets: RSVP and ST-2*. Currently, the RSVP model is more favored than the ST-2 model and the work under way in both the ATM Forum and the IETF revolves around mapping the semantics of the protocol to a network's QoS features.

RSVP   RSVP[82] stands for ReSerVation setup Protocol. It is a network controlled protocol for real time services in connectionless networks. RSVP is used after the data path is set up to deliver QoS requests to each switch or router along the path. This is a key point of RSVP that is often overlooked, it is a signaling protocol and not a routing protocol. Each node along the data path processes the QoS request, possibly reserving resources for the connection and then forwards the request to the next internetworking device along the selected path. RSVP is a very robust protocol and is designed to support multicast and unicast data delivery in a heterogeneous network environment, but it is clearly designed with IP in mind.

Some high level terms used to describe RSVP are as follows:

- *Flow*   A sequence of packets with the same QoS requirements
- *Session*   A dataflow with a particular destination IP address and port

- *Flowspec*   Information contained in the reservation request pertaining to QoS requirements
- *Filterspec*   Used to specify flows that can be received

RSVP is a receiver-oriented protocol, with receivers sending QoS requests upstream toward senders. The protocol operates by the source sending a message to the receiver specifying the path that joins the two computers. The receiver then sends a reservation message "upstream" along the path that signals traffic and QoS requirements. The protocol also supports a message type that allows the receiver to query the network about existing QoS state before it formulates its actual request. The RSVP flows are illustrated in Figure 7.7.

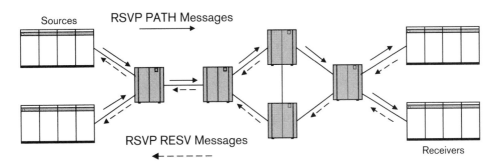

Figure 7.7   RSVP flows

This reservation style is in stark contrast to the ATM signaling model, where QoS parameters are specified at connection setup by the sender. An additional contrast is that RSVP provides "soft" resource reservations, meaning that the QoS is not guaranteed and may be changed. Resource reservations time out and must be refreshed periodically. This requires applications to refresh their resource reservations periodically. In contrast, ATM resources are allocated at connection setup and remain intact for the duration of the connection, until connection tear-down.

The integrated service components used by hosts to determine and signal QoS are:

- *The setup protocol*   Used by hosts/routers to signal QoS into the network
- *A Flowspec*   Which defines traffic and QoS characteristics of a traffic flow
- *Traffic controls*   Controls traffic flow within host/router to meet required QoS

The interaction of these components is illustrated in Figure 7.8.

In developing the RSVP model, the int-serv group designed a description of the traffic pattern contained in the reservation request sent by the host or router. This

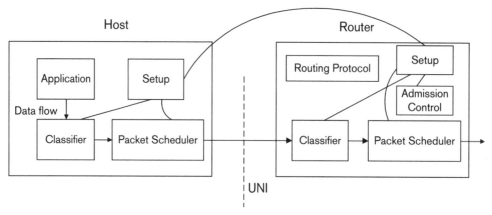

Figure 7.8   Flow spec

description is called the *Tspec* and is specified by a set of parameters which is very similar to ATM's traffic models. (See Chapter 8.) The Tspec is communicated to the network to specify the rate of data transmission, then used as a traffic shaping descriptor. The Tspec is defined as a "token bucket" with a value for the bucket size and the data transmission rate. Data sent by a host or router cannot exceed the value of $rT + b$, where T is a time interval. The concept of the Tspec is illustrated in Figure 7.9.

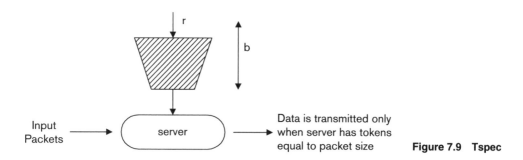

Figure 7.9   Tspec

The RSVP protocol is also designed with two reservation styles that assist multi-sender sessions, and select a subset of senders identical to the IP multicast model. ATM supplies only point-to-multipoint connections with a single sender. The reservation styles supported are:

- Distinct Reservations which require separate reservations for each sender
- Shared Reservations which can be shared by multiple senders and also allow receivers to dynamically change list of senders (i.e., change channel)

Finally, the last area of contrast to ATM's semantics with RSVP is: routing negotiations, which was designed to be independent of other network components. With RSVP, QoS negotiations occur after the data path has been established. ATM resource reservation and route setup occur at connection setup time.

There are a number of potential problems related to integrating ATM and RSVP:

- ATM resource reservation is sender-based; RSVP is receiverbased.

- ATM's point to multipoint connection management is controlled by the sender.

- ATM maintains a "hard," unchanging connection state. RSVP maintains a "soft," changeable state that must be continually refreshed.

- ATM QoS resources are set up at connection-time, RSVP QoS is independent of connection setup.

- ATM has a single QoS specification for point to multipoint sessions. RSVP supports different QoS specifications per receiver.

Although solutions to many of these problems are being developed, the major challenge is to develop implementations that will efficiently determine setup time and network resource used by ATM networks that are the result of differences between the RSVP and ATM models of operation.

ST-2   ST-2 [86] is an Internet QoS protocol that coexists with IP. Due to its strengths, there are several multimedia transport protocols that operate using ST-2 including Packet Video Protocol (PVP) and the Network Voice Protocol (NVP).

The ST-2 QoS model is similar to the ATM QoS model in many ways. The main features of ST-2 include:

- *Sender-oriented*   Senders set up simplex flows to receivers at call setup time.

- *Hard State*   ST-2 maintains unchanging hard state along the connection path as ATM does.

- *Receiver-oriented joins*   ST2+ supports this feature to reduce the burden on senders.

- *Dynamic QoS*   QoS parameters can be changed, unlike ATM QoS parameters which are fixed until call tear-down.

- *Unidirectional QoS resource allocation*   ST-2 QoS flows are simplex, unlike ATM, which uses bidirectional QoS and uni-cast and unidirectional for multicast.

- *Heterogeneous receiver QoS*   Receivers in multicast flows can have different QoS specifications, unlike ATM which is homogeneous.

As with RSVP, there are some difficult problems with integrating the ST-2 QoS mechanisms with ATM. For example, the data stream in an ST-2 connection is one-way, with a reverse direction channel for control messages. This is adequate for ATM point-to-multipoint connections, but wastes the reverse flow connection for a standard point to point ATM virtual circuit. An additional difficulty is that dynamic QoS changes are allowed in ST-2. This can pose a problem when the QoS change means exceeding current ATM QoS. UNI 3.1 does not support QoS changes. It should be noted that the ATM forum is developing techniques for dynamic QoS changes after connection setup, but the difference will challenge implementors until a standard is finalized.

QoS capable API   The above discussion has focused on protocols that are used to communicate QoS information to or within a network. In most cases, applications will be unaware of which protocol is actually used to reserve resource but will interface to the protocol via a standard Application Program Interface (API). One troubling concern to application developers is that this area has received little attention until recently and to date only the Windows Sockets (WinSock) API is clearly mature, thus favored by software developers. Below is a brief description of some of WinSock 2's features.

WinSock is the API specification used to implement TCP/IP data communications on the Microsoft Windows platform. WinSock 2 extends the WinSock v 1.1 API for TCP/IP networks by providing an interface designed to support real time multimedia communications across several types of communications infrastructures.

WinSock 2 is designed and developed to enable applications that employ real time multimedia communications like video conferencing. Besides QoS, there are several features in WinSock 2 that assist applications with real time multimedia communications, such as overlapped I/O, circular queues and buffer flushing.

Important to applications developers is the ability to use the WinSock API as a standard interface, shielding them from the details of the resource reservation protocol. The final solution and applications development space will resemble what is shown in Figure 7.10.

Discussion and comparison of QoS approaches   The major features of IP, ATM, RSVP, and ST-2 are shown in Table 7.2. Obviously, there are challenges in integrating IP, ATM, and QoS into a seamless environment. The problems are being worked on in the appropriate forums and while some approaches are favored, it is too early to tell the details of which solutions will be chosen. It does seem clear that as a QoS protocol ST-2 is more adaptable to ATM than RSVP. However, it appears that the IETF is converging

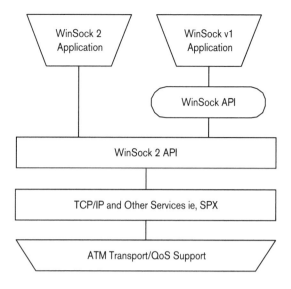

Figure 7.10   API Layer

on RSVP as the QoS mechanism for the Internet. Nevertheless, there are a number of outstanding areas that need to be resolved in an integrated IP/ATM internetwork with QoS:

- *Integration of QoS specification*   A QoS model that is applicable to IP, ATM, and integrated networks is needed. This is required to provide true end-to-end QoS in an integrated network. Mappings between QoS implementations in different portions of the network are necessary to realize this goal.

- *Dynamic QoS will continue to be a problem for ATM networks*   While there may be alternate methods for solving this problem, they are by no means elegant or efficient solutions. It would be very useful to have dynamic QoS support within ATM.

  In the short term, it is most likely that new virtual circuits will need to be created as QoS changes during the lifetime of a flow.

- *Sender-oriented multicast*   QoS in ATM is sender-oriented with a QoS specification common to all receivers. It is unrealistic to assume that all recipients of a multicast group, especially a large group, will require identical QoS.

Therefore, multicast servers will most likely fill this role for the next several years. In essence, these servers act as middle men and adapt QoS to meet the various requirements of receivers. An example would be a video broadcast in which some receivers are attached to the network via ISDN, therefore requiring relatively low bandwidth compared to the direct ATM attached hosts.

Table 7.2 Comparison of features of IP, ATM, RSVP, and ST-2

	IP	ATM	RSVP	ST-2
Connection style	Connectionless	Connection-oriented	—	—
Multicast support	Yes	Unicast	Yes	—
QoS state	—	Fixed	Dynamic	Fixed
QoS orientation	—	Sender	Receiver	Sender
QoS setup time	—	With connection	After connection	With connection
QoS changeable	—	No	Yes	Yes
Multicast receiver QoS	—	Uniform	Heterogeneous	Heterogeneous

7.3.2 Adaptive protocols, working with today's networks

Although integrated IP/ATM networks with QoS mechanisms are not available, there are adaptive protocols available that can provide benefits. Adaptive protocols run on best effort networks and adapt transmission rates independent of the network, to make optimal use of resources. Although they do not provide Quality of Service and reservation capabilities, adaptive protocols can function to optimize available network bandwidth to yield better application performance. In a client/server network, an adaptive protocol would simply use ATM as a high quality high speed transport system in which IP would function as a network layer addressing/routing system.

The features of adaptive protocols include:

- Adaptive protocols with existing best-effort networks. They can be useful as an interim solution for integrated services while integration of IP, ATM, and QoS is being developed. They are fully compatible with existing IP over ATM implementations.

- Adaptive protocols do not require Quality of Service mechanisms, but can make use of them if they are available.

- Adaptive protocols do not require the application to specify its behavior. It can be difficult for some applications to specify requirements because they may be variable or unknown. In this case applications tend to overspecify network requirements, resulting in under-utilized network resources.

- Connection oriented protocols such as TCP that perform poorly for transmission of many forms of continuous media (MPEG). Sequencing and retransmission can be an obstruction to application performance. Adaptive protocols replace TCP transmission behavior with application-specific behavior.

An example of an adaptive protocol is the Video Datagram Protocol (VDP)[96] developed at the University of Illinois. VDP is an end-to-end protocol for MPEG transmission that runs on IP. VDP has been used to implement Vosaic (video Mosaic), the Mosaic browser with support for real time MPEG audio/video. By customizing VDP transmission to optimize network bandwidth without causing congestion, VDP applications can achieve a fortyfold increase in application frame rate compared to using TCP transmission for video.

7.4 The future of client/ server technology

Client/server computing has dramatically changed the way applications are built, but where is the client/server model leading? In the past, application technology has been based on a monolithic approach, where each application is used for a single purpose and maintains its own data formats and files. Remote Procedure Call technology allows the application to be split into client and server. Integrated applications, like Netscape Navigator, have enabled the use of multiple servers and data types to be gathered from various servers and used simultaneously within a single application. Now audio, video, and real time interactive data are making their way into integrated applications, pushing the integration of real-time data delivery within the network.

There is another fundamental change on the horizon, called component based applications. In the same way that Internet browsers integrate multiple data types into a single application, component software technology will integrate multiple application components into an application interface.

Component-based software allows large, monolithic applications to be replaced by a number of small application components, that cooperate to accomplish their task. The model is similar to the object-oriented model, where each object (component) is responsible for itself, and objects (components) are plugged together to form the application. The components are managed by a software framework that coordinates the interaction of the components. This model is very similar to the Java-applet model within many network browsers. The power of the component model comes from the ability to replace single components within applications. For example, a faster network video display component can be replaced within a component based conferencing systems without requiring any other changes to the application, and without requiring a new release from the vendor.

Component-based application systems under development include: OLE from Microsoft, OpenDoc from Apple/Component Integration Labs, and PDO from NeXT. Component-based distributed applications will continue the trend toward of using the network for both data and application component delivery. Both the delivery of components and data will require the real time services of an integrated IP/ATM network. Guaranteed QoS will be required to ensure that distributed applications with components, and data being delivered in real time, perform adequately, even if a particular application does not use real time data.

7.5 Summary

New applications have extended and expanded the client/server model of computing, leading to integrated applications with text, graphics, audio, and video. The HTML and related standards for Internet communications make this possible by facilitating the creation of portable documents, including data from multiple locations. Java, and plug-in technologies are adding to this base to create live, interactive, real time interactive, and network portable applications.

The real time interactive applications along with audio and video client/server applications on the Internet demand real time data delivery within the network. IPv4 does not provide support for real time applications, and ATM was designed with real time support from the start. Unfortunately, most applications are written to run on IP networks, and not directly on ATM.

Although IP over ATM exists, via LAN Emulation and RFC 1577, there is no widely available full integration of IP, ATM and Quality of Service. The IETF is working on real time service models to support real time applications in an integrated environment. RSVP and ST-2 are being studied as QoS implementations over an integrated Internet, but neither of these QoS models conveniently supports IP, ATM, and multicast. While the integrated Internet model is being developed, applications can make use of custom, adaptive protocols to maximize network and application performance.

This chapter demonstrates that providing support for the next generation of applications, including QoS, multicast, and IP compatibility, is problematic, but not insurmountably so. Although the IETF and ATM forums are working hard toward a solution, a number of issues must be addressed before IP, ATM, and QoS can be interconnected into a single, seamless environment. However, it is encouraging that the standards bodies are coordinating work on the solutions since this cooperation illustrates the widespread faith in ATM.

7.6 References

82 R. Braden, L. Zhang, et el, "Resource ReSerVation Protocol (RSVP)-Version 1 Functional Specification," ISI/PARC/UCS, July 1995, `http://www.isi.edu/rsvp`

83 C. Adie, "Distributed multimedia survey," `http://cuiwww.unige.ch/OSG/MultimediaInfo/mmsurvey/`, January 1993.

84 C. Adie, "Distributed multimedia survey: Standards," `http://cuiwww.unige.ch/OSG/MultimediaInfo/mmsurvey/standards.html`, January 1993.

85 D. Le Gall, "MPEG: A Video Compression Standard for Multi-media Applications," *Communications of the ACM,* April 1991, pages 34(4), 46–58.

86 L. Delgrossi and L. Berger, "Internet Stream Protocol Version 2 (ST-2) Protocol Specification-Version ST2+," *RFC 1819,* August 1995.

87 G. K. Wallace, "The JPEG Still Picture Compression Standard," *Communications of the ACM,* April 1991, pages 34(4), 30–44.

88 "HP Precision Risc Architecture Video Instructions," Available at `http://www.dmo.hp.com/wsg/strategies/parisc3.html`.

89 L. Kohn, G.Maturana, M. Tremblay, A. Prabhu, and G. Zyner, "The Visual Instruction Set (VIS) in UltraSPARC." Sun MicroSystems White Paper.

90 "Mbone frequently asked questions," `http://www.research.att.com/mbone-faq.html`. Document in progress.

91 National Center for Supercomputing Applications, `http://www.ncsa.uiuc.edu/General/Internet/WWW/HTMLPrimer.html`. WWW document, December 1995.

92 National Center for Supercomputing Applications, `http://www.ncsa.uiuc.edu/SDG/Software/Mosaic/NCSAMosaicHome.html`. WWW document, Febuary 1996.

93 Netscape Communications Corp., `http://home/netscape.com`. WWW document, February 1996.

94 Sun Microsystems, Inc. Java, `http://java.sun.com`.

95 Virtual Worlds Consortium, `http://www.hitl.washington.edu/projects/knowledge_base/vrm.html`. WWW document, February 1996.

96 Z. Chen, See-Mong Tan, R. H. Campbell, Yongcheng Li. `http://choices.cs.uiuc.edu/Papers/New/vosaic/vosaic.html`. WWW document, October 1995.

chapter 8

Traffic management and performance of client/server over ATM

As described in the preceding chapters, ATM networks are designed to carry traffic generated by a wide variety of applications. These applications have different traffic characteristics and network performance requirements that can range from 64-Kbps voice encoding to a 100-Mbps scientific visualization. In order to efficiently support this multiple application environment, ATM possesses a sophisticated set of traffic management functions and procedures.

This chapter presents information useful for network planners, managers, or individuals interested in the performance of applications over ATM networks. The chapter covers aspects of traffic management and performance in ATM networks which are intended to be both practical and applicable to several different network models. Traffic and performance management techniques are important with ATM networks because they allow users to maximize the benefits that the network can provide. However, the concepts of traffic and performance management with ATM are not trivial because of ATM's complexity.

Traffic management concerns two areas:

- An application's ability to understand what facilities are available to it on an ATM network

- A network manager's understanding of traffic parameters used to govern the flow of data through an ATM network

Performance management is concerned with real time reactions to congestion in the network. It addresses the techniques that the network has, for coping with, or preventing congestion.

The material on traffic and performance management is divided into three sections. The first section covers ATM traffic management parameters, service classes, traffic descriptors, and resource sharing. The second section details reasons for performance degradation in ATM networks. Finally, section three addresses techniques for dealing with congestion in ATM networks.

8.1 Traffic management introduction

ATM traffic management must meet the challenge of providing high quality service while maintaining maximum network utilization. For example, a network that has reserved bandwidth for every connection's maximum needs will give high quality service. However, this may yield low utilization because no statistical multiplexing gains can be made. When a network is used without over subscription, the effect is to treat the system as Time Division Multiplexing (TDM). With TDM, resources are permanently allocated but may never actually be used. An example of this on a TDM network would be during the silent periods of a voice phone call in which unnecessary voice sample data (for example, silence during transmission) is still being transmitted between the two parties.

ATM attempts to achieve higher utilization in two ways. First, by statistically multiplexing multiple similar traffic types onto one connection. Second, it achieves higher utilization by segregating traffic of different priorities and guarantees delivery of the higher priorities (e.g., protecting a video VCC from a data VCC).

The goal of statistical multiplexing is to attempt to run several different data streams through one physical link. Because the hosts are not using the network at all times, statistically, there is a good chance that their data will be successfully passed. If all of the sources were to transmit simultaneously, serious congestion would occur. The effects of congestion on an ATM link are shown in Figure 8.1 which shows the throughput realized by a host as it increases its load into a congested ATM network. When the total available bandwidth on a link is over allocated, then the link utilization can be very high. However, high utilization may come at the price of poor quality service that is perceived by the hosts who are concurrently transmitting data and, thus, congesting the link. If these hosts are not well equipped to deal with congestion, they will continue to overload the link and effectively destroy each other's data. Bursty data applications that use ATM networks today are especially prone to congesting the network quickly. Compounding the problem are the higher layer protocols that detect data loss and request retransmissions, thus further congesting the network. These applications tend to make over-allocation a difficult engineering problem. Over allocation is appealing since it can ensure that expensive resources like ATM switches and WAN links, are used to their fullest potential.

Statistically over allocating or under allocating resources is effective for prototype networks but lacks scalability. Because of the difficulty in foreseeing future bandwidth requirement of a network, an application must be capable of intelligently reacting to congestion. A major focus in the ATM Forum is to devise schemes that can dynamically change the rate computers transmit data to make certain equal sharing of the bandwidth among all of the hosts.

The ability to dynamically control the rate at which hosts transmit data into a network is very important for maintaining high quality service. In the B-ISDN protocol stack, control over the rate of traffic transmission into a network is the responsibility of the ATM protocol layer. The ATM layer controls the rate that traffic enters the network by "shaping" or pacing its flow. The parameters used by ATM layers to pace its traffic

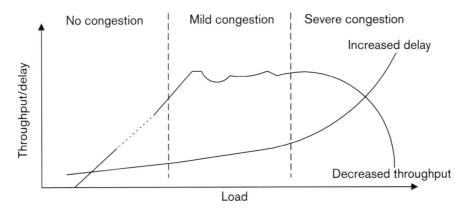

Figure 8.1 Effects of congesting

are those defined for the virtual circuit at call setup time, or when the PVC was created by a network administrator.

The main objectives of ATM layer traffic management are to:

- Provide predictable behavior to help achieve performance objectives
- Minimize network congestion
- Maximize the efficient use of network resources
- Independently operate from either the data being carried or the AAL being used

When designing the ATM layer management functions, the ATM Forum's goal was to devise a scheme that could support all existing or future B-ISDN traffic types. In addition, the intent was to develop protocols that did not overtax the host implementing the software, while meeting high standards for quality of service guarantees. The product of this work was the definition of a collection of traffic models that describe source flows (i.e., models of similar traffic streams), and schemes to transmit data into the network that is compliant to the model's definition. In the following sections, the service classes will be discussed from the viewpoint of their effect on traffic management.

8.2 ATM services classes

In addressing the issue of providing high quality of service, the ATM Forum's starting point began with considering the types of applications used on the ATM network. ATM service described, from a high level, the types of traffic the source would generate. Characterizing the applications has been important because each type had very different traffic profiles. For example, circuit emulation generated a steady stream of cells, as opposed to LAN traffic which had a strong "on/off" pattern. The ATM Forum concluded that the traffic from various applications supported on the ATM platform could be segregated into four categories. In order for ATM to provide high quality service, each of the following models would need to be supported.

- Constant Bit Rate (CBR)
- Variable Bit Rate (VBR)
- Available Bit Rate (ABR)
- Unspecified Bit Rate (UBR)

The next section will examine these classes in terms of their traffic profiles.

8.2.1 Constant Bit Rate

Constant Bit Rate traffic has a deterministic bandwidth requirement that makes it easy to provision/engineer. CBR sources are similar to a virtual wire, and generate cells at a consistent rate, fully occupying the allocated bandwidth at all times. The source rate corresponds to a known peak emission rate measured in Cells Per Second (CPS). Conforming cells are typically guaranteed high priority because they are the product of latency-sensitive traffic such as video, voice, and circuit emulation. Loss of cells, or large delay, will have a substantially negative impact on these applications.

8.2.2 Variable Bit Rate

The second traffic model developed by the ATM Forum is the Variable Bit Rate model in which sources can generate traffic at random rates. VBR is designed to operate on ATM links shared by multiple users. VBR traffic is modeled by a maximum and average value. During active periods, cells are transmitted into the network at a constant rate, but are governed by a peak rate. The maximum rate that the VBR source can transmit traffic is the Peak Cell Rate (PCR). The duration of on/off period is characterized by the Sustainable Cell Rate (SCR). This bursty traffic model is intended to be used for transmitting LAN packet data or Frame Relay over ATM. The degree of VBR burstiness can be quantified as: *Burstiness = PCR / SCR*

As the value of PCR/SCR increases, the traffic from the given source is more bursty. Sources that are very bursty can be statistically multiplexed, but congestion can be extreme and occur quickly.

Because VBR sources alternate randomly between periods of transmission and idleness, the probability of traffic from two sources colliding is minimized, as is shown in Figure 8.2. A network designer can make an educated guess of what the offered load will be and attempt to realize statistical bandwidth gains by "overbooking" the links. By statistically multiplexing multiple VBR connections onto a single ATM link, and buffering the overload, the users can get the impression that they alone are allocated the entire link capacity.

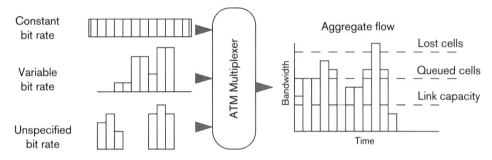

Figure 8.2   ATM traffic multiplexing

The VBR model is not without its drawbacks. The values of PCR and SCR, while valuable in characterizing a theoretical traffic type, are of questionable value in practice. Because the PCR is allocated when the virtual circuit is created, it is a constant for the duration of the connection. The source should never transmit above this value even if some event after call setup requires higher bandwidth. This has the effect of unnecessarily throttling the source in the absence of network congestion. A second problem with the VBR model is that it is very difficult to characterize a traditional LAN in terms PCR and SCR. Because load can change from second to second, not many network managers can pick one of their legacy LANs and declare, "That's a 5,000 cell/second PCR, 2000 cell/second SCR LAN."

In order to overcome the problems of static allocation of bandwidth and guessing which values are appropriate for a network, an adaptive technique for traffic management must be used. There are two techniques traffic sources used to cope with the problem of dynamically adapting to congestion. The first involves turning off all shaping and allowing higher layer protocols, like TCP/IP, to deal with congestion. To do this the network operator would set the link bandwidth = PCR = SCR. In essence, this turns off all egress shaping and makes the switch behave like a buffering ethernet. The second technique is adaptive rate flow control. The ATM Forum's specification for adaptive rate flow control is the Available Bit Rate protocol.

8.2.3 Available Bit Rate

With adaptive flow control, the network is capable of supporting high quality video (CBR) service along with data (ABR) services. Telecommunications typically call for fixed bandwidth allocations since voice communications generate a constant data stream. Conversely, data communications has a long history of using protocols, like TCP slow start [97], that adjust to network congestion. Slow start will sense congestion by detecting packet loss, then reduce the size of bursts of traffic transmitted. The ABR specification is an example of the ATM Forum developing a networking technology that can be simultaneously used by telecommunications carriers and enterprise data networks.

ABR is designed to implement an adaptive mechanism that modifies its output speed depending on feedback from the network. By using an adaptive protocol, VBR's problem of determining in advance what load will be offered is eliminated. Applications are able to make use of all available bandwidths on the network but slow down when congestion occurs. With ABR, hosts sharing the network understand and correctly respond to the feedback messages, so they will realize a fairer distribution of resources, and higher quality service.

An ABR source dynamically varies its transmission rate by reacting to special cells, called Resource Management (RM) cells. RM cells are constantly generated by traffic sources at a regular pace, regardless if congestion exists or not. When a source receives a RM cell indicating a congested state, it reduces its transmission rate by one half. Then, the host attempts to slowly increase its output speed until it is receives another RM cell indicating congestion. This interaction between the ABR source with RM cells results in appropriate adjustments in the transmission rate to avoid congestion.

In order to make certain that the source is obeying the RM requested reduction, it is necessary to police the transmission of the ATM switches (Section 8.6). In addition, the ATM switches will need to be able to monitor their buffer utilization and each port will need to create RM cells where applicable. A more detailed description of ABR is deferred to Section 8.8.

8.2.4 Unspecified Bit Rate

The UBR service class is the ATM Forum's attempt to model a traffic type that is very similar to LANs. The UBR class is best effort and offers no quality of service guarantees. Data is transmitted by the hosts with the understanding that the network will do its best to carry the information to the destination, but the data may not make it. The UBR service can be considered the same and VBR when the PCR and SCR are equal. However,

UBR is typically given a lower priority than VBR if the two coexist. The UBR service class is attractive because it is very simple to support on ATM switches. The switches do not need to perform any resource reservation, or precall setup bandwidth allocation algorithms. UBR is also attractive from the host perspective since it does not require any prior knowledge of traffic characteristics and is similar to traditional LANs. Because UBR places no ATM layer processing requirements on the ATM devices, it relies on higher layer protocol to react to congestion.

8.3 Quality of Service parameters

When a call setup message is received by an ATM switch, a call acceptance function determines if the network can support the requested connection without degrading the performance of existing connections. Each call setup specifies the service category (CBR, VBR, ABR, UBR) and traffic characteristics. These parameters in the call setup message are used by the switch to characterize the data and determine if it has adequate resources to provide the requested quality of service. The traffic parameters are also used after the call has been established to monitor the call of traffic contract violations.[99]

Quality of service is negatively affected by three parameters:

- Cell Loss Ratio (CLR)
- Cell Transfer Delay (CTD)
- Cell Delay Variation (CDV)

8.3.1 Cell Loss Ratio

The CLR is determined by the percentage of traffic that successfully traverses the ATM network from source to destination and is a measure of Lost Cells/Total Transmitted Cells. Cell loss can be caused by faulty transmission links, congestion, misrouted traffic, or a ATM switch failure. Most of these causes are difficult to avoid and typically can only be prevented with redundant switch architectures, and correct engineering of network resources.

Any cell loss is undesirable but particularly so when cells are lost on a voice or video connection which is usually noticed by the user as a break in the continuity. CLR negatively affects data transmission in several ways. Typically, LAN data packets are segmented into several cells before being transmitted. When cells are lost on the ATM network the entire packet must be discarded. Higher layer protocols detect the lost packet and request retransmission of the data. If the network is still in a congested state, the retransmission only adds to the congestion and may be lost as well. Additionally, multiple sources that lose traffic, then simultaneously request retransmission may get synchronized. When sources are synchronized, a large scale patter of on/off bursty of packet into the network can occur.

8.3.2 Cell Transfer Delay

CTD is the total amount of time required for a cell to traverse the network from the source to the destination. CTD is introduced on a connection in a number of ways. First, when a network is congested, cells are buffered in ATM switches. The time spent in queues adds latency. Even when the switch is not congested, it will add some CTD when processing the cell from the input to the output port. Second, the physical link distance adds CTD. For example, a link from Washington, D.C., to San Francisco will typically have a CTD of about 30 ms. An additional cause of CTD is the time required for a host to segment a packet before transmitting it on the ATM network and the time required by ATM switches to correctly route the cell.

CTD can negatively affect interactive video applications because a long delay (e.g., 250 ms) hinders the semantics of human conversation. With long CTD, words have a tendency to collide and force the participants to use uncharacteristically long pauses between exchanges. Long delays are possible when the link between conference participants passes through several switches and crosses long WAN connections.

Higher values of CTD can also negatively affect data communications. Long CTD can negatively affect sliding window protocols because these protocols have been developed to transmit data, and then wait for an acknowledgment. The amount of unacknowledged data in transit is called the window size. If the window size is set too low, the protocol never gets the opportunity to fully utilize the link bandwidth. The source will transmit a burst, then stop while waiting for the acknowledge. If the hosts were adjusted to be aware of the long CTD value, the host would increase its window size in an attempt to maintain constant data transmission. While CTDs are always to be expected, a lower value yields a higher quality of service.

8.3.3 Cell Delay Variation

CDV is a measure of variations in arrival times of cells at the source. CDV is caused by queuing in switches and multiplexing of traffic. CDV has a negative impact on performance since some applications do not adjust well to changes in the rate that they receive data. For example, a video decoder that is displaying video at 30 frames/second will expect a consistent stream of data from the network. However, if the input rate slows down, then the decoder will have to adapt and display fewer frames/second. As the input rate increases, the decoder may have to display more that 30 frames/second. Dynamic modifications like these are possible in workstations, but would be highly undesirable in ATM cable television set top boxes. The cost of the additional RAM to cope with CDV in millions of homes would be unacceptable.

In order to provide a higher quality of service and reduce the quantity of variation in the cells stream, some ATM switches are capable of supporting egress shaping. A switch that is capable of shaping on its egress port will attempt to modify the output traffic so that it will have a very consistent pattern [98]. This is illustrated in Figure 8.3.

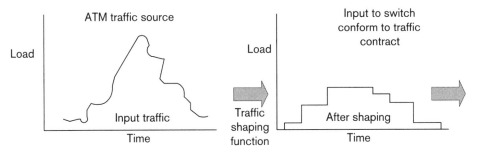

Figure 8.3   Traffic shaping

CDV, also called *jitter*, can have either a positive or negative value. A positive value occurs when time between cells is decreasing. Conversely, negative CDV occurs when the time between cells is increasing.

Two methods of measuring CDV have been established by the ATM Forum:

- 1-Point CDV measures variability in the cell stream as it passes a single point. The measurement is the difference between the cell's actual arrival time and when the cell should have arrived based on network delay.

- 2-Point CDV measures variability in the cell stream as it passes two points: the source and destination. This is the difference seen between the two endpoints and the calculated CDV imposed by these two endpoints. 2-Point CDV is very hard to measure in practice and is typically not used.

Key points a network manager must consider with CDV are reducing its value by minimizing buffering in the network and segregating traffic types by desired quality of service (i.e., voice from data).

8.4 End-to-end traffic management

In order to secure high quality service, every aspect of a connection, from the hosts, through switches, to links, must work together well. All components of an ATM network must have clearly defined parameters and understand each other's role [100]. The goal of end-to-end traffic management is to obtain a system such that:

- Hosts will have a clear understanding of their traffic pattern
- It communicates them to the network
- It receives permission to transmit at those rates
- It can be policed to check that the traffic conforms to the contract

The components of the connection can be subdivided into pieces shown in Figure 8.4. The parts that make up Figure 8.4 are distributed among software, hardware, and policy. The four major traffic management elements are:

- Traffic parameters, a description of the traffic
- Connection admission control, software for resource allocation
- Conformance monitoring or policing, hardware check on traffic
- Queue management, hardware to maintain quality of service

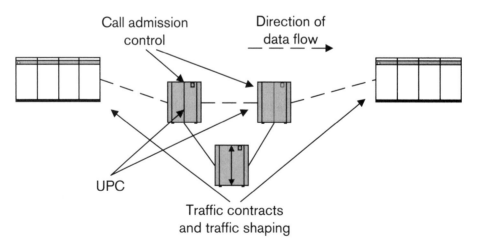

Figure 8.4   End to end traffic management

8.4.1 Traffic parameters

The traffic parameters are a set of values used to characterize an ATM connection. At call setup time, the originating host must have some knowledge of the type of connection it is about to make and the type of data that will be carried on that connection. These parameters, when communicated to the network in a call setup message, are referred to as the *traffic contract*. It is important to understand traffic parameters because they form the basis of a quality of service request.

When a host requests certain parameters, the network will use the parameters to characterize the source when executing a call acceptance algorithm. The actual parameters in the request are the traffic descriptor and the Cell Delay Variation Tolerance. The combination tells the network what the load will be and how high is the expected quality. When an ATM network accepts the call setup messages, it has agreed to allocate the necessary resources, and guaranteed the quality of service for the duration of the call. If changes are necessary, a new call setup message and traffic contract are required.

8.4.2 Source traffic descriptor

The source traffic descriptor is a collection of values that the originating host specifies. It describes to the network the anticipated bandwidth needed for the connection. The number of values constituting the source traffic descriptor differ depending on the type of service class being used. In the worst case, VBR, there will be three descriptors utilized to quantify the maximum and average load. The minimum number of descriptors required would be just the peak rate associated with a CBR connection. The source traffic descriptors that define a virtual circuit are:

- Peak Cell Rate or peak transmission rate
- Sustainable Cell Rate which represents the average bandwidth required
- Maximum Burst Size which represents the maximum number of cells that can be transmitted at the PCR, while still being considered compliant with the SCR
- The following descriptors are used for ABR only:
  1 Minimum Cell Rate (MCR) represents the minimum bandwidth required for the connection and can be as low as zero. Once accepted by the network, this value is always guaranteed.
  2 Available Cell Rate (ACR) is used to represent the current state. The value is not transmitted in a call setup message, but is maintained by an ATM client to signify what bandwidth the client believes it can utilize at that moment.

3 Maximum Cell Rate represents the highest rate that the host will ever transmit data. The ACR will fluctuate as it tries to approach the maximum rate. The maximum rate, which is conveyed at call setup time, will never exceed the PCR.

In an ATM call setup message, depending on the service category, the above descriptors will be set for each direction. ATM virtual circuits can be asymmetric, so the values may be different for the reverse flow in a bi-directional connection.

8.5 Call admission control

Call Admission Control (CAC) is an process executed by ATM switches as they receive new call setup messages. The intent of CAC is to determine if adequate resources exist in the switch to support the requested quality of service, and if the requested quality of server will adversely affect currently established calls. CAC uses the traffic descriptors discussed above to make its best estimate of whether the switch can carry the data between clients. Typically, CAC process allocates virtual bandwidth to connections that it accepts.

The algorithm actually used by CAC is not ATM Forum defined and is left to the switch vendor's discretion. However, in the case of inter switch routing, where switches must guess at the best path to route a call, the ATM Forum has developed a Generic CAC algorithm that may be applied by a switch to any switch, to determine the likelihood of having the call successfully accepted.

8.6 Conformance monitoring and enforcement

In order to maintain the quality of service agreed upon when traffic contracts are established between users and the network, it is necessary for the ATM network to monitor the user's traffic. The monitoring of traffic being transmitted into the network is sometimes referred to as ingress policing. With policing, the ATM switch checks the stream of cells entering a UNI to ensure that the host "behaves" and complies to the traffic descriptors.

When the network commits to establishing a virtual circuit, it agrees to transport all compliant cells of the circuit. Compliant checking is termed Usage Parameter Control (UPC) and involves validating several aspects of the virtual circuit. As shown in

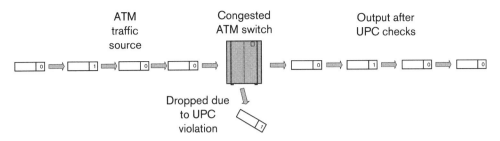

Figure 8.5   ATM usage parameter checking

Figure 8.5, the validation is usually performed by special purpose hardware and software on ATM switch ports.

UPC is used to:

- Check the validity of the VPI/VCI values
- Monitor cells to determine if they conform to the traffic descriptors
- Tag, discard, or pass non-conforming cells

The objective of UPC is to perform the check in a timely manner and not be more stringent than the theoretical conformance definition of the Generic Cell Rate Algorithm (GCRA). This allows a host to clearly understand the criteria used to examine the traffic it has generated, so it can then apply the same criteria to its own traffic prior to transmission.

Verifying input traffic or monitoring the conformance definition consists of one or more checks of the GCRA. The GCRA provides rules for checking each of the traffic descriptors and a leaky bucket mechanism is an implementation of the algorithm. If a connection passes the GCRA test, then it is compliant with the traffic contract. It should be noted that there is a certain degree of leeway when testing compliance. A network service provider can set the definition of compliance to include a connection that passes some number of cells over their negotiated values, but below the providers threshold. The threshold is set by the provider whose main concern is ensuring that the traffic entering his network is segregated and does not interfere with the virtual circuits of other customers.

8.6.1 Leaky bucket algorithms

A leaky bucket is the analogy most commonly used to visualize the UPC checks performed on each value of the traffic descriptor. Each leaky bucket has two parameters:

- The increment parameter which is the value the bucket increases per unit time, or the fill rate of the bucket.

- The limit parameter which corresponds to the capacity of the bucket or number of cells that can burst into the network.

When several traffic descriptors are associated with one virtual circuit, as would be the case with VBR, multiple leaky buckets are cascaded with the output of one bucket feeding the input of the next in line. The leaky bucket scheme is shown in Figure 8.6.

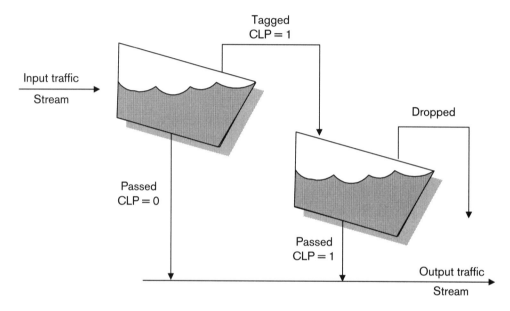

Figure 8.6   Dual leaky bucket algorithm

The first leaky bucket checked is always associated with the PCR. A token is placed into the bucket at the same rate cells are arriving on the ingress port. The bucket is then allowed to drain one unit leak per unit of time. As cells are burst into the port, the bucket fills quickly. If the bucket should overflow, the input stream is noncompliant. Compliant cells are passed to the next leaky bucket, for example to check the SCR compliance. The fate of the noncompliant cell is left to the discretion of the switch. A switch can either discard the noncompliant cell or "tag" the cell. The term tagging refers to setting the Cell Loss Priority (CLP) bit in the cell header. This bit then signifies that the cell is lower priority. The tagged cell is allowed to proceed to the egress port, providing capacity exists. When tagged cells arrive at the next downstream ATM switch, they are considered lowest priority and dropped should they fail a leaky bucket test.

To provide higher quality of service, each queuing resource may implement a threshold above which tagged cells are discarded. For example, in a case where a switch has a 1000 cell buffer, and a discard threshold of 500 cells, a tagged cell will be discarded if it arrives when the free buffer size is less than 500 cells. Nontagged cells are allowed to enter the queue until the queue is completely full.

8.6.2 Traffic shaping

From the discussion of the GCRA and UPC, clearly the most favorable input stream to an ATM network is a smooth and consistent one. For this reason, it is critical that the ATM software (i.e., traffic shaping) on the traffic source, correctly understand the GCRA and generate traffic that is at least compliant, but best if shaped to be smooth. Often, in data communication, a host will be required to modify the output stream to comply with its traffic contact. To make sure that the cells conform, the sources implement a traffic shaping function on the data before it leaves the ATM network interface card. An example of necessary shaping would be when a customer was buying a 6-Mbps WAN ATM service from a carrier. If the customer wanted to make certain that his traffic was not dropped by the carrier due to ingress policing, the cell stream from customer's equipment must shape its traffic.

Traffic shaping is the process of scheduling the entry of a cell such that the inter-arrival of cells on one VC does not violate the ATM switches GCRA. For example, a CBR host will shape its traffic using the PCR traffic descriptor, hence, its offered load will be scheduled at one cell every 1/PCR units of time. A VBR source shapes its bursts at the PCR rate and it must additionally shape its traffic to make sure no more than the MBS will be transmitted at the PCR. An ABR source requires dynamic shaping at all times. The ABR mechanism complies with the traffic contact by adjusting its output to match the value the network will support at that moment.

8.7 Queuing strategies

This section addresses how different ATM switch architectures affect quality of service in the context of the traffic management parameters described above. When an ATM switch experiences congestion of its statistically multiplexed traffic, it will attempt to place the overflow traffic into a buffer for temporary storage. When the load on the switch decreases, the buffered traffic is allowed to drain. Depending on the switch architecture, there are three points where buffering can occur (See Figure 8.7).

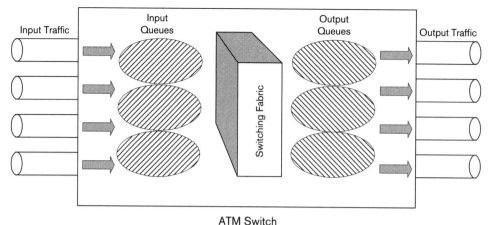

Figure 8.7 Switch traffic buffering point

- Input buffering where traffic is collected at input ports while it waits for outputs to become free.
- Centralized buffering where traffic is collected in a central location between the input and output port.
- Output buffering where traffic collects in a buffer at the switch egress when the offer load is greater that the output link speed.

8.7.1 Input buffering

A switch using an input buffering scheme is designed with a queue on the input port that stores cells when output port resources are overloaded. Input buffers are attractive because implementation is relatively simple and the components can be built from low speed memory.* However, there is a potentially serious problem with input buffered switches.

When traffic arrives on an input buffered switch that is congested, it will be placed in a queue. If there are cells arriving on the input that are destined to different outputs, they will all be placed in the same queue, as shown in Figure 8.8. The problem arises when a cell destined to output port A blocks the path of a cell destined to port B. Even though there is no congestion on the B port, its cells must wait until the A port resources are freed. The problem is called Head of Line blocking (HOL) and can

---

* Regardless of whether the switch is input, central, or output queued, the buffer are physically just RAM.

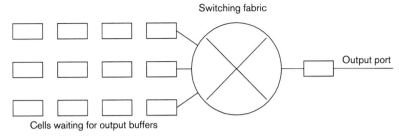

Switching fabric

Output port

Cells waiting for output buffers

Figure 8.8   Input buffering

seriously limit the switch's capacity. Techniques for improving the performance exist, but require complex high speed circuitry that examines each cell in the queue.

8.7.2 Centralized buffering

Centralized buffers, sometimes called a shared memory switch, are another method of coping with congestion and avoiding HOL problem. With central buffers, traffic destined to a congested output port is held in a central buffer pool. The pool is like a large waiting room with multiple exits. Specialized hardware is then used to scan the pool and copy cells to their correct outputs.

The advantages to centralized queuing are no HOL blocking can occur and, in some cases, multicasting support is made easier. The disadvantage to centralized queuing is that it requires very high speed memory in order to keep up with output port speeds. Currently, there are very few commercially available shared memory switches. They are typically only available in large carrier class products.

8.7.3 Output buffering

An output buffered switch that performs cell queuing at its output ports is shown in Figure 8.9. Cells are switched immediately when they arrive from the input to output ports. This design avoids HOL blocking at the expense of more complex implementation because

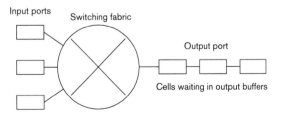

Input ports   Switching fabric

Output port

Cells waiting in output buffers

Figure 8.9   Output buffering switch

multiple input ports can send out to a single output port simultaneously. Output port buffered switches are the most common in switch designs. Many bus-based switches, like the Fore System ASX series switches utilize output buffers and achieve acceptable performance with this architecture.

8.7.4 Queue size

There is a long history and several differing opinions about the best size for queues. The size of the queues has a significant impact on the switch's capacity and quality of service. For CBR services, queue sizes should be small and queuing should, in general, be avoided. By keeping queues small, the total amount of time cells spend waiting to be transmitted is reduced. This will have a positive impact on reducing transfer delay and cell delay variation. For applications using CBR service, like voice, it may be better to discard a cell than allow it to sit for a long period of time in a queue.

Typically, data applications do not have tight constraints on delay and will benefit from large queues. Research on the Internet indicates that the minimum queue size for data applications should be equal to, or greater than, the delay bandwidth product. Therefore, the minimum switch buffer size can be determined by multiplying the delay (i.e., 60 ms for a US cross country connection) by the desired bandwidth. The rational for this value has to do with the closed loop congestion control scheme used by TCP.

If multiple TCP flows are converging on an inter-networking device and data is being lost due to congestion, the sources will not be notified about the congestion until the time required to send a packet from the source to the destination, and back again has passed. This time is called the round trip time (RTT). One RTT will pass because the source will generate a packet that may be dropped in the first switch it encounters. When the source is notified by the destination that data is being lost, it will reduce the rate it is transmitting. However, there will still be outstanding packets from the source on the network. The total number of packets will be equal to, or less than, the product of the link delay and the bandwidth of the connection. Therefore, by providing a buffer of this size, the effects of congestion loss can be mitigated.

8.8 Coping with congestion

The above description of the closed loop feedback used by TCP illustrates why its congestion management scheme will work over ATM, in addition to traditional frame based technologies. However, there are several network layer protocols that do not have native support for congestion control. In order for these protocols to work well over ATM, they need to rely on the network to provide this functionality. The next section will analyze schemes developed to improve the quality of service realized by data application over congested ATM networks. The two schemes presented are Available Bit Rate, and Early Packet Discard. Both may be very useful in coping with congestion. Though, it is unlikely that the ABR specification will be realized in ATM hardware before EPD is widely deployed.

8.8.1 ABR requirements

The rationalization for the ABR specification is that data was extremely bursty and could not be carried via VBR or CBR without causing unacceptable utilization, loss, or jitter to delay sensitive applications. Data applications typically cannot characterize their traffic in terms of SCR and maximum burst size. Enforcing these values leads to cell loss, performance degradation, and under utilization of network resources.

Data application bandwidth requirements can vary dynamically as time passes, therefore static resource allocation is not an efficient solution. The applications require as much bandwidth as available on an as needed basis, but can cooperate with the network when congested. In addition, bandwidth allocation should be fairly distributed between users.

ABR is intended to provide bandwidth on demand by allocating the unused bandwidth on the network to applications as they need it. Ethernet is a good analogy to ABR because on an Ethernet network, resources are dynamically shared between several hosts. When the network is idle, hosts can communicate at wire speed. When congested, hosts will be notified via collisions, and reduce their transmission rate.

With ABR, two parameters are used to specify the connection:

- *Peak Cell Rate* The maximum rate that the host will ever attempt to transmit data. The default value is the link rate.
- *Minimum Cell Rate* The minimum rate which a host will always be able to use. The default value is zero. When the minimum rate is set to zero, the network does not always promise that bandwidth will be available.

8.8.2 ABR implementation

The ABR specification can be implemented in several different ways. The simplest method for switches to indicate congestion is by setting the explicit forward congestion indicator (EFCI) in the header of the data cells (See Figure 8.10). When a switch is congested its sets EFCI and when it is not congested, it leaves EFCI unchanged. This mode of ABR operation is called "binary mode."

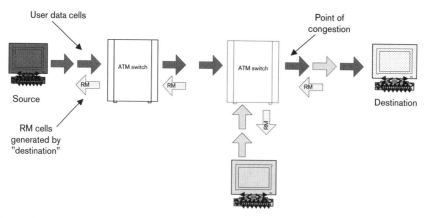

Figure 8.10   Explicit forward congestion indication

When the destination end station receives cells with EFCI set, it uses a resource management (RM) cell to send a message back to the source telling it to slow down. Later, when data cells arrive that do not have EFCI set, the network is not congested, so the source can increase the offered load. The source is notified when it receives RM cells indicating no congestion.

When ABR is implemented in binary mode, the end stations are responsible for implementing most of the protocol. The switch only needs to determine if it is congested then set EFCI bit accordingly.

In the second ABR implementation technique, the switch can explicitly tell the source which rate to use at any give instant. This "explicit rate" method allows much finer control than the simple "congested" or "not congested" EFCI approach (See Figure 8.11).

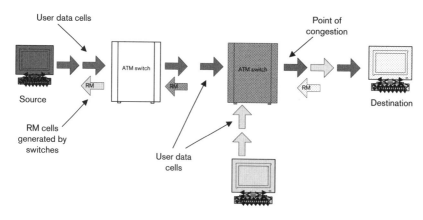

Figure 8.11   Explicit rate ABR

Instead of requesting a decrease or increase, an explicit rate switch will specify exactly how fast the source can transmit. As RM cells pass through the switch, it sets a field that indicates how fast the source can send. For example, the explicit rate switch may specify, "send at 10 Mbps," when there is no congestion. Then when bandwidth gets scarce, it might tell the source to send at 2 Mbps, or even lower. The explicit rate switch changes these estimates millisecond by millisecond and provides feedback to the source.

To a switch manufacturer the choice between the two options, EFCI or Explicit, is influenced by the complexity and increases in switch construction difficulty. ABR with explicit rate is definitely more complicated than the much simpler EFCI. Most switches available today either already support a form of EFCI, or soon will. Explicit rate does require careful design considerations to make sure it complies with the specification.

An additional component to the ABR specification is called "virtual source/virtual destination." (See Figure 8.12.) ABR normally uses an end-to-end control loop between the source and the destination, including all ATM switches in between. With virtual source/virtual destination that control loop is segmented into multiple control loops that are under control of the ATM switches. Introducing switches as virtual source/virtual destinations permits tighter control and improved isolation between network segments.

8.8.3 Issues with ABR

There are some outstanding concerns with ABR that will remain not well understood until more practical experience using the protocol has been gained. Two major concerns are the reaction time of the protocol and its interaction with existing transport

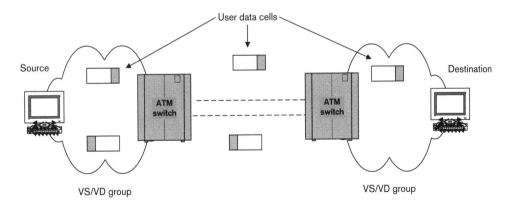

Figure 8.12   Virtual source/virtual destination

protocols. The concern of the reaction time has to do with the ability of the ABR hosts to quickly respond to RM cells when increasing or decreasing their offered load. For example, the speed a host "ramps up" its load to the network will determine how fast it gets bandwidth on demand. If the host ramps slowly, then the quality of service will be poor. If the host ramps up too quickly, the switch buffers will overflow. A final serious concern with ABR is its inability to work when used with multicast VCCs. Because ABR utilizes a closed loop feedback mechanism with the loop formed between the source and destination, it is not possible to have different transmission rates on a one-to-many multicast circuit. If multiple receivers share the single multicast VCC, then their feedback loops will be merged and their RM cells cannot be differentiated by the source. If the source can not determine where the RM cell comes from it will not be able to apply the ABR protocol to scale back its transmission rate and the system will fail. The only plausible option is to create unique virtual circuits for each destination.

8.8.4 Alternatives to ABR, Early Packet Discard

The problem of congestion can be addressed with standards based technology like ABR, or avoided with nonstandard intuitive techniques. Early Packet Discard is one example of a nonstandard technique for coping with congestion that has been shown to work well in production networks. EPD works by discarding entire network layer frames, instead of cells in congested switches. The ATM switch knows how to drop a frame because it relies on the data packet being encapsulated in AAL 5. When a packet is segmented with AAL 5, the last cell has a special bit set to indicate that the packet has been completely sent. If the ATM switch is experiencing congestion and needs to discard cells, it can now use this AAL 5 marker to drop cells that belong to only one packet. (See Figure 8.13.)

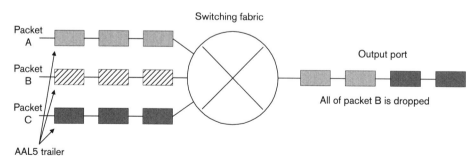

Figure 8.13   Early packet discard

Dropping entire packets is very effective in increasing the total throughput on an ATM network. Figure 8.14 and 8.15 illustrate this point. In the figures, several ATM sources are attempting to transmit data through a common port and for demonstration proposes, intentionally cause congestion. The *Y* axis represents the total possible percent throughput, and the *X* axis is the TCP window size. As the TCP window increases, the hosts will attempt to transmit more data without an acknowledgment, thus increasing the load.

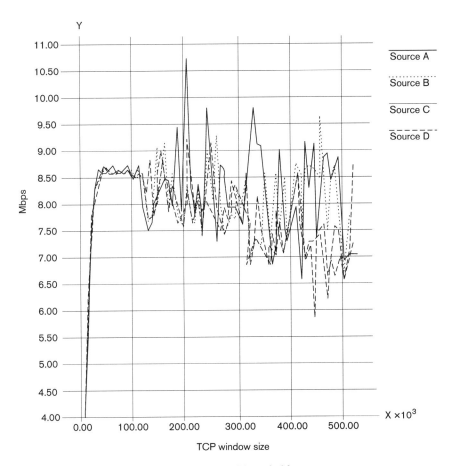

Figure 8.14   ATM congestion with EPD capable switching

Both graphs are similar until congestion, which occurs at the first knee, or a window of 30 kilobytes. After the congestion point, the EPD capable switch drops entire frames, which correctly place TCP into slow start mode. TCP slow start reduces the rate at which traffic is transmitted when it has detected a packet drop. The slow start

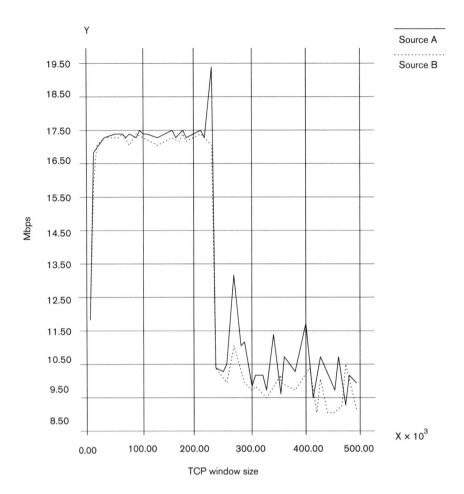

Figure 8.15   ATM congestion without EPD capable switching

algorithm then gradually ramps the offered load back to line rate, or until a point when more packets are lost. This cyclical behavior of gracefully striving to achieve high output bandwidth then slowing during congestion yields very good performance. As can be seen in the graph that without EPD, the result of letting several packets collide in the switch is serious congestion, with fairly random performance.

In addition, EPD has the advantage that in times of bursty congestion only one virtual circuit at a time is losing traffic. The performance of EPD can also be improved with per-VC queuing or per-VC accounting. By controlling the buffer utilization on a per-VC basis, the entire buffer does not overflow at one time. With this scheme, if one VCC starts using too much bandwidth, the switch will begin discarding cells on that VCC. Unlike ABR, EPD also has the advantage of functioning on a multicast VCCs.

A drawback to EPD that it is tightly coupled to the AAL 5 protocol. If a host decides to use a different AAL, EPD will not have the ability to determine the end of packet marker and will fail to improve performance. EPD also relies on higher layer flow control like that provided by TCP. TCP is a mature protocol with good end to end flow control, but not all transport layer protocols can make this claim. Therefore, protocols that are not well suited to running over-congested networks may not benefit from EPD.

8.9 Summary

It is becoming increasingly more evident that large scale deployment of ATM switches will soon be here. Consequently, network managers must understand both the complexities of ATM's traffic management, and their host's requirements for quality of service. More customers with high performance connectivity needs are emerging and have both greater interest and high expectations of ATM network performance. However, ATM's performance gains can only be realized via a tight coupling between applications and the network. If the technology is not used correctly, the performance gains will be severely affected and in extreme cases lower performance, versus frame based networks, will be realized.

While the opportunities for large scale deployment of ATM are great, so are the challenges in making ATM networks support a diverse number of services such as video, voice, imaging, and data. Each of these services has distinctly different traffic characteristics. The optimal performance of an ATM network depends on accurate modeling of traffic from the various sources combined with appropriate switching architectures that provide the means of supporting these services.

The challenges for the next generation of network planners and application developers are to understand and optimize the tools available with ATM. The ultimate goal is to construct systems that far exceed traditional paradigms for communication and capitalize on the capabilities that ATM technology offers through its bandwidth, scalability and flexibility.

8.10 References

97   D. Comer, *Internetworking with TCP/IP*, Englewood Cliffs, NJ: Prentice Hall, 1991.

98   C. Partridge, *Gigabit Networking*, Reading, MA: Addison-Wesley, 1994.

99   D. McDysan, *ATM Theory and Applications*, New York, NY: McGraw-Hill, 1995.

100   R. O. Onvural, *ATM Performance Issues*, Norwood, MA: Artech House, 1994.

index

ATM-ready hub 188
AVA/AVD 245
Available Bit Rate (ABR) 160, 187, 251, 268, 284, 286
    meaning of 187
Available Cell Rate (ACR) 273

B

back-ends 36, 59, 86
bandwidth 148, 158
    scalability 150
bit timing 165
Broadband Integrated Services Digital Network (B-ISDN) 145, 156, 264
Broadband Intercarrier Interface (B-ICI) 161, 186
broadcast 194
    addresses 200
Broadcast and Unknown Server (BUS) 81, 174, 201
    initialization 176
browser 126
    applications 238
    protocols 238
buffering 180
burstiness 266

C

C++ 33, 49, 107, 241
CAD/CAM 81
Call Admission Control (CAC) 274
Call Control capability 93
carrier sense multiple access with collision detection. *See CSMA/CD*
carrier-provided ATM services 183
Category 3 UTP 182
Category 5 UTP 182
CD-ROM 21, 81, 100
Cell Delay Variation (CDV) 270
cell delineation 165
Cell Loss Priority (CLP) 164, 276
Cell Loss Ratio (CLR) 269
Cell Relay Service (CRS) 3, 89, 94
Cell Transfer Delay (CTD) 270

centralized buffering 279
centralized maintenance 218
CICS 115
class of service 167
classes 132
Classical IP Over ATM 208, 212, 233
    as developed by IETF 193
client 59, 107
Client Control Flows 229
client/server
    advantages and disadvantages 122
    architecture 107
    computing 19, 30, 48, 72
    computing defined 8
    computing, transitioning to 73–75
    future of 259
    mainframe-based applications 74
    methodologies 18
    technology 3, 18
clients
    defined 8
CMIP 27
code
    reuse 130
    sharing 135
Common Intermediate Format (CIF) 246
Common Object Request Broker Architecture (CORBA) 13, 28, 35, 59, 70
communications architectures 25
computer-based training (CBT) 21
computing evolution 7–8
concentrator 186
    remote 187
configuration 176
    management 116
Configuration Flows 229
conformance monitoring 272
connection admission control 272
connectionless 83, 94
connection-oriented 83, 94
connections 194
consistency of interface 135
Constant Bit Rate (CBR) 92, 160, 183, 187, 251, 266
    meaning of 187

VC switching 186
VCC 205, 284
vertical applications 44
very large scale integration (VLSI) 146
video communications 247
video server 197
video/audio teleconferencing 236
Virtual Channel Connection (VCC) 166
Virtual Channel Identifier (VCI) 163
virtual corporation 54
virtual destination 283
Virtual LANs (VLANs) 152, 215
    with ATM 216
    with multiprotocol over ATM 218
Virtual Path Connection (VPC) 166
Virtual Path Identifier (VPI) 163
virtual reality 237
Virtual Reality Modeling Language
        (VRML) 241
virtual source 283
Visual Basic 49
Vosaic 243
VP switching 186

W

WAN 26, 71, 148
weakly consistent replication 120
wide area
    communication 93
    connectivity 88
Wide Area Information Server (WAIS) 126
Wide Area Networks (WANs) 14
windowing services 69
Windows NT 32
Windows Open Services Architecture
        (WOSA) 60
WinSock 2 256
work group 218
World Wide Web (WWW) 4, 125, 236
WORM jukeboxes 81

X

X.25 packet switching 83
X-servers 65
X-terminals 65